WHEN THOU SITTEST IN THINE HOUSE

WHEN THOU SITTEST IN THINE HOUSE

MEDITATIONS ON HOME LIFE

by

ABRAHAM KUYPER, D.D., LL.D.
FORMER PRIME MINISTER OF THE NETHERLANDS

WIPF & STOCK · Eugene, Oregon

Wipf and Stock Publishers
199 W 8th Ave, Suite 3
Eugene, OR 97401

When Thou Sittest in Thine House
Meditations on Home Life
By Kuyper, Abraham and De Vries, John Hendrik
ISBN 13: 978-1-60899-171-6
Publication date 11/2/2009
Previously published by Wm. B. Eerdmans Publishing Co., 1929

A Word Preliminary

THE family is the wondrous creation of God, from which all our human social life has of itself unfolded.

Compare national existence in Israel with that in Rome and Greece, and nothing is more strikingly evident, than the far higher place of honor, which the family in Israel occupies.

From Israel this beautiful trait has passed over into the Church of Christ, and in every land where the Cross has been planted, family life has made gains in loving tenderness and uniting power.

Among Christian nations family-life is of higher repute among Protestant than Romish nations. Prussia is ahead of Austria, England of France, the Netherlands of Belgium.

But the sense of home-life was most strong among the nations of the Reformation in Switzerland, Scotland, Netherlands and in America.

Even among these our Netherlands was in the front rank from of old.

In our quiet, substantial domestic social life was the strength of our middle classes and the nerve of strength in our national life.

At present there is less to boast of, however, along this line. Awayness from home has increased. Life in public interests and by night sitting in the clubhouse and bar-room has gained ground.

And therefore the confessors of Christ in the land are called of God, by heroic confession and seriousness of life to save the security once confided to our keeping, and which threatens to be lost, for our own circles, and thereby for the fatherland.

Hence the wish, so frequently expressed, that some volume might be written, suitable at the beginnings of new homes to be placed in the hands of those newly married.

Even church authorities felt the need of this at the solemnities of weddings.

As a sample I wrote and gathered the meditations, which are contained in this volume.

The wondrous Creator of the Family command His blessing upon it, that reading and rereading in many a home might sanctify domestic life, heighten the tone of life, and make you sit down in your house, ever richer and happier in the treasure, which in that glorious fellowship God gave you.

KUYPER

Amsterdam, July 1, 1899

HOWEVER *one may read the "signs of the times" with respect to home-life among us, it is still the exception, where human greatness, in its best sense, does not trace its beginnings to the home of the opening years of life. To the reported saying of the Jewish Rabbi: "God could not be everywhere, and therefore He made mothers," may properly be added, that for a similar reason God made fathers. For with the fathers and the mothers rests the future of the world.*

In the hope and with the prayer that the object which the Author had in view when he wrote these "Meditations" on Home-life may reach a broader realization, by their appearance in an English dress, this English version is offered to the actual and prospective fathers and mothers of this and other lands, by the

TRANSLATOR

Walpole, Mass., April 2, 1929

Contents

WHEN THOU SITTEST IN THINE HOUSE

I

In the Beginning

THE NEW HOUSEHOLD

ALREADY in the first word, with which Holy Scripture begins, there is a far deeper significance than the superficial reader thinks. "In the beginning," narrates not merely, that first the world was *not*, but only afterward *came* into being, because God created it, but it also implies, that God *has made a beginning*, and thereby has appointed in all His creation the distinction between the beginning of a matter and its *further course.*

This distinction is familiar to us and we well understand, that one's birth is different from his further life, and likewise that one's *conversion* is something else than his later life of *faith and sanctification.* To us this distinction between the beginning and the further course of a matter is as clear as day in all our ways. Yet this deeply penetrating and all our life dominating distinction is not come of itself, but has been appointed of God, and therefore there is so much more in it, than we commonly think.

For this patent fact, that all things on earth have not merely their career but also their beginning, is important in this way, that the wise of the world have long tried to demonstrate, that the world has had *no* beginning. Yea, it is of such great importance, that to the man of deeper insight, all the difference between the wisdom of the world and Holy Scripture is, that Holy Scripture always points again to that beginning, puts

all the emphasis upon that beginning, and from that beginning derives every further progress, while on the other hand the wisdom of the world is ever bent upon obliterating that beginning, to bring it to naught and to deny it, in order to proclaim the *lie,* that the world has *always* been and is as *eternal* as God.

When you take a grain of corn in your hand, there is in that small grain the capacity, to develop itself into a blade and to produce the ear of corn. But so long as you hold that grain of seed in your hand, nothing comes of it. Only when that seed is dropped into the furrowed earth and is buried, the working begins. So by casting that seed into the earth you yourself appoint the *beginning* of its development. If you do not do this, but leave it lying on your table, there is no *beginning*. This only comes when you do something to that seed, which happens only once, and therewith is ended. But if the beginning is once made, the further course follows of itself.

Jesus Himself has outlined this so strikingly in the parable of St. Mark 4,26, when He spoke of that man, "who first cast seed into the earth"; and afterward "slept and rose night and day, the whiles the seed sprang up and grew, he himself not knowing how."

Here too that selfsame deepgoing distinction is sharply and clearly indicated. The beginning is that that man "casts the seed into the earth"; and the further course follows of itself, without the man knowing how.

WHAT is true of all the world, and in all nature, is also true in our human life.

We look forward with concern to many things, but experience teaches that all goes well, when once the beginning is made.

The first step, says the proverb, costs, but the further steps follow of themselves.

He who has to make up a document, or write an important letter, feels how difficult it is to make a beginning, but also how much easier it succeeds, after he has begun.

He who is not accustomed to speak, and must appear in public, feels his heart beat when he must begin, but after he is once started, he comes to himself, and all feeling of apprehension leaves him.

When ten together must do something, the question always is, who shall be the first to put his hand to it, and when he is but begun, following and coming after on the part of the others is so much easier.

So we feel and observe time and again, how much more there is to the beginning of a matter, than to its further course.

The beginning is of so much greater importance, demands so much more exertion, asks of us so much more. And is not this the case, because that single beginning properly contains the propelling power for all the further course?

He who builds an house must first lay the foundation, on which further building can proceed, and knows that order and solidity of foundation guarantees the entire further construction.

So is all beginning the laying of foundation, on which further building can proceed; and for this reason all beginning is so difficult.

He who is godly, senses therefore so deeply, how much hangs on it, whether he makes that beginning *with* or *without* God. Hence the solemn word of consecration, that lies in the soul or on the lips of God's child, at the moment of every beginning: "*Our beginning* (help) is in the Name of the Lord, Who made heaven and earth" (Ps. 124, 8).

God appointed the beginning of all beginning, when "in the *beginning*" He made heaven and earth. And so he who is godly seeks for every beginning he has to make, his power and strength in Him, Who became the origin of all beginnings, when He created heaven and earth.

This implies not merely, that all power is with God, but also that from God is all beginning, and that God's child will make no beginning of anything without God.

It can not be sufficiently deplored, that so frequently most important beginnings are made so thoughtlessly and without God.

This is especially noticeable at the beginning of a *household.*

Two people fall in love with each other, and propose to marry; and after they are married, to begin a household.

One may say, that few things can be begun of so preponderant and so all dominating an importance. Founding a household is instituting a family; laying the foundation for common living together until death; the creation if you will of a small domestic circle in life of one's own, of which everything is to be expected, and

by which the future of man and wife, and presently of children and children's children is governed.

The importance of this matter is so commonly realized, that it is made the occasion of feasting, for which long preparations are made, and large sums of money expended, such as no one thinks of doing at other times. And we grant, that he who lives a consecrated and godly life, will not make so important a beginning without God.

As a rule the happy couple present themselves in the midst of the congregation, to invoke the prayers of all and to hear the blessing of the Lord pronounced upon their marriage. They who are married without this, can be counted.

But when you ask, whether in such days, or at such moments, it is sensed, felt and realized, what it means, to make such an extremely important, all one's future dominating beginning, we put an interrogation mark, upon which all too frequently follows a disappointing answer.

On such days one is so busy. There is so much diversion and distraction. The urge of enjoyment is so strong. And when in the sanctuary they kneel side by side and plight each other their troth, alas, how few they are, who at that moment did anything else, than take part in a solemnity, of which they thought it so wonderful to be the central figures.

Alas, of how many it must be deplored, that they *let* themselves be married more for the sake of others and after the rules of tradition, than that they themselves made a *beginning*, the beginning of a new life, of an altogether new future.

This unpremeditated acting, such doing in which the deeper consciousness has no voice, the heart no part and God no recognition, is bound to bring its own pitiful consequences.

The beginning is there, the new life begins, and to this too applies the rule, that it will be, as the pace was set.

It is of exceeding importance, therefore, that husband and wife, already on the first day of their living together, give themselves account of their new future, which they face, and therefore not let themselves thoughtlessly be carried along, but so to appoint things, that a happy life together, consecrated to God, can grow out of it.

For from that first beginning, that is formed on the day of marriage, flow all sorts of other beginnings. A beginning is made with the household; a beginning of the life of the husband with respect to his wife; a beginning of the life of the wife with respect to her husband; a beginning of their living together with respect to their several relatives; a beginning with the way in which together they shall serve God; together will care for the poor; together will order their day's work; together will act on occasion of difference of insight; together direct their finance; together take measure with respect to their servants; together regulate the style of their life.

Much of this begins on the very first day; while in the days that come after, ever and again they face new choices, new crises, the adoption of new habits and usages, which, once begun, presently become silent law and order.

And can it be acceptable to God, when all this is

left to chance, when all this is done without thought, when half playfully and sportively the household and the domestic life are left to make of themselves, what they will, rather than that consciously, as result of counsel and forethought, everything is regulated according to God's Word and according to the standard of His Holy Gospel?

But this is what happens, when no heed is taken of the difference between the beginning of a matter and its further course.

For though blessing is invoked, how can that blessing come, when such important moments and days are spent, not as by two human beings, who take thought and accept God's Word as rule, but as by two birds, that together build their nest.

Seek the blessing, it is well, but seek it from Him Who Himself has appointed a beginning to all things, when He made heaven and earth, and for this reason called you, as created after His Image, to the sacred task, of appointing, in a human way, a beginning in your life, to form it, and to do it with all the seriousness, which so holy a matter demands.

Who will be to blame, when presently the consequences of the unmeditated and playful beginning bring their bitter regrets? When there is confusion instead of order. Waste instead of stewardship. Anger and ennui where there might be happiness and domestic joy. And where in this way, far from building you up, edifying, comforting and sanctifying you, the home-life spoils your character, inflames your passion, and quickly ruins your heart.

In case of conversion at a later day, much of what was spoiled can be righted; but is it not far more joyous and beautiful, from the beginning to have chosen the right path?

And would not father and mother take a nobler stand and go out more free before God, if, when their children are married, they would provide not merely clothing and furniture, but would also urge upon them the one importance, of making the beginning of their marriage in the name of the Lord, i.e., by the appointment of all things according to the closely thought-out demand of His holy Word?

II

When Thou Sittest in Thine House

HOME-LIFE

THE "house" is no invention of man, but a creation of God in our behalf.

The question, whether, had Paradise remained, we would have had houses, need not trouble us. It is enough, to call to mind, that our Savior speaks of a *Father-house* in the heavens; of one mighty, all-embracing Father-house; the "Father-house with its many mansions."

In Israel our Lord Himself dwelt in an house on Zion, the house of the God of Jacob; and as now Zion's temple lies in ruins, believers are built as living stones into a spiritual house which is an habitation of God.

Yea, Scripture goes yet further, and does not hesitate to call God Himself an house, even as He is called a fortress and a high tower, as the Psalmist prays in Ps. 31, 2: "Be Thou, O God, a strong *house* unto me, for me to dwell in" (Dutch version).

He who is familiar with the Word knows, how high, throughout Scripture, *the house* and life in the house, are held in honor.

Even in Scripture you can observe, how the honor of the house is allied to the honor of God, and how "the curse of the Lord comes into the house" (Prov. 3,33), when the soul wanders off in strange paths and abandons her God.

But this contrast is still more strongly evident, when you look out upon the world without God, and hear, how in that world that has gone astray the foundation of the home is undermined, till finally it must be ruined.

This is not new, for already centuries before Christ Greek philosophers have elaborated ideas, that attack the very existence of home and family.

In this respect also the bold language of our times is not new.

Then as now it was told abroad, that marriage is an unnatural tie, and only free love responds to the ideal. Then as now plans were rife, to take new-born infants away from father and mother, and bring them up in large state houses for children and large boarding schools. Yea, even the home meals were to be sacrificed, and all people together were to sit at long tables in great halls.

This is the spirit from below, which stands over against the Spirit of the Father-house.

And to this extent you can say, that the home, and family-life in the home, is a symbol of salvation, and that the underestimation and presently the abolishing of the home is the sure sign of the working of demoniac powers.

THE "house" stands to this extent even over against "the world."

Just as Moses makes the contrast: "When thou sittest in thine house" or "*when thou walkest by the way*" (Deut. 6, 7).

Going out or staying home, are even now the words which imply two proper spheres of human life. And he who knows the Scripture, knows very well that it does not confine us to our house, but rather calls us out of our house, that in the world also we may serve our God. But this makes it no less a fact, that a good many more souls are lost in the world than in the house, that the Holy Spirit is considerably more grieved in the world than in the house, and that the danger of moral poisoning and of getting away from God menaces far stronger in the streets, than when you sit in your house.

So is the house a haven of refuge, a tent of salvation, in which you withdraw from before the evil storm of the world, and in this sense too it may be said, that the house brings you nearer to God, and that almost all going out from your house menaces to estrange you from your God.

You know the man and his character by it, for one dwells and literally lives in the world, while the other dwells and lives in his house. Both are on the street at times and at other times sit in their house, but with this difference, that the man of the world lives outside and merely sleeps in his house, while the other truly goes out, but presently to come back to his house, as to the center of his life.

EVEN between people and people you observe this difference.

When you come to Italy and other southern European countries, you find that every one lives in the street. The houses are less attractive and are not planned, to spend the day in them. But there are everywhere large halls, where, when work is done, every one repairs. Mostly even one's midday meal is taken out of doors, and on a summer's day you can certainly see half of the population sitting in the squares.

In countries where the Christian Gospel in its soberer form exercised power this was altogether different.

In Scotland and in the Netherlands, home-life is almost the all-in-all, and life in the street and by the way has only taken form in this last half century.

In villages and small towns it is not so far yet, but in great cities the custom has more and more gained ground, that he who can afford it, eats and drinks away from home and spends the evening in all sorts of public places, preferably with wife and children.

"Going out" that magic word for those who had long to stay at home, is becoming more and more the urge, we would almost say, the passion that rules life, not only with men, but equally with women.

He who still "sits in his house" a good deal of the time, is scorned as a "house-sparrow," and already there are many families, where, when the weather permits, both afternoons and evenings almost no one can be found at home.

Every one is out.

FROM another angle you find something of this even in very Christian homes.

One has friends, dear brothers and sisters, Christian associates, and the temptation is: to spend time in their company, to the neglect of home and dear ones.

Already in the church of Christ in Paul's day this was observable.

At Corinth believers would leave their houses, that they might come together with their friends in a large hall, and there have a common meal, a kind of love feast. Each brought his own food and drink, and so they were not in their houses, but in the hall of feasting.

But Paul would have none of it, and he asks: "Have ye not houses to eat and to drink in?" (I Cor. 11, 22).

And when later he observed, that certain believers devoted themselves to the things of the Kingdom in such a way that they neglected their homes and their families, he did not hesitate, to witness against this, by his sharp saying: "He who does not provide for his own, is *worse than an infidel*" (I Tim. 5, 8).

No, faith in Christ Jesus should not loosen the ordinances of God respecting life, but sanctify and draw them closer.

Not by letting home-life down in appreciation, but by exalting and consecrating the same, one opens for himself the way to the Father-house that is with God.

Our "house" is so much smaller than the "world." It is as an oasis in the wilderness of earthly barrenness, as an island in the world-sea.

At home we do not lose ourselves as we do outside. There we are more master of ourselves. There we *are* more ourselves. And the small dimension of the house is more proportionate to the small dimension of our small personality.

In the house it is quieter, more restful and calm.

The wind of the day does not blow there so strongly and the noise of life has no entrance there.

Therefore you hear at home, what you do not hear in the street, and at home you can overhear far better the voice of your conscience, the anthems of God's angels, the voice of your God, that calls to you.

At home you are used to your surroundings, hence by what there you see and observe, you are not so diverted, not so distracted, not carried so much outside of yourself.

On the street others in a sense direct your life for you, but at home you direct your life yourself.

At home there are fixed customs and usages, that have been practiced by your relatives, by your generation, in your own family, and this fixed manner of life offers you a support, suits your nature and inclinations, is in harmony with your entire inner existence, and thereby holds you in paths of holier sense.

At home there is more *truth.* In the street, in the open, and with the great public almost everything is camouflaged and dissembling. Always a smile about the lips. Always the urge after interesting conversation. But at home the mask is laid aside, and you know the man as he is.

In the street is cool politeness, as the head is uncovered before one another and mutual bows are exchanged, but at home is the habitation of love, the glow of affection.

Above all, when you go on the street, everything tends to break up fellowship of soul with your God; while in your home you pray, at home God's Word lies open before you, at home with your own you can sing the praises of your God.

That God's people might be wise and not fall into the snares of evil.

When so much coöperates, to undermine the power and the blessing of home, in our circles the foundations of the home-life must be strengthened.

III

No Vain Repetition of Words

FAMILY PRAYER

WE read in S. Matthew 6, 7: And when ye pray, use not vain repetitions, as the heathen do: for they think that they shall be heard for their much speaking.

Does Jesus mean by this that every prayer must be *brief*, and that a somewhat *longer* prayer already by itself is judged on account of its length?

Certainly *not.*

For in St. John 17, the Savior Himself has set a pace in sending upward an extensive prayer; moreover, the Evangelists tell how sometimes for hours together Jesus continued in prayer. Also in the Old Testament Solomon's prayer for instance at the consecration of the Temple can by no means be called short.

And yet by His warning against the "vain repetition of words" Jesus certainly means to say, that too great length injures prayer. For He adds the elucidation, that the heathen "think they shall be heard for their much speaking"; and the prayer which He himself puts in the lips of His disciples is one of not three minutes.

Yet it is not difficult to straighten out this seeming contradiction, provided you but put the emphasis upon this "vain repetition of words," which is presently followed by "their much speaking" (St. Matt. 6, 7).

If you observe this, you will see that Jesus has nothing to say about the duration of your prayer, nor about the length of it, but that He objects exclusively, and very definitely, to the *verbosity* of your supplications; at least in so far as those words are nothing but "vain repetitions," or as we would say a concatenation of hollow sounds.

This evil crept in with all heathen forms of worship. They kept up prayer, but they had lost God; and so their prayer was bound to be devoid of that earnest character of outpouring of soul and of real supplication.

Consequently their prayer became formal; a duty which they performed. He who was most proficient in this counted for most pious; hence that muttering of endless prayers, every time repeated again, and this of course had nothing in common with real prayer, while with them it passed as such.

From the Heathen world this *formal* service of prayer had gradually crept in.

And against this Jesus warns.

Ye, children of Abraham, do not follow the Heathen in this. Keep yourselves from desecrating the holiest that is given us on earth. No muttering of vain sounds. Let your prayer be real *prayer.*

AND yet this warning of Jesus has failed of the mark; and formal, verbose and long drawn out prayer has passed from Israel and from the Heathen world over into the Church of the New Covenant.

In the churches of the Reformation this is not as bad as in the churches of Rome; but yet with us also this evil undeniably cankers on; be it in different form.

The Church of Rome uses few *long* prayers. Her

prayers are mostly short and sometimes even very short. And in this we might learn of Rome.

But Rome's fault is, that she lets the same prayers be prayed too much and too often one after the other. One knows the paternoster. A string of beads with a crucifix attached. And by these beads one counts how many paternosters, Ave Maria's, and angelic hails, etc., have been prayed.

However well intentioned this might be, it is bound to assist mechanicalness, and so it does. One begins seriously and with good purpose. But soon the thought of prayer is lost. The mouth mutters, but the eye wanders. And long before the task is ended, the latest trace of real prayer is utterly gone. Something that in Romish countries is even seen in the priests, who, seated in all sorts of means of conveyance, aside from their other religious literature, also say their prayers; and thereby noticeably make the impression that the spirit indeed is willing, but the flesh weak.

This gives rise to a false religious sense, as though it merely implies the act of having prayed, and not the outpouring of soul before God.

And so it is again *words*. A repetition of *words*. A verbosity which is vain.

YET well as it may be, to have our eye clearly open to this shadow side of *Rome's* practice of prayer, it would be self-righteous, if we were to imagine that Jesus' warning against vain repetition of words had nothing to say to us Christians of the Reformation.

The contrary is true.

Our practice of prayer suffers pitifully from heterodoxy and in many ways is tainted with sin.

We, of the Reformation, aimed *high.* Even too high. And this in a twofold way. First that we almost always use *free* prayers, and few written prayers. And again that the demand is put not only to the Minister of the Word, but also to every Elder, to every Deacon, and to every father in his family, to offer, what is called *prayer aloud.*

This is aimed high, because all leading in prayer is high art, and one which brings great temptation with it.

To pray aloud is something self-contradictory. To pray is to deepen oneself in fellowship with the Eternal Being; and to pray aloud is to practice fellowship with people around us. And so it comes to pass, that one truly prays earnestly and zealously, but forgets those who are around him, and so makes them to be listeners to *his* prayer, rather than that he prays with them and for them. While on the other hand the leader in prayer thinks so much about the people for whom and with whom he prays, that he forgets to think of God, and so prays not at all. In which latter case the great temptation arises, that he who leads others in prayer becomes ambitious to make "nice prayers," and so is more anxious how he may please his fellow worshipers by his prayer, than how his prayer may be acceptable *unto God.*

This temptation is for, oh, so many an unblessed fountain of all sorts of sanctimonious and pharisaic show.

How often you see that when such people pray for themselves alone, they are so quickly done. It then lasts but for a moment. But when there are others present, or when they lead them in prayer, it seems as though their prayer has no end. Everything must be brought into it. The same things must be repeated and repeated under other forms. It all carries the impression, even upon those with whom they pray, that they but want to show, how long and earnestly they can pray.

This needs by no means to be always sinful intent. There are those who in ordinary conversation are always dreadfully prolix. There are those who, especially in prayer, find it difficult to come to an end. There are those with whom, especially in prayer, through lack of self-control, tediousness has become a second nature.

But with due respect for all this, there is always this sin in it, that they ask too much, what *people* will say about it, and too little, whether *God* will take heed of their supplication.

"To be heard of men" makes them lose their reward with God.

An evil, to which sometimes some Ministers of the Word have so habituated themselves, that it cleaves unto them till their death.

If you would be on your guard against this, there is but one efficient means, and that is that you *exercise* yourself in prayer.

One thinks, that a child can pray. And so he can. But a child prays as a child, because he thinks and speaks as a child. But when you have become a man, you should put away childish things, and learn to pray as *a man.*

And this is a glorious, but also a very difficult art, which is not acquired by praying aloud too soon before others, but upon one's knees before God.

Many would find it impossible, like Jesus, to spend hours together in prayer.

One has so little to say in his prayer, simply because all day long he has thought so little of God. Because even in prayer one has so little fellowship and communion with the Eternal. And also because one feels so little his own deep need and lets the love of fellowship operate so faintly in behalf of others.

Many make even no transition.

They fall on their knees. They pray. They are done. And immediately life resumes its ordinary course.

And that should not be. There must be a transition. One must first inlive in the glory of the sight of God's majesty, that by the indrinking of that glory the flower-bud of the soul may open.

And only he who has so *learned* to pray by himself in private, and continuously persisted in this practice, till at length he entered into it, will be able later on, so to pray aloud, that it remains real prayer with him.

But to pray in public requires still something else.

Namely, that in the fellowship of those who pray with you, you lose yourself; that you carry their need on your heart; in a priestly way enter into their life; and as having become their interpreter with God, from the heart and soul of all, for them and with them, you call upon the Eternal.

IV

It Had Been Evening and Morning

THE DAY

WITH us evening is part of the day, while in the East, as soon as evening comes the day is done.

You see this with the Jews in our midst, who do not begin their Sabbath on Saturday morning, but on Friday evening. As soon as the sun is set it is Sabbath.

While we say: "Every morning and every evening" the Scripture says: "Every evening and every morning." and so runs the narrative of creation. First: it had been evening, and after that: it had been morning, the first day (Gen. 1, 5, Dutch version).

About this difference there need be no dispute. It is because we do not count the night. Morning and evening makes for us a long day of sixteen hours, and then come eight hours of the night, of which we make no count. In the East, on the other hand, count is kept with the night and so must begin with the evening.

The Eastern language is therefore more mysterious.

When there is no sun, with us there is no count. Only when the sun rises, there is life, and till the sun sets, it goes on. And what lies in between remains uncertain.

But in the East come first the evening and the night, as those hidden times, in which God works, refreshes us in sleep, and prepares us for the life of day. And only then comes morning, when this Divinely prepared life, this Divinely wrought strength comes out, spreads its glow and glistens.

But whatever order we follow, it always is, with Westerling and Easterling, that our lifetime is no leak that tick, tack, restlessly drips on; but that the course of time is *divided,* that time is *broken,* that there is a *wave-beat,* which continuously goes up and down, and that by a wise appointment of God the whole earth, and our life in this world has obtained two sides, two forms, two ways of existence, life by *day* and life by *night.*

Hereby to your soul's perception everything there is to you is every time ended, and then begins again anew.

This makes all of life surveyable.

It does not stretch itself out before you as an endless crudeness, but has lines, boundaries and mile-posts. You can calculate it backward and forward. It goes so far, then it goes under, afterward again to begin anew. The day, and then the night, and after that again the new morning, when life is once more granted you, renewed, and once again begun.

A slowly sounding clock-stroke not from the tower, and not from your mantelpiece, but which rings out toward you from all of nature and finds an echo in your own soul's perception.

Fatigue and weariness at eventide. And at waking again the feeling of strength and freshness, wherewith you meet the new day.

By itself this is nothing but a phase of your natural life. But is it therefore without spiritual meaning?

That going up and down of the stream of light and life was already there in the creation, when God brought it forth, and no human eye was yet able to close and open itself to the light. Then it had been evening and it had been morning, the first day!

There is a reckoning in that going up and down, and as soon as that reckoning teller enters into your life, he puts an ever and again recurring question to you.

Again a day is done, and what is the portion of your life's task, that this day you have brought to a finish? Again a night is passed, in which God once more has filled the empty quiver; what shall be the task, to which you will devote the strength received by grace?

A life without division would be endlessly to postpone everything and never to accomplish anything.

But as time is divided, not only into years, into months and into weeks, but also into days, and that day is divided into an evening and a morning, God the Lord urges and stimulates you, to think of your life, to reflect upon it. Why do I live? Why do I exist? God does not give me my life, my time, my day, my morning and my evening for naught.

During the long hours of night He performs on you the wondrous work of renewing your strength, of refreshing your head, of quieting your heart into peace, and of relieving you of care and anxiety.

In the night He enriches you. Not merely on your land, where He makes the grain to ripen, but also in your own person, in your blood, in your nerves, into which He pours out new strength. And so in your life of thinking and willing, in your inner existence of soul, in your life of grace, He, with Whom there is no variableness, neither shadow of turning, also by night, when His hiddenness is over your tent, continues His work *on* you and *in* you.

And now you regain consciousness. You awake. You feel strong again. You are not merely rested, but you are also newly equipped. What now? What shall be the fruit of that long day? And what is the calling, the task, to which you set yourself?

So, when it is again morning, the Lord asks of you, and when presently the day is done, that silent inquisitor returns again, and examines you, and compels you to look back upon the path that you have traveled. Not now: "What *will* you do?"—but: "What *did* you do?" Is the task, to which God called you, *done?*"

AND with what result?

Is it not, that, oh, so many must complain, that not half of the day has been put to use, and that the other half has been squandered in idle talk and in trifles? That certain things were done, for which one was responsible, but more from habit, or because they happened to come along, but without leaving a trace, that you understood anything of life, or knew how to put your time to usury, or realized what it is, so to number one's days, as to apply one's heart unto wisdom.

Alas, so many, when they die, have almost lived for naught. Of what it is, to accomplish something in life, they have never known the secret. And when at last their thread of life is spun, they remind you of a palm tree in the desert, whose fruit was of no use, because there was no one who has gathered it.

Their life was there, the powers were there, but

they were not employed, their life was not applied. It had all been dissipated and wasted.

This is no less than a life's sin. A life that has been sinned away. For in sin everything sinks away that you do not direct to the mark, for which God gave it.

And especially God's children might well be on their guard.

The Italian speaks of his *dolce far niente,* i.e., of blessed idleness; but under cooler heavens, where work is so much easier, you need no lantern to look for lovers of that "blessed idleness."

Everything that requires effort and exertion is avoided. If one *must,* one works, but oh, the relief when it is done, and "blessed idleness" can again be begun.

Do not say, that he who does manual labor for his living, slaves from morning till night; for let a man, who at first had to work hard, become more affluent, and at once he is done with work.

Not work for the sake of *a living,* but work for the sake of *God's will* is here in question. Of the perception, that God calls you to something, puts a task upon you, wants something of you. Of your *Divine* calling, as our fathers named it.

Ask yourself, how few there are, who in their morning- and evening-prayer so interpret their life, keep count of it, and pass constant criticism upon it.

Moreover, that one particular work is not all the labor yet, to which God called you.

He gave you not merely muscles and muscular strength to dig or handle a hammer, but He also gave you other powers. Or is your *head* empty, is your *heart* a shaken-out bag?

And did God give you those powers of head and heart for naught, without a purpose, to be neglected, not to be disciplined, and so to leave the field of your inner life lie fallow before His face?

Does not this indicate a calling? Does not this speak of a life's task? And is there not all too frequently bitter complaint about lack of thought, about heartlessness and sometimes utter want of inner activity, because that labor of head and heart is not put upon you as a duty and also gets no *wage?*

Oh, when you walk about in a churchyard, and consider how many dead are there at rest, who came and went, without having developed a thought-life in their head, a loving and devoted life in their heart, to what ignoring and destroying of divine power do not these graves bear witness.

Yet God had prepared so wondrously the head for them and the heart.

And it went all for naught.

Power that is wasted, something of divine mightiness in a child of man, but not by him considered.

So, that God received no honor from it.

It had been evening and it had been morning, so it echoes, in still deeper sense, continuously also in your life of grace, if at least you have been privileged to enjoy the lovely reflection of the Sun of righteousness.

A work in divine strength. Even the noblest power of grace. Exertion of strength on the part of the Holy Ghost who is in you, to make you as God's child to grow and wax strong and bear fruit.

This your life of grace is also a matter of time. In

the morning you wake up with it, and in the evening you dispose yourself to rest with that grace-life in your heart.

Thus here, too, the question is, whether you understand what your calling is, whether you see the course, which you have to run, whether the: *Lord, what wilt Thou have me to do?* ever and again resounds in your soul, and whether you take heed to yourself, to be aware of real advance, whether you gain in holier mindedness, and observe, that you live not for naught, but that from your grace-life something proceeds, something shines out, something that can refresh the brethren, and be an honor to God's name.

Even with this question we are not content.

When after an absence of three or more years you meet again an old acquaintance, you sometimes receive the comfortless impression that he is still precisely what he was before. No step has he advanced, if only he has not retrogressed, and gone backward in grace.

And therefore this thoughtless gliding along from day to day must have an end.

Every time it is evening and becomes morning again, the account must be straightened out before God on one's knees.

What have I lived for, what shall I live for, live also as child of my Father in heaven?

So only on one's knees can it become seriousness, on one's knees the battle can be fought, and the fruit of that struggle shall be peace, because it rouses you out of your spiritual indolence.

V

The Night Also Is Thine

THE NIGHT

As in reading a book you skip a part that does not interest you, so there are those who between the days of their life simply skip *the nights.*

So a day does not have twenty-four, but sixteen or seventeen hours. They keep count of time from their rising in the morning until they pillow their head by night; but the night, that lies in between, does not count. This is especially so with persons in good health, who sleep at once when they touch the pillow, and, though they may have dreamed, know nothing of it. To such as they the night is simply a something that goes out of their life. When they go to sleep they are lost in unconsciousness, and when the sun is above the horizon again, they raise their head above the waters of self-forgetfulness. This is yet more strongly the case with little children, who as roses have slept all night long, and at awakening have no faint perception of the length or duration of the time that they slept.

The sick, *they* know about it. And no less they of weary head, people whose nerves are overstrung, or whose head is crowded with carping cares. When one struggles to get to sleep, and cannot succeed, or if lost for a moment in unconsciousness, at once wakes up again with anxious fear. Then especially a long winter's night seems almost endless, and the first ray of light that enters in by the window brings a feeling of deliverance.

For those, too, who watch with the sick, such a night can creep along with oppressive slowness. But by far most people, especially they who labor with their hands, know nothing of this. In the evening they are tired. They long with their garment to drop the cares of life from their shoulders. And though they live through the night, into what the night is, they do not enter. But with men of deep spirituality, like a David and Asaph, it is altogether different.

The night, too, is a subject of deep thought, of the night count is kept, and the honor of the night is brought to our faithful God and Father.

"I laid me down and slept, and rose again: for the Lord sustained me" (Ps. 3, 5).

As Asaph exclaimed: "The day is thine, the night also is thine, O my God" (Ps. 74, 16).

Do you not perceive the higher seriousness of life in this?

The night of sleep is usually a *third part* of your life's day. With retiring and rising again, each day *eight* of the twenty-four hours. He who may reach the age of seventy-five years, loses by sleep twenty-five full years, counting day and night together.

And would you be unmindful of that third part of your life, take no heed of it, have no eye for it, and act as though you had no knowledge of it?

"Teach us to number *our days,*" prays the Psalmist, "that we may apply our hearts unto wisdom" (90), and the "Teach us also to number our nights," is included in it.

Also at night, when you lie down in unconsciousness, you are there, you exist after soul and body, and something takes place in you, and something with you. When you rise, you are not just as you were, when you laid down, but altogether different, refreshed in thought and refreshed in strength.

The night is even of so much importance, that it is none too strongly put, when we say, that by day you live on the capital, which you lay up by night. In other words: that *impoverished* as to strength you go to bed, and in the morning *rich* in power you go into life again.

Let there be a night when sleeplessness tormented you, or one, which in your folly, as Job 17, 12 has it: "You had changed into day," and in your inability to apply yourself to work and in the depressed condition of your nerves, you realize what it is, for a single night to have missed the supply of strength from the Fountain of Life.

And with this for the most part we only think of our physical strength. Of the healing of our tired muscles by rest. Of the healthy tension of our weakened nerves by that surcease for hours together of all excitement. Of the cooling of our blood. Of the relaxation of our whole body by lying down, the freedom from the weight of our garments, and the gentle equable warming of the skin and the opening of the pores.

But apart from that renewal of physical strength, there is still something more in sleep. Sleep also affects your *spiritual* existence.

Even in every way.

Sleep affects your thought, and many a one experiences the truth of the French proverb: *La nuit porte conseil,* i.e., in the night we form our best plans. It is folly, of course, when a schoolboy puts his book under his pillow, but it is not folly, that a lesson learned at night, and is only half committed, in the quietness of night sinks into us more deeply, and thereby is more firmly imprinted in the memory. And apart from this, as every one knows, when in the evening the head refused to work, and was utterly disabled, and the spring of thought ceased to flow, in the morning that same fountain flows fresh and abundant again and makes thoughts stream toward us.

But even to this the inworking of sleep upon our spiritual existence does not limit itself.

"In the night seasons," the Psalmist sings, "*my reins also instruct me*" (16, 7). And from the remembrance of many a dream every one knows, how at night, while we sleep and the body rests, great activities can be going on in our inward man.

Sometimes it seems as though, at midnight, some one enters into our soul, to put in order there again, what by day was spoiled, to refill the lamp with oil, and inwardly to prepare us for the life-task of the following day.

AND truly this is no self-deception, it is reality.

Every evening when you go to sleep, you let yourself go, and there is some One else who takes you up in the arms of His compassion, and that some One else is the Lord your God.

It is He alone, Who at the entrance of night takes you from yourself, during the long hours of night to protect and to refresh you, and in the morning renewed again to return you to yourself.

But in the night He has possession of you; it is He Who carries and keeps you; Who takes you in hand after body and after soul to mold you. And so all the night long your God is busy with you, while you are not in the least aware of it.

By day you are also in His hand, but by night in a different way and far more effectively, for in the night God takes you away from yourself, independently of yourself to fashion and to purify you, to equip you with new capital of physical and spiritual strength, and after that to bring you back again to conscious life.

The world calls this Nature, and undergoes it without giving itself an account of it, as the bear ensconces himself in his winter-sleep.

But to him who honors and fears God, there opens in that life of night more and more a world of rich meaning. For him that life by night obtains the significance of an extremely important chapter of history. And more yet than by day it is by night that God's child learns to observe the work, which God works on his body and to his soul.

A third part of our life, i.e., every night, like the small boat from the water is pulled on land, so are we taken by God out of the stream of life. In the night He repairs the suffered injuries. And when in the morning the cock crows, that same God brings us without damage back again into the waterway of life.

Now you can say: "If this is so, it all goes on outside of myself, and can imply no instruction for my soul," but this is not so.

All Scripture and experience of the saints teaches differently.

Not merely does the psalmist say, that at night his reins instruct him, but time and again the Scripture brings you the active attestation of he man who meditates in the law of the Lord *day and night* (Ps. 1, 2), or the declaration: "The Lord will command his loving-kindness in the daytime, and in the *night His song shall be with me*" (Ps. 42, 8).

For sleep is indeed sleep, and when one is once "gone" in sleep, one does no more conscious thinking; but it makes a difference how, and with what deliberations and thoughts one goes to sleep, and what sensations rise in us at waking.

And the more godly among the children of God have ever striven, before retiring at night, to loosen their thoughts from the world, by reading of the Word and by prayer to connect their thoughts to the things of the eternal Kingdom, and in lying down, before they slept, to seek fellowship with the Eternal Being.

So going to sleep is even most rich and most blessed, and is as it were a sinking away into a night, from which on this earth one might not awake. This imparts discipline to the soul. It prepares the soul. So that when at last death does come, he can not so greatly surprise you.

In this way your going to sleep is no longer a surrender of yourself to your pillow, but a conscious surrender of yourself into the hand of your God, Who for that whole night long takes you away from yourself, only at dawn of the new day to give you back to yourself again.

What is said in the Moravian evening hymn: "Let me sleeping wait on Thee. Then my sleep shall peaceful be. Holy thoughts inspire in me. Dreaming let my joy be Thee," is somewhat strained. Most rarely indeed have we fellowship with Jesus in our dream. For we know Him no more after the flesh. In the dream everything is representation, outward appearance. But this aside, this prayer breathes piety and devotion. A deep appreciation of the fact, that night also is a part of our life, that of the night honor must come to our Lord, and that night must not separate us from our God, but must bring Him closer to us.

The day is Thine, the *night also is Thine.*

That in the end is the main thing that counts.

He who can go to sleep, and all night long let himself be healed and operated upon and refreshed by his faithful God, and can rise again in the morning, without a thought of what during all those hours of night God has done in him and for him, is a Christian with a faded religion. If he does company with the Lord's people, his piety is offensively superficial.

He on the other hand who has an eye for this great work of God, which goes on through all those hours of night and is effected, will praise God and thank Him, O, most truly, for all help accorded him *by day,* but no less warmly and earnestly for the supply of strength and grace, that was accorded him *by night,* after soul and body, whereby alone success of life became possible on the new day.

More yet.

Night is the instrument in God's hand not only to strengthen our body and to pour fresh oil again into the stiffened joints of our spiritual existence, but night must also renew our *faith* and no less our *fellowship with our God.*

The sprinkling of the blood of the Lamb of God must every morning be upon you.

VI

The Winter, Which Thou Hast Made

WINTER

Of Nova Zembla Tollens sings: "Here the *Prince of Winter* has erected his throne."

Yet at heart this is ungodly and fundamentally heathen speech, as though there were a Prince of winter, who brings ice and snow and hoar-frost. A language that contrasts strongly with what in Israel a David and an Asaph sang: *Our God* gives snow like wool, *He* scattereth the hoar-frost like ashes, *He* casteth forth his ice like morsels: who can stand before *His* cold?" (147, 16, 17).

This is the language of piety.

Winter also is nothing but a wondrous creation of the almightiness of the Lord.

In cold also, which changeth the face of the earth, our God is made great.

More briefly still, with Asaph confessed in Psalm 74: *The winter also, which Thou hast made.*

Neither is winter accidental; what it brings with it is no mere play or whim. In winter also there is *formation.* One great thought expresses itself in it, which temporarily puts its fetters about all of life, and penetrates even smallest particles.

The same God, Who created Paradise without seasons, presently has broken up the one vast paradise-wealth into four seasons, and as by magic imparted unto each of them a glory of their own, as well as a shadow-side.

And in that succession of the seasons God gives you instruction, every year again the same instruction of His majesty and might, and of the turn from life to death and from death unto life again; an instruction in images as rich in meaning as compelling to action; for you yourself go on with the seasons and undergo the stimulus of the same.

IN Israel *our* winter was not known. Only from Hermon glistened the never melting snow; but for the rest cold was never so biting, and the Jordan was never so solidly floored as ice builds it upon our rivers.

And yet, Scripture brings us, children of the north, in many ways a richly varied interpretation of what winter provides.

Snow, that covers the earth, however beautiful, is an image of death, and the first that Scripture tells you of it is in the white of leprosy "*leprous, white as snow*" (Ex. 4, 6).

And yet, because from death is life, that same snow is likewise the image of purging from sin. "Wash me, and I shall be whiter than newly fallen snow" (Ps. 51,7). So in anguish of soul David prayed, and Isaiah brought us the word of Divine promise: "Though your sins be as scarlet, they shall be as *white as snow*" (1, 18).

So the snow-garment became the image of heavenly spotlessness. There are *treasure chambers,* from whence that heavenly whiteness descends. He who knows

God will for "no rock of the field leave *the snow of Lebanon*" (Jer. 18, 14). When the majesty of the Lord appears, "His garment is *white as snow*" (Dan. 7, 9). That gleaming white glistens on the angels of God when they appear at the opened grave of Jesus. Of the Savior Himself on Tabor it is said: "His raiment became shining, exceeding *white as snow*" (Mk. 9, 3). And John on Patmos saw Him once more in that *snow white raiment.*

But snow is not merely the image of death and the image of spotless heavenly purity, there is also a working in it comparable with the working of God's Word.

You know the passage in Isaiah (55, 10) that oracles of this: "For *as the snow* cometh down from heaven, and returneth not thither, but watereth the earth, and maketh it bring forth and bud, that it may give seed to the sower, and bread to the eater, so shall my word be that goeth out of my mouth."

This is what we said above, that in winter there is a formation, a creation, an action on the part of God.

Winter is not merely there, no, God Himself has formed it.

"WHO can stand before His cold?" asks the Psalmist, and the cold wherewith God can cause all life to freeze apart is terrible. At the North- and South-Pole the cold is so dreadful, at its worst, that no human breast can draw breath. And by thermometers put down on tops of highest mountains such cold has been observed, which renders all life impossible.

But what is this compared with that cold which

in the uttermost parts of His creation God has weaned of all glow and glitter?

So there is grace in the moderation wherewith God, here on earth, changes for you heat and cold. At one time He could scorch you, at another He could freeze you. That He sends you cold thus tempered, is protecting, preserving grace.

But without serious warning no winter ever goes by; there are always aged among us, or weak-lunged, or susceptible natures, who cannot stand even that tempered cold, and for whom winter is a messenger of death from God.

"If they might reach spring, there would be hope; but winter is bad," so runs the discouraging word, and every year through snow and frozen ground grave after grave must be dug, to lay away those that have succumbed before God's cold.

ENTERING so deeply into life, all unobservedly that "cold of God" changes the whole character, the whole manner of our life.

In summer we are as birds that fly about. Almost no one stays at home, every one goes out to enjoy the air and the sun. But in winter all remain indoors, to escape the inhospitable out-of-doors. This enriches the home life. At the fireside one finds again that happy quiet world, which in the busy outside world had been so largely lost.

The mood which makes one turn indoors, instead of out-of-doors, affects our personal life.

The seriousness of life impresses itself more deeply

upon the soul. There is more time for serious literature. Conversation is more restful, and thereby less superficial. Even church life in winter assumes richer proportions. There is more housework done. It even may be said that a life with continuous summer makes us spiritually poorer, while winter every time again deepens our life.

Herein also winter is a servant of God, going forth to consummate His work in us, and blessed is the heart, the home, the people, where each coming winter may realize this end.

From *without* to *within*.

And the more the cold increases round about us, the better is the soul warmed to the seriousness of life.

YET these gains of life in winter should not make you cruel and indifferent to the suffering of winter.

When the skate is clasped to the foot, and merrily young and old glide along the ice-floor, there is something refreshing in the humor wherewith our human heart defies the terrors of the cold.

What suffering winter brings, is therefore not less striking. When work grows less and presently is at a standstill. When cold limbs ask for double covering, and, to satisfy hunger the last blanket had to be taken to the pawnshop. Because of the cold, there is more food required, and yet, how many there are, with whom wages in winter are least. Oh, the woes of winter for the poor, who have nothing laid by are so bitterly hard!

"Who can stand before God's cold?", asks the Psalmist, and you may be thankful when God gives you a good house and a warm garment and comfortable covering, to be able to stand before His cold.

But bear in mind, that there are those who will succumb, unless pity comes in to help.

For He formed the winter for this end, that the suffering of the impoverished should rouse those who are warmed and fed, and that the love of God should beam forth cherishingly from the hearts of men, to shield against His cold.

So then according to the Covenant sworn to Noah, and in him to us all, this change of seasons shall not cease, until our Lord's return, and every time after heat the cold, after summer the winter shall come to you "*from the Father-hand of God.*"

Not summer from God, and winter from the Evil One, but summer *and winter* formed by Him.

Formed, to show you, how as with one turn of magic He can change the whole face of the earth and make it glisten with a beauty all its own; prelude of what it once shall be, when the old fashion of the world shall have passed away for good, and there shall be a new earth and new heavens.

Formed, to concentrate your life more upon yourself, to deepen it in you and to tune it to higher seriousness.

Formed, in all sorts of images to make you understand eternal things.

Formed to quicken pity in your soul and generously to open the hand for the brother who would succumb.

But formed also, to be to you a *memento mori,* i.e., to place before your eyes in great and mighty outlines the withering and dying of what was once flourishing and beautiful, and to say to you, that the winter of life already came or presently shall come upon you, and that from that winter-sleep there dawns no other spring, than in the eternal morning, for such as are in Christ Jesus.

VII

Thou Renewest the Face of the Earth

SPRING

SCRIPTURE does not know *Spring* by name, any more than *Autumn;* only once, at the very end, in Jude's brief epistle (12, Autumn trees, Dutch version) it is noted more in passing, than described in its dying glory.

The country accounted for this. In Palestine the transition from winter to summer, and from summer to winter took place more quickly, more as it were at once, and the almost six months' absence of rain, of itself led to placing over against one another the *rainless* half year and the half year that began and ended *with rain,* as the two great seasons of the year.

From April till October there was dew, but no rain. That was called *summer.* Before and after this fell the former and the latter rain. And that season was called *winter.*

A striking contrast, as everything else in Israel and in the revelation to Israel appeared in bold sharply outlined antithesis. Death and life. Darkness and light. Impure and pure.

So here the season of the year *without* and the season of the year *with* rain. "Thou, O God, hast made summer and winter" (Ps. 74, 17).

But though there is no separate *spring* in Israel as interlude between winter and summer, the Scripture is very well conversant with the spring-idea and the fact of spring. Israel came to this loveliness of spring with the *feast of firstfruits.* To the Covenant people the triumph psalm of Passover was one with the song of spring.

The people themselves had been quickened by Jehovah from the *sleep of death,* which once they slept in Egypt, *that was their Passover.*

So the land, flowing with milk and honey, which God gave them, passed every year into *winter-sleep.* But when the sun poured forth richer beams again, it returned to life, and that was its *spring.*

Spring not three months long, but concentrated as in one span of time, and centered in that single act of God's almightiness, of which in Psalm 104 so exultingly the Psalmist sang: "Thou sendest forth Thy spirit, they are created: and Thou renewest the face of the earth."

So the faithful in Israel lived through these transitions with their God.

They did not shut themselves in, and were not afraid of light, as though the life of nature did not concern them.

On the contrary, scarcely had the moment come of the rich renewal of life in God's creation, but from their villages and hamlets all those that were at liberty went out through dales, by the side of brooks, across the hills, to Zion's sanctuary.

And though at the Passover, the lamb that was slain, and therewith the deliverance from Egypt, that had come, and the deliverance from Satan's bands, that was to come, appeared more prominently in the foreground, yet God's goodness in the life of nature was not forgotten, and for the people and in their name, the firstfruits of the land were offered unto Jehovah.

But what they refused to do, was, that they would make no *distinction.*

They would not in the sanctuary taste the mysticism of God's presence, and presently amidst the wealth of nature forget Him.

No, they lived through that transition from season into season with their God.

It was not nature that had gone asleep and had wakened again. All that you call nature is nothing of itself and can of itself do nothing. And in nature also, and in her mighty transitions, there is nothing that God does not work.

His almightiness works therein, His omnipresence dwells therein.

He, the Lord our God, doeth all these things.

When from leafless branches spring-birds sing again, it is God Who sends them.

And when soft winds blow from the South, and what seemed dead begins to bud again, it is God Himself Who sent forth His Spirit, and as with His own hand renews the face of the earth.

As in the hour of creation the earth was first without form and void, but, as God's Spirit brooded over it, presently all life went forth, so, from a distance always, it is every time when spring returns.

First the land bare and the flowerbed unkempt.

But God sends out His Spirit.

And now what seemed withered sprouts and buds, what seemed faded colors itself, what was dull begins to glisten, and what was silent as in death begins to sing.

And when God so makes nature live again, *it is spring.*

THIS appeals to the human heart.

Most of all because winter is unnatural to you. For though winter is as one who is *beautiful* in death, it is dead, and our heart calls for life. Winter drives us out from God's free nature, in which an inner voice declares, that we are at home. Winter even attacks us as an enemy, makes suffering of cold and want, and carries every year a vast number of his vanquished ones to the pit of the grave.

Hence winter *depresses.* Limits and distresses us. And when at last his power breaks, young and old are glad to speed the parting guest.

Winter held us closed in, now doors and windows reopen, and busy hands are at work in every house to remove winter stains from floor and walls. Everything must be clean, and be made to shine and glisten. A whole house embracing cleaning.

And where winter compelled us to protect our sensitive bodies with heaver clothing of less artistic outlines, now that spring returns, even that winter garb is laid aside, and they who have the means, provide themselves with a *new outfit.*

A feeling of freedom and delight must thrill through heart and members.

It is our God Who prepares us joy again.

But this is not all.

Our inner and our outward life hang together.

Nature and grace mutually affect one the other. In the visible God puts a speech of the spiritual life.

It is God Who sends out His Spirit and renews the face of the earth, for, according to Scripture, the Holy Spirit is active in the work of creation (Gen. 1, 2), and likewise in the work of the renewal of life when spring comes (Ps. 104, 17).

It is not the Father in nature, and the Holy Spirit in the soul, but it is God Triune, Father, Son and Holy Ghost, Who in all your life, after the inward- and after the outward-side, reveals His wondrous Divine power.

So that sleep of *nature* speaks to us of a sleep in the *spiritual* world, and spring in God's creation of a waking up again of those who fell asleep, that Christ might give them Light.

There is a rise and fall in nature, from the emptiness of winter, to the horn of abundance in autumn, and so there is a rise and fall in the faith-life, from the barrenness of the desolate soul to the wealth of gladness in God's hidden walk.

Therefore Passover is placed at the opening of spring.

Thus from Easter and spring together goes out one voice of God's urgent compassion, to lift every one of you out of your condition of depression, to pour out upon your dullness the glow of fresh oil, to tune what was silent in you to a song of praise, to make the withered branches bud again, and where deathliness had covered the soul, to make the life of faith gloriously active again.

When winter is severe, every one feels that it

neither can nor will continue such for long, and everything in you prophesies that Spring is at hand.

So no one can say peace, when it is winter in his soul. Winter sleep of soul is equally unnatural and resists grace.

He sins, he hardens himself, who rests content in that winter sleep of soul.

See, the Sun of righteousness shines out gloriously again from the Throne of grace.

And therefore, awake thou that sleepest, and arise from the dead, and Christ shall give thee light (Eph. 5, 14).

EVEN to such as have never yet known the sweet and the beauty of a spiritual spring in the soul, every return of spring is a voice of their God.

Your first spiritual spring is your conversion to Jesus, your turning to the living God, when He sends out His Spirit to you also, and renews the face of your heart.

To this first conversion every soul is called, especially those who in infancy received the mark of Holy Baptism. It is dreadful to see, how many grow up in Christ's church, and reach maturity, without ever having opened the windows of their soul, that the light of the Son of God might shine in upon their inner life.

And for this conversion your time is always ready.

But in spring is a speech of God, which reproaches you with double sharpness for continuing in your barrenness and deathliness.

God lets you see with your eyes, how life *can* spring from death.

And when you hear the rustling of life, in the hardness of your heart will you resist yet longer?

THUS in that return of Spring there is an impulse to life for all men.

There goes out from Spring a new animation to life, to lift up the hands which hang down, and to strengthen the feeble knees (Heb. 12, 12); to stimulate every one to a taking hold of oneself; to make exhibition of nobler seriousness, of diligence, of greater zeal in everything that is good.

Spring tells you that seed must again be sown, that presently the full corn-stalks may rustle. And so each is his own position in life, in his calling, in the department of work appointed him of God, must harness again the weakened elasticity, reach out again toward the ideal, be impelled to mightier activity and to greater perseverance of action.

It must become Easter and Spring together, not merely round about you, and in your soul, but also in your allsided life.

A seeking anew, with new urgency of the things, that are above, and *in* those things, that are above, a taking of one's stand with rejuvenated, with renewed, and therefore with heightened, with sanctified power.

VIII

The Hasty Fruit Before Summer

SUMMER

Rightly viewed the Scripture knows but *two* seasons of year: summer and winter.

You hear this in the Divine utterance after the Flood: "Henceforth, while the earth remaineth, cold and heat, summer and winter shall not cease" (Gen. 8, 22).

So in Psalm 74, 17, in silence passing spring and autumn by: "Thou hast made *summer and winter.*"

And in the vision of Zachariah (14, 8) is said, that "living waters shall go out from Jerusalem, and that these waters shall be in *summer* and in *winter.*

Spring and autumn are transitions, they form no antitheses. There is heat or cold, there is life or death, there is light or darkness, and everything that lies in between, may differ in degree, but is no third new something.

When Jesus says: "Now learn a parable of the fig-tree, when his branch becomes tender, and putteth forth leaves, then know *that summer is nigh*" (Matt. 24, 32), and from Matt. 21, 19, you observe, how already *before Passover* the fig-tree was in leaf, it is clear, that "the nearness of summer" means what we call spring.

That this antithesis between summer and winter is altogether the outcome of the curse, and is come upon us exclusively on account of sin, is difficult to accept.

The curse certainly operates definitely in the intense cold of severe frost, and in the sultriness of *excessive* heat which makes breathing difficult.

Frost that is too severe in winter kills man, even as sunstroke at too great summer-heat, is always death by reason of the curse.

So there is ground of acceptance, that the curse has intensified the antithesis between summer and winter; but from this it does by no means follow, that this antithesis originated from the curse.

Already at the creation, before sin came in, you come upon the antithesis between day and night, between light and darkness, and it is evident that the antithesis between cold and heat, and also between summer and winter is of one piece.

Night cools off, day brings a softer atmosphere.

And so we may accept that the antithesis between summer and winter, i.e., between two periods of time during the course of the year, in which now cold predominates, and again heat prevails, belongs to the ordinance of creation.

SUMMER abounds in wealth of nature, but winter also exhibits a glory of its own, and in both of these God glorifies His majesty.

If you subtract from winter the cutting sharpness of the wind, and the stiffening of nature by reason of too great severity of cold, winter has a beauty altogether its own and an attractiveness which nothing else can supply. There are days in winter, so tempered in cold, with high, clear skies, that in beauty of kind is by nothing excelled.

To suppose that this winter beauty would forever have remained hidden, if man had not fallen, falls short of the glory of God's work.

That a result of sin has its aftermath in winter as it now is, even as in summer, which frequently loosens every restraint of human elasticity, is clear; and it also appears from John's Revelations, in which the Tree of Life blooms twelve months together and bears fruit, that in the state of glory this antithesis also, even as that of day and night, of light and darkness, falls away; but this does not take away the fact, that in this provisional dispensation, both summer and winter were made to give us a speech of God's majesty; and it is this speech, that goes out not only from winter, but also from summer, to all nations and to all parts of the earth.

THAT speech of summer is the language of brightness and ardor, of fullness of life and of super-abounding wealth.

The nights are short, and even in their brevity less dark. The day is long begun before you leave your couch, and reaches almost to the hour of retiring.

Artificial light is little needed, and fire, indispensable for the preparation of food, is put out as soon as possible.

So in summer there is far less suffering. The lot of the poor, in winter oft so bitter and so hard, in summer is far more enjoyable. Human need grows less. Food is more abundant. Even all fruit and vegetables do not pass by the dwelling of the poor. His frugal home no longer shuts him in. Windows are opened wide. In streets and byways one runs out and even sits down, to enjoy the freer life.

The misery of the sickroom is lessened with the coming of summer.

The consumptive, who fetched the summer, revives again with the feeling of recuperation. Unless an epidemic breaks out, hospitals depopulate.

All suffering of troubled humanity summer can not dispel, but summer brings moderation and amelioration of pain.

Even where fullest enjoyment of summer is not possible, the warm, softer season of year renders almost every one's lot in life more bearable.

SUMMER has also this wondrous good to its credit, that it accustoms us again to life in and with *nature.*

Compelled by necessity, life in our homes is for the most part artificial, and in many respects unnatural. Too narrowly enclosed. Too greatly crowded. Too greatly separated from God's rich creation.

But when summer is come, nature entices us again out of doors. The full impression of God's glorious creation is upon us. Nature fondles us to her heart and affects us benignly by her soft embrace.

We become as children again, who revel in what God gives us to enjoy.

And this life with nature rejuvenates physical

powers, enriches the blood, and opens the heart to purer sensations.

The motion and struggle of spirits takes a surcease during the summer months, as though we refuse to disturb the pleasure, which God grants us in the wealth of summer.

Schools are closed for many weeks. Children are at liberty. Parents and children, brothers and sisters live together again the livelong day.

Even the heavy-hearted feel moods of cheer come upon them. The end of it all is that life is lived in a happier way.

True, thunder sounds time and again from on high, and lightning darts through the clouds, as though to remind man of God, and in the midst of so great wealth not to forget Him, but even that thundershower leaves a blessing behind, and when the skies clear, and the sun breaks out, for everything that hath breath, there is fuller happiness.

But harvest is not yet. This follows in autumn days. At least the harvest of the finer fruits. So everything together bears the character of preparation for the harvest that comes later.

In the wealth of summer, the work of God which aims at fruit, goes restlessly on.

There is brightness, there is richness and splendor, there is fragrance and choice of blossom and flowers, but in all this life aims at a still higher something.

The wealth of summer is not simply for its own

sake, but finds its consummation only when presently the full harvest is brought in.

Herein lies the admonition to seriousness.

In our human life there may be much beauty, and much may be granted us to enjoy, but in that beauty and in that wealth our life must not lose itself.

The most beautiful and richest life is worthless, when in the end nothing buds but leaves.

Presently the heavenly Husbandman comes to gather fruit from us.

And woe unto him, in the hour when his life is cut off, on whose branches fruit, well-ripened fruit for the barns of heaven, is wanting.

YEA, there is more.

Though summer is only consummated in autumn harvest, yet the Scripture speaks of a summer fruit, and of a "hasty fruit before summer" (Is. 28, 4).

Such is God's ordinance in nature, that already in summer itself there is fruit ready to be gathered, and so is His ordinance with respect to you, that already in the summer of your life fruit shall not be wanting.

The spring of your life is your youth, and harvest reminds you of old age, but the summer of your life is the years of your full manly strength.

From you, therefore, it is demanded that the years of your manly strength are not merely marked by harmony of character, and enriched by the unfolding of your God-given talents, but that they shall cast off those desired summer fruits, in behalf of your environment, of yourself, but above all for the glory of God.

In the summer of your life something must ripen for the great day of harvest, when the angels shall put forth the sickle into the corn; but there must already now be fruit ripened, a summer fruit that can be picked already on earth, a fruit received from God, and therefore in deep humility laid on His altar.

And when the years run their course, and every time again summer comes after spring, that new summer always comes back to you with the old inquiry: whether at length you will become wise not merely to make a show of leaf and blossom, but also to be mindful of *the fruit of your life,* which must ripen to the glory of God.

IX

The Grass Withereth, the Flower Fadeth

AUTUMN

IN some parts of England Autumn is still called "fall." The common word used overseas for the waning part of the year is the familiar word "*autumn*," an expression derived from the French. But however widely this French word gained the field, the original word is by no means passed away, and in ordinary conversation one still uses the descriptive, significant word of "fall," precisely the same word, that is used for the fall of Adam and Eve in paradise.

Autumn is the fall, the slow insinking of the season, the time of year of the failing series. Spring climbs and goes upward, in summer to reach its highest point; autumn, on the other hand, goes down to seek its lowest point in winter.

If winter is the delineation in nature which God gives of death and of the grave, autumn shows us on the part of God the languor of disease, that pulls down and consummates itself in dying.

This delineation of God in autumn images the decline of vital forces in the visible. "As for man, his days are as grass: as a flower of the field, so he flourishes. For the wind passes over it, and it is gone; and the place thereof shall know it no more" (Ps. 103, 15).

It images the decline of the spiritual life in the soul. "He shall be like a tree, whose leaf shall not wither. The ungodly are not so, but are like the chaff which the wind driveth away" (Ps. 1, 3).

It images the decline of wellbeing and prosperity: "Ye shall be as an oak whose leaf fadeth" (Is. 1, 30).

Yea, it even images the decline that awaits all the glory of the world: "The heavens shall be rolled together as a scroll: and all their hosts shall fall down, as the leaf falleth off from the vine" (Is. 34, 4).

And finally it is the image of the judgment that cometh: "I will surely consume them, saith the Lord, there are no grapes on the vine, yea, the leaf is faded" (Jer. 8, 13).

Though thus, with the exception of Jude, verse 12, the Scripture does not mention autumn by name, because in Israel the seasons were differently divided, yet Scripture knows well the nature-image, which we call autumn, and describes it by like terms, as *the fall, falling, the falling off of the leaf.*

ACCORDING to one's age, impression differs, which spring and autumn make upon us.

When we are young, for the language, for the speech of spring we are all ear. We drink in with full draughts the fragrance of spring. We perceive how really in spring alone nature outside of us tunes in perfect accord with the speech of our own heart. Autumn, on the other hand, fills every one who is not young with sadness. The appearance of autumn is not the expression of his life. He lives through the fall as a necessity from which there is no escape, but not as a pleasure. Because spring still sings in his own heart, autumn can not accompany him in the song of his soul.

But when you are in the decline of your days, and your locks grow thin, even as the foliage of the oak, your impression is quite the opposite. Then spring still refreshes you, but more as a joy that has had its day, that comes upon you strangely, and you are in your element only when the leaves begin to turn yellow, presently to fall. Then autumn is to you the significant season of year, which agrees with your own life and condition. And more than from spring and summer, from autumn there goes out to you a language, to which of itself the echo resounds in your own state of mind and heart.

Yea, as in autumn you see the fall before your eyes, so actually it happens in your own life.

You were child, and have been young: the summer of your life is come; and now you are getting old. Not at once, but imperceptibly and slowly. The eye sees no more so sharply, your movements are less quick and easy. You seek a place to sit down, where before, when you had to sit down, you longed to stand. The mind unfolds less luxuriantly. For what used to give you pleasure, you have no more taste. The blood once so young flows more calmly through the veins. You feel, how the yellowing of the leaf in nature is the image of your own withering.

This continues till the wind lifts itself, and the autumn storm in accident or sickness drives through your branches. And then with you, too, falls the leaf and the foliage begins to be transparent. And time and again it tells you, that from the period of decline you have passed over into that of demolition.

Till finally the last autumn days come, which will

presently lead you into the sleep of winter, those cold, anxious days, of which the preacher sang: "When the keepers of the house (i.e. the hands) shall tremble, and the strong men (i.e. the legs) shall bow themselves, and the grinders (i.e. the teeth) shall cease, and those that look out of the windows (i.e. the eyes) shall be darkened. When the doors shall be shut to the street (i.e. the ears), and you shall be afraid of that which is high, and fears shall be in the way, and the almond tree (i.e. the gray head) shall blossom, and as a grasshopper you shall be a burden to yourself. For man goeth to his long home, and the mourners go about in the streets" (Eccl. 12).

Then, when with you it comes to this, the autumn of your life runs to its close, that on your deathbed winter might come upon you.

Well for him, who by faith hidden in his Savior, knows that for him after that winter the spring dawns of the eternal morn.

YET this end of the autumn is not all of it, and this season of year is also preceded by a period of transition, sometimes with a beauty of its own.

When the first autumn storms have spent their fury, there follow sometimes quiet beautiful days, which affect you beneficently, and entice from you an utterance of admiration. Not least in our land this autumn loveliness comes out in its soft colors in a most charming manner, and not least from these autumn tints have our national painters borrowed their most fruitful impressions.

Spring and summer are at times highly colored even to weariness. The tints are few, the colors overwhelmingly many, often too brightly hued.

But in autumn it seems as though these high colors are dulled and changed into soft tints.

Thereby contrasts are less strong. Everything fuses more readily together. And of itself a wondrous harmony is born.

This is brought about in part by moisture in the air, which breaks the force of the light-beams, and in part it is the weaker life-force in nature itself, which makes it stand out less sharply defined.

And thereby God reconciles us to the loss of summer.

Extreme heat no longer oppresses us, and there is no cold as yet to drive us indoors.

Evenings are no longer very short, and yet not too long to be wearisome. Days begin to shorten, but not yet so short as to prevent going out.

So in every way autumn occupies a sort of middle ground, and maintains a certain poise, a certain harmony, which puts you into a restful state of mind and relaxes you after the tension of the summer.

And not only that by so doing God reconciled you to the decline of the year, but that by this autumnal beauty He also reconciles you to the decline of your own days.

By autumn He shows how even in later years you still have a calling of your own, by your character, your disposition, your expression of life, to develop something in you, that thus far has remained hidden, to wit: the beauty of calm, of what is restful, of what is softly tinted. No more distraction but poise. As far as possible among men, completed harmony.

He who in old age is still irascible, is still driven by his passions, or shuns the middle way, to walk in sidepaths on the outer edge, makes an unpleasant impression.

A soul, a human heart, a character, that in old age still exhibits a fiery temper, striking colors, wild tossings, and has not come to poise, provokes first your disgust, after that your anger and finally your laughter.

Autumn rebukes such an one, and passes judgment upon his wasted opportunities of self-discipline.

Like autumn with its softened tints, so in your old age should be the tenor of your inner life.

If such be not the case with you, as man with a human heart you stand ashamed and confused before the face of nature.

STILL a third mark of autumn is that of nobler, finer harvest.

Even the word *herfst* with us is derived from that third mark; for it is the same word as the English *harvest.*

And harvest is the gathering in of all ripe fruit; and in this general sense there is a harvest in every season of the year, winter alone excepted.

In spring harvest of the first vegetables, early fruit, in part even grass, that shall turn into hay.

In summer you continue the harvest of the grass, of green vegetables, to end it with the ingathering of the grains.

Thus harvest by itself is no distinguishing mark of autumn. On the contrary as such it is common to spring, summer and fall.

But the nobler mark of autumn is, that then harvest is not gathered from the land, but from what grows on vines and branches; grapes and all sorts of fruit from trees.

As high as the tree top lifts itself above the ground in which it roots, so high in quality stands tree fruit above the fruit of the earth. In paradise fruit of the tree was man's food.

This mark of autumn, too, brings you in your older days an admonition of deep seriousness.

There must be fruit on you also in the decline of your days. Not purposeless must be the life of your old age, but a giving out of nobler and finer fruit of soul, of head and heart, than that wherewith thus far you had refreshed the members of your family, your environment, and your compatriots.

The time of spring greens is now past. Time also is gone, when grain in full measures is carried away from your field.

Now your family, your associates and friends expect yet nobler, finer fruit.

The fruit of calm wisdom, the fruit of quiet harmony, the fruit of purer love, the fruit of ripened faith, the fruit of unshakable hope.

There are old men and women of years, who are still intent upon money and with money are busy in their hidden thoughts; who grumbling and peevish are burdensome to all; and instead of being much to others, demand from others everything for themselves.

Oh, withered souls, when on your autumn dish you

see the noble fruit of vine and peach tree as it were smile on you, by that bunch of grapes and by that noble peach, become at length wise.

Wise for yourselves, wise for your fellowmen, wise for your God!

X

On the Day of His Birth

OUR BIRTHDAYS

Of only two "birthdays" Holy Scripture makes mention. In Genesis of a birthday festival prepared in honor of Pharaoh, and in the Gospels of the wild festal day in Herod's palace, so gruesomely stained with the blood of the Baptist.

And when alongside of this memory of what the Pharaohs and Herods celebrated on their birthday, you put the dreadful words wherewith first a Job, and presently a Jeremiah curse the day "on which they were born," can you ignore, how from this striking combination there goes out a voice of seriousness and of warning with respect to our birthdays?

Birthdays can be days of commemoration, which diffuse a friendly glow upon life, spread a soft sheen from the Holy Ghost in the soul, but they bring us this beautiful effect so rarely.

In a sumptuously celebrated birthday there lurks a danger, which is not so visionary, for our heart so open to temptation.

We then are feasted; in the estimation of every one the home-life and the life of the circle of our friends moves itself all that day long around us as a center; we do not hide ourselves, but naturally stand in the foreground; our friends approach us with words of congratulations, even with verses in rhyme; the post brings good wishes from far and near; he who never receives a telegram, receives one on that day; everything is astir in our behalf; for us are those flowers: for us all this commotion; and also the presents, which we exhibit with a certain pride, enrich our treasure.

And where that day of our personal glory so comes and goes, would you think, that that day could pass, without having the heart throb with a somewhat higher tension, and making us feel somewhat more strongly than at other times our already so sensitive *self?*

Prudence in early training sounded a warning therefore already from of old against too elaborate a keeping of the birthdays of our dear little ones.

Especially with those little ones, who do not yet understand their birth, who cannot yet make their only just beginning lives a subject of thought, and have not yet undergone the impression of God's faithful Father-care, a too sumptuously celebrated birthday rarely did anything else, than hurt the tender flower of simplicity and waken vain sensations in the still thoughtless heart.

IF on the anniversary of our birth, things were right with us, together with warm thankfulness and deep shamefacedness, little else than quiet seriousness should possess our soul.

It is our *past,* from the hour of our birth, that forces itself upon our memory: it is our *present* that demands candid and thoughtful valuation of our condition, as well before God as in the world; and questions with respect to the future, call for serious resolution.

On a day of this sort, if it shall be well spent, our whole existence should to our self-perception concentrate itself as in one point of time.

But measure after this not too high a claim, what most birthdays come to, and are you not disappointed?

Think of the birthdays of others, which you have helped celebrate in the domestic circle or in the circle of your friends. Think of your own birthdays. Ask yourself how many years you are of age. By this you will know how often you yourself have left such a day behind you. And then ask yourself, what fruits these high days in your life, taken as a whole, have brought with respect to the forming of your character, to the direction and course of your life, to the enrichment of your soul, and to the hidden walk with God.

And confess, is there then not all too much remembrance of busy, excited days, which scarcely left you any time for turning in upon yourself?

Remembrances of almost nervous excitement, of overwrought expression of face, of sumptuous feasting, and of a weary retiring, to pay the following day the toll of jaded and dull feeling to the overstimulation of the festal day?

WITH followers of the Lord this self-complacency and high tension of spirits undoubtedly undergoes some slight moderation.

He who lives by the Word, and links the course of days with his morning and evening prayer, will also on the day that commemorates his birth seek that Word, and find no rest until he has finished the soliloquy on his knees before the face of his God.

He who is so rich, that, while he himself seeks after God, lives in a family, that is interested in the same high ideal, will in the midst of festal joy undergo the hallowing grace, that at the morning meal and at the banquet the Word comes to lift up the soul, and in prayer and praise honor is brought unto God.

Oh, by the grace of God there is in a family that honors God's Testimony, still so strong a preponderance, to put bit and bridle on what inclines to excess.

But though we readily acknowledge this, and give thanks for it, should not in our Christian families, more than in the circles of the world, the self-accusation be overheard, that so many a day of birth-commemoration by far the greater part was stolen from God and set apart for adulation of our own self?

Have you never known the painful struggle, when on such a day, at the hearing of the Word, the soul *would* listen, but *could* not, and *tried* to pray, but was *distracted*, by reason of the fullness of heart and head of all sorts of things that diverted and overstrained to the point of confusion?

Or, since the other side of this medal is not lacking, did you not observe, how on such a day that was anticipated with so much interest, disappointment made the heart shrink, and in bitterness strained the eye, when you saw, how little notice was taken of you, and you were nettled that less was done for you than for another, whom you counted on a line with yourself, yea, when even the birthday gift pained you, when it showed how the question, of what would conventionally do, had far more governed choice and purchase, than that other, how you might be made glad.

WHAT constitutes joy in the home, at the return of a birthday?

Is it the gladness of heart, that we possess one another, and still possess, and in this possession are so aboundingly rich? Or rather sometimes that a day of relaxation dawned, an uncommon day, which brings a change in the routine of life, a day on which something more than on other days comes to all the members of the family to be enjoyed?

Who then has an open eye to the reality which it sees time and again, and handles as with hands, that the feeling of richness in the possession of one another, in, oh, so many families, has scarcely any part, and how, when in the morning congratulations and good wishes have been extended, the heart and head of all goes out almost exclusively to the things that have been planned?

Sometimes even such days of splendid glory end in sin. When more money was wasted than circumstances justified. Lightsomeness gave the keynote to conversation and at the festal board. And at that board itself wantonness overcame reason.

Though in Christian families, thank God, instances of this sort are extremely rare, that reformation with respect to birthday celebrations ought to be seriously taken in hand by many a family, may be denied, by him who has no pleasure in seriousness, but to this all who fear God will heartily consent.

Above all on such a day our place is *at the altar,* and on that altar of worship more than on other days *love and praise* must be mingled as an offering unto God.

For does not the commemoration of our birth point back directly to that birth itself, and therewith to Him, upon Whom our mother in her travail cast us, and Who by His wondrous counsel and wondrous power of creation formed us and called us into being, after having thought of us already from eternity, before He opened our eye to the light of day?

The days and years that since went by, are they not the exhibition of the goodnesses of our God, Who, where so many thousands were cut off early, spared us, permitted us to live, and all the days of our life fed and watered, clothed and covered, protected and cherished us in His love?

Should not on such a day the remembrance of all this sound as with one mighty voice in the ear of our soul, as the call of our God, wherewith He never ceases to entice and draw us into His blessed fellowship?

Must not our existence and our life, our character, our strength of life, our calling in the service of the Lord, the question whether your foot stands in the gate of the heavenly Jerusalem, be thought upon on such a day with doubling of seriousness?

Yea, shall not he who lives not miles apart from his heart, but close by his soul, on such a day of deep seriousness, also think of his sins? In face of the question what God was to him, shall he not relive what he has been to His God? And shall self-ashamedness, which thereby comes upon the heart, on that day, which reminds us of having been born in sin, not drive us to the

Fountain, that has been opened to the house of Israel for sin and for uncleanness? (Zach. 13, 1).

NOT that therefore this day of gladness must be turned into a day of sombernesses. What is enjoyable in life, God gives us to enjoy. And the abundant joy of our birthdays is a means in God's hand, to strengthen the tie of blood and make a silver lining to glisten around our home-life.

Also here the *use* alone must be sanctified, that the *abuse*, which so readily enters, may be resisted.

In better days one did well, on such a day to remember the poor or to contribute means for the maintenance of the holy cause of our God.

Sometimes even one's own joy inspired him to heighten joy in poorer families, where frequently the birthday was devoid of all extra delight.

Here, too, is inequality, which may not be susceptible to radical improvement, but from which love should inspire us to remove the all too sharp antithesis.

In many ways what is spent and wasted in higher circles on birthdays is *superfluous*, while on the other hand in lower circles such days frequently pass *without joy*.

So it is human sympathy, when they who confess Jesus on their own birthdays refrain from superfluity, and take pleasure to pour light upon this day of commemoration in the circles of our poorer brothers and sisters.

Much is done for children of the poor at Christmas, and in this we rejoice. Something is done for them when they are sick, and that is splendid. But he who knows the children of our poor at close range, may well plan on their birthdays to surprise them.

They do not ask for much.

The hand of a child is soon filled.

And especially when that childhood is poor, and is with, oh, so little, made rich.

XI

And He Builded a City

COUNTRY- AND CITY-LIFE

FROM of old it was a point of interest, that in Holy Scripture city-life is first mentioned among the descendants of Cain.

With the report, that Cain builded a city, we need not think of a city in the sense, which this world has now. In our eye it would scarcely have deserved the name of a village. But this much may be inferred from this remarkable report, agreeable to the ancient significance of the word, that he had fixed dwellings built for his rapidly increasing family, and that he surrounded these simple structures by some sort of moat, to defend himself against wild beasts or against enemies. The Dutch marginal reading is, that Cain "sought defenses for himself."

From fear, from anxiety, from unrest, from a feeling of unsafety the first city was born, and not without reason it is ascribed to Cain's *evil conscience*, that he was the first to take refuge behind moats and walls.

Yet the second mention of a city in Holy Writ shows, that the idea of a city implies yet something else. With the building of Babel's tower the idea appears far more in the foreground, of dwelling together in one place, rather than scattering across the length and the breadth of the land.

But also that second time this building of a city is

mentioned in a *less favorable* sense, even such, that the plan of settling down in Babel was foiled.

Also later on there cleaves to Babylon the continuous idea of a power, that makes itself great against God, while on the other hand Paradise provided country-life, the patriarchs wandered about in tents, Israel dwelt in Goshen, David was called from behind the flock, and in the days of our Lord's sojourn on earth the country people hail Him with Hosannas, while the city people of Jerusalem, at the instigation of the priests, call for Jesus' blood.

The country-people, as we would say, have adhered to Jesus, in Jerusalem they have killed Him.

THIS somber shadow has rested upon city-life till our own times, and it can even be said, that only in our days that shadow has become real dark.

Cities like Paris and London contained most of human misery and extremest human wickedness. The scenes described not so long ago by General Booth in his "Darkest England" are truly repulsive. And though it must gratefully be acknowledged, that in our smaller cities it has not gone such lengths, still one would have to be a stranger to our own conditions, if he had no eye for the profound difference, which both from the religious and the moral standpoint exists among us between city- and country-life.

We are not blind, therefore, to the many sorts of sin, which disgrace country-life; though we grant that frequently it is mere absence of temptation, which renders country-life more uneventful, more restful; but in almost all lands the rule still holds that the faith once delivered held its ground most firmly among country people, and that peaceful home-life there still develops all its power.

The constant touch of nature, and the more regular habits of life, which every stay in the country brings with it, operates refreshingly and thereby purifies.

You see this in the ardent longing of city people, to get away to the country.

There overstrained nerves become calm, health becomes stronger; and after the rule that health of body works beneficially upon the health of the life of the soul, presently, invigorated after soul and body, they come back within their city walls.

Winter bleakness repels; only in spring and summer we enjoy life to the full, and in connection herewith the cities are sought in winter, but in summer, every one who is able, goes to the country.

City-life, however, by itself should not on this account be considered sinful.

Though the idea, to build a city, was first original with Cain, do not forget, that in the vision of Patmos the glory that is to come appears with the descent of the New Jerusalem out of heaven, and that what was shown John, to give him the highest idea of that glory, was not a paradise, but the city with its foundations and precious stones and gates of pearl.

Already under the figurative dispensation of the Old Covenant, the Tabernacle, the habitation of God, first goes through the wilderness, and to the days of

Solomon the holiness of the Lord dwells in a tent; but the course of Revelation ever points forward to the time, when the Lord shall find His rest in Jerusalem, and that the place, which He had chosen for Himself, was upon Zion's mount.

Not in the country, but in the city of David, the majesty of Jehovah revealed itself in the holy of holies. There were the thrones of judgment set. There God appeared shining in His beauty.

So one can say, that in Scripture the idea of *a city* is not lower, but rather of higher standing.

As the glory of Eden pales before the glory of the New Jerusalem, so far stands country-life beneath life in the city. But on account of sin, we are not able to enjoy this richer life, without falling into all sorts of temptations, and therefore life amidst nature holds us nearer unto God than life within city walls.

It is noteworthy, that the first Christian churches were not organized in the country, but as in Palestine, so elsewhere, in cities. All the apostolic epistles are addressed to Christians dwelling in those cities. To those in Rome, in Corinth, etc., and only afterward was the blessing of the Gospel carried out to outlying villages and hamlets.

THE strong tendency of our times, to move into the cities, and to make the population of great cities number millions, is readily understood, but from the side of Christians should not be encouraged.

For that which feeds this tendency, is not the desire to enjoy the higher standard of life, but rather the urge, to lose oneself in the masses, and so to be freer in one's movements, and have the chance to indulge in pleasures of every description.

Not to live after the *higher* standard, but to enjoy oneself more broadly, they who have the means, move into the great cities, and so the smaller towns are more and more emptied of their old-time families, that ennobled the town life, and the country is more and more robbed of those old-time lairds, who by the fact of their living in the midst of their people, were in so many ways a blessing to them.

And this tendency from our side should not be encouraged. He who free and independent has to choose his own place of residence, escapes, oh, so much temptation and distraction and fosters so much more easily the sense of piety among his own, when he shuns the sinful commotion of the city, and holds himself united with the more substantial folk, which you find in the country.

If on the other hand you are not free in your choice, and He Who disposes the place of our habitation, has appointed you a work in a city, then let that city-life quicken God's children, in their own and in their children's behalf, to double watchfulness, and greater frequency of prayer.

The suction of the stream of city-life is so strong, and woe be unto us, when for ourselves or for our family, we deem that temptation can have no hold on us.

In every city the confessor of Christ must be in all his manner of life a protest against the unholy spirit, which for the most part poisons our city-life. Christian life also in our cities can be at higher levels than in our villages. It is richer, it is more intense, it develops greater power. But this finer result is only obtained, when the children of God are clearly conscious of their position, of the danger that threatens, and of their higher calling.

They must not allow themselves to be poisoned by city-life, but by their example and that of their family, must be as a leaven in the midst of the masses; salt, that prevents corruption.

A fixed rule, that holds good for every one, is not here given either.

In the midst of city commotion God's child can come to higher spiritual life than in our quiet villages, and in the country God's child can be spared many a temptation.

Here, too, it can be said: *All things are yours*, life in our cities and life in our villages.

Provided it is not forgotten, that upon this "All things are yours" there ever follows: "And ye are Christ's."

His property and in His service.

XII

Male and Female Created He Them

MAN AND WOMAN

THERE are a few, simple, but extremely important facts in life, that mock at all human self-willedness and scorn all arbitrariness. One of which is the great creation-fact, when God created man, He created them *man and woman.*

Think these three small words out of existence, and imagine, that it would have pleased God, to create man after the rule that applies to the angels, of whom Jesus said, *that they neither marry nor are given in marriage,* —and all history, all life, yea, the fashion of the world would be irrecognizable.

Imagine a world of men only, and everything that in barracks, offices, in great throngs, gives offense by reason of the absence of what is gentle and tender, would weigh on all of our human life with the heaviness of lead. The whole world would be nothing but one great barracks, one endless market-place, one concourse which would never end.

Or imagine a world of women only, and by lack of firmness and strength, endless mobility, softness and tenderness, and the never-ceasing hum of talking lip, making all life seem as a soft undulating sea, with the evening wind dancing and moving upon its waters.

In either case it would be a life without marriage, without family-homes, without brotherly fidelity and sisterly love, without ties of blood, without wooing and repelling, without change and antithesis, one monotonous human sameness.

Of course we pass the inquiry by, how in that case the child of man would have been created. Why He, Who created Adam from the dust of the ground and formed Eve from a rib of Adam, could not have been able to call us one by one into being without coöperation on the part of the woman and without the will of man.

Did not He so create the world of His angels and seraphim, the world of His cherubim?

With conception and birth, as now it proceeds by His ordinance, it is He and always shall be He Who creates the soul of every one, and "embroiders the body" from the still "unformed substance." See Ps. 139.

Such a world without distinction of sex is indeed thinkable.

And it has its use, for one moment to lose oneself in such a world of endless ennui, because nothing lifts us up to praise and thanksgiving more than this, that in reality it is not so, but that God created us *man and woman.*

BUT that antithesis should then be taken in its *deep* sense, and not, as often is the case, exclusively in connection with the body.

It is by no means true, that man and woman differ merely by longer or shorter hair, by more or less muscular strength, by greater angularity or more roundness of form.

It is not written: "God created, male and female,

as to body"; but it reads: "God created man *in his own image*," and then follows immediately: "male and female created He them" (Gen. 1, 27).

Thus the distinction between man and woman refers, even first of all, to the soul, the hidden inner being. And that the body differs, is not least because the real distinction lies in the body, but also because in the body, if it shall be well, must lie the expression of our inner existence.

He who is not entirely weaned from knowledge of man and faces, observes this again and again.

Though we may know nothing of a person, the outward appearance of one will inspire us with confidence and open our heart toward him, and the face of the other, as well as his bearing, will repel us and close our heart against him.

Body and soul are strongly distinguished, and it is not true, as reported even among Christians, that our soul itself has formed its own body; and neither can it be said, that there is no relation between the two.

God gives to every one an own body, and apart from sin every one would have just such a body as would suit his soul, and be adapted to his inner existence.

Thus when it reads: "God created them man and woman," it is first of all our duty to think of the difference that marks the inner being. The inner disposition of the soul of a man differs from the inner disposition of the soul of a woman.

On either harp the same number of strings are strung; but they are differently arranged; they differ in length and weight; and they are differently played upon by the soul of a man than by the soul of a woman.

THIS antithesis runs now no longer true.

Here, too, sin has come in between the two and worked disharmony.

On the harp of the soul, of man and woman both, strings have been loosened, others have been covered with rust, and some have snapped.

And since with one this went this way and with the other that, the mutual relation at times is so strongly modified, that you meet women who make you think of dressed up men, and men who have much in common with a disguised woman.

So sin always does.

It tears us out of our standing. It breaks equipoise. It disturbs harmony.

Hence all the discords, which the ear continually catches and which presently pass your own lips.

There is no longer beautiful and pure accord.

It is all become chaos.

It is evident with children, for when they are together you hear more than one girl say, that she would rather have been a boy. When they grow up as boys and girls, not infrequently you find a girl, who behaves as a boy. And among married women, it is not rare for a woman to think: I will be what my husband ought to be.

Altogether lack of reverence for Divine ordinance.

And yet, even in this aberration the trace of the Divine ordinance still shows itself.

For almost never do you find a boy who wants to be a girl, but the girl a boy; thus in their folly confirming the Divine appointment, that God created them, not woman and man, but man and woman.

Adam first, and only after him and from him, as his helpmeet, Eve.

For of course in that simple statement, "God created them male and female," there is order.

Where there are two, as long as these two stand side by side as equals, there is neither tie nor junction.

You can plant two poplar trees side by side, but you cannot put two animals together, and far less two people.

To create a tie and a connection between these two, order must be established over both. One must be first, and the other second. Two cannot simultaneously occupy the same place. One stands in the front, and therefore the other stands behind.

With two one must always have the precedence.

No ship has two steering-wheels or prows, but one prow and one rudder, and in the ship each has a place and calling of their own.

In the world of music there are *high* and *low* notes, which each as such have their own place and order.

In the world of colors one color precedes the other.

An ordinance of God for His entire creation, which also applies to man and woman, because God created them male and female. The man first, and *after that* the woman.

But here, too, sin has worked effects.

With the man, from his precedence to borrow a cause for despotism, and to assume an authority, to which he has no right, since it is stolen. And on the other hand with the woman, in that she takes no pleasure in the *second* place according to the rank of order, and is bound to take the first place, which God has withheld from her.

Especially in our days this tendency is strong.

Still to believe that God said to the woman: "Your

husband shall rule over thee" (Gen. 3, 16), our modern age turns into ridicule.

AND in this respect also the harmony, originally ordered by God, and broken by us, shall once be restored, and when in eternity the redeemed shall enter upon that new state, in which there shall no more be given or taken in marriage, from the two-sided disposed human heart, after its male and after its female fundamental type, God's honor shall be chanted, in purest accord.

Then the subjectivity of the woman to the man shall cease. For that subjectivity is not original in the creation, but follows from God's judgment after the fall into sin.

Then there shall merely remain precedence, but a precedence like that of Christ to His Church, the less to seek self and the more to give self.

Mutual completion. Two halves of one whole which belong together. Fusion and solution of duality in higher harmony.

OF this the prelude can already on earth be enjoyed.

Not in the way of the chivalric gallantry of the Middle Ages, which in semblance elevated woman, only to humiliate her the more deeply, but in the way of Christian wedlock and of the Christian family.

Then from the side of God there is authority over both.

Then both man and woman feel a deep sense of

their own calling. Of *manly* calling the man, of *womanly* calling the woman.

Then both know their own place and have no desire to vacate it, neither will they allow themselves to be driven from it, and the life of faith itself tends, to develop in man strength, fidelity, courage; in woman gentleness and tenderness.

So does God's ordinance provisionally revive again, and begins again to bless the partners in holy wedlock.

And not the married alone. The relation between brothers and sisters also becomes different and better. And in these circles, blessed of God, even the *general* intercourse and relation of man and woman mutually become measurably again what they should be.

Then the foolish notions of the world lose flavor and taste. Healthy relationships according to the Scripture obtain power again and consecration.

And in the end, both become richer and happier, because they act together again after the ordinance of Him, Who created us *man* and *woman*.

XIII

Which Were Expressed By Name

MAN IN HIS CALLING

To hide behind dark figures in the *background,* or, without being called, to stand bravely and heroically in the foreground, are the two extremes between which our natural impulse continuously moves back and forth.

On one side timid fear so much as to hear one's name mentioned, and on the other side even ardent desire, where it concerns a noble cause, to have a place among *"the men which are expressed by name"* (2 Chron. 28, 15).

You know what happened in Samaria under Pekah, the son of Remeliah.

God let Pekah loose against Ahaz, the godless descendant of David, who broke the covenant and as king led the already apostatized Judah in the cruel worship of Moloch, which he was the first to introduce into Judah.

In Samaria they bent the knee before Baal, but close by Jerusalem, in the valley of Hinnom, David's descendant knelt before Moloch, which was far worse.

Therefore God let the king of Samaria loose against the apostate Ahaz, and Pekah, with his well-disciplined army slew Judah's neglected troops so dreadfully, that of Judah there fell one hundred and twenty thousand in one day.

That was the vengeance of God upon Judah's apostasy, and Pekah was God's instrument.

But in his recklessness Pekah spoiled his own cause.

Not enough, that he had humiliated Judah in so bloody a way, his victorious army would enrich itself further at the expense of Judah; not merely by spoils, but also by carrying away into slavery two hundred thousand men, women and children, even in so shameful and heartless a manner, as to drag many of them naked along the way.

And with this shameful spoil the army of Pekah, drunk with victory, returned to Samaria.

THIS was shameful, it was criminal, it was an outrage against the ties of blood, which ever yet bound the men of Samaria to Judah.

Oded, the prophet, at once therefore set out to meet the victorious army, to stop them in their senseless course.

That they had vanquished Judah, was right, so the prophet said. The Lord Himself had delivered Judah, by reason of its apostasy, into Pekah's hands. But to make slaves of the children of Judah and Jerusalem, was to defy the God of hosts to His face. This they must not do, but at once give these captured Jews and Jewesses leave to return to their own cities and towns. For, unless they would so do, the fierceness of the wrath of the Lord would be terrible upon them.

Yet the army did not let go its spoil. The march went on. Already the boisterous and insolent host, with their degraded train of slaves, was approaching the capital city.

Even of Pekah it is not said, that he gave counter-order.

It seemed, as though Oded's voice had not been heard.

THEN there formed itself, as we would say, a commission of four brave men.

Their names were Azariah, Berechiah, Jehiskiah and Amasa.

These four came together.

Deeply indignant over what took place, feeling that thus God's right was trampled under foot, and determined at the risk of death, to foil so wicked a purpose, they agreed, without further delay, and entirely on their own responsibility, to meet the returning host, and to demand the immediate release of the captives.

This action called for dauntless courage, for ten to one, the insolent army would meet them with scorn and contempt, and either push them aside or because of their interference place their heads at their feet.

You well know, in those days not much store was set by a human life more or less.

Yet danger does not scare them. They go out from the gate of Samaria, they go along the highway, by which the army must come, and boldly and bravely meet it face to face. They offer no supplication, but briefly state their demand: "Ye shall not bring the captives hither. It would bring guilt upon us over against the Lord. Our trespass is great already. Would ye commit this trespass also and add yet more to our sins?"

And see, the effect of this heroic address is wondrous.

The whole army gives way to these four men. They halt. They stand as though bewildered. Not only do they release the two hundred thousand captives, but also make immediate surrender to these four men of the priceless spoil, which they had plundered.

God blessed this heroic act.

The spirit of the whole army is changed. It is as though the general and other officers recognize that they have been outdone, and in a moment they all put themselves at the service of Azariah and his three friends, and instead of entering Samaria with shouts of triumph, under the blue skies begins a sacred work of brotherly love.

Read how beautifully and touchingly in Scripture this is narrated: They took the captives by the hand, and with the spoil clothed all that were naked among them. They arrayed them, and shod them, and gave them to eat and to drink. And over and above all this they annointed them. And all the feeble of them they put upon asses, and so, as in arms of love, they carried these two hundred thousand men, women and children to Jericho, the city of palm trees, back to their brethren. And only when that labor of love to the brethren was ended, did the victorious army, with Azariah and his three friends in the lead, and with quieted consciences, return to Samaria, where was the palace of Pekah.

So Azariah, and Berechiah, and Jehiskiah, and Amasa were the first four *good Samaritans,* and even as the Samaritan in the parable, they were seen in Jericho, the city of palm trees.

YET it is not their compassion, which has assured Azariah and his three friends these many centuries a place among "the men which were expressed by name."

What distinguishes them, and places them in the full light of history, is their personal courage, their personal initiative, their resolute attitude, their stand when every one trembled, their risk of everything for the sake of their fatherland.

Truly they performed an act of mercy, but presently multitudes have done this with them. You understand, that these four men did not personally clothe the two hundred thousand captives, fed and assisted them. But what distinguished them from all the rest, was their initiative; their daring stand against a menacing wrong; their courage to hold the people back from a dreadful national sin, that would have become a judgment upon the people.

Their act tended to practice compassion, but it was first of all a deed of love of country, in a sacred sense of political tendency. They dreaded the judgment, which, by reason of so great a sin, would come upon people and fatherland, and therefore with heroic courage they resisted the king and his generals and his army.

They believed, they confessed, these men, that their land and their king had an account with the Lord of hosts; that the anger of the Holy One of Israel would inflame against the people; and it is this approaching disaster, that these sturdy men, by their heroic initiative, have diverted from people and native land.

Like as Phinehas did, when he thrust the javelin through the body of the adulterous servant of Baal-Peor (Numb. 25), so, not by killing, but by saving, did

Azariah and his three friends, in the name of their God, make *personal initiative* glisten.

THIS sacred impulse, not to wait for others, not to sit still, and not to shrink back from trouble nor danger, comes of itself from the fear of God, and has therefore always been the earmark of true Christianity, wherever it has struck root.

Of course such action is never justified, except when the Lord calls. But the faithful servant of Jehovah does not wait for visions nor for inspirations, so as to allow himself while waiting by passivity to be unnerved.

Where strong faith operates, that impulse works immediately, and only when faith is weak and timorous, does that impulse remain wanting.

Then one hides himself, then one withdraws himself from everything, and lets God's flood inundate God's country.

So doeth not the sturdy Christian. He builds dikes. He constructs sea-walls against the flood and strengthens them by cofferdams when waters swell. Where there would be no ground to build on, he creates land by drainage, and when it is drained he thanks God and praises not himself but ascribes to God the glory.

To this sacred impulse alone the Dutch in times long past owe the restoration of their national existence. So long as that noble impulse operated vigorously, the cause of God has flourished in the land. And what in this century also has been won from the ancient enemy, God's people in every land owe almost exclusively to the Azariahs and the Berechiahs, who did not dally but took hold, did not sit still but heroically showed themselves men of action.

This nobler spirit has come upon whole sections of land in all parts of the world, and you can make whole rosters of all sorts of groups of people, who have united themselves, and bravely made advances, in the name of the Lord to stand against *unbelief* and *revolution,* and to continue propaganda of principles so sacred to their heart.

Yet it is by no means yet the case, that courage and compelling power of a sacred conviction has made itself master of all hearts.

There are still many that are "at ease in Zion." "Peace, peace," sounds the song of slowness, "peace, for no harm is near!"

One loses himself in his affairs, and the needs of the cause of the Lord do not concern him.

Everything is expected and hoped for from the men who are in office. One leaves it with those who appear to have been appointed.

Always others, never yourself.

And if the spirit of the lukewarm and the slow to act had also unnerved Azariah and his friends, the trespass would have been committed, and the heinous wrong in Israel would not have been arrested.

XIV

A Virtuous Woman

THE HOUSEWIFE

Our translators do not speak in Proverbs 31, 10, of the "virtuous," but of the "real" housewife, and there is some difference here. In our times at least one thinks of a "virtuous" housewife as one who is reliable, good-natured and home-loving; but he who speaks of a *real* housewife, means not merely an honest and good person, but one who is truly meritorious *as a housewife.*

And such was the meaning of the Proverb-poet.

In this beautiful song, in which Lemuel outlines the picture of the real housewife, almost no mention is made of the quiet virtues of this woman.

It says "that she feareth the Lord," but this, too, is not taken subjectively, but objectively. A woman who shows in her *housekeeping* that she does not pursue vanity, but feareth the Lord, she shall be *praised.*

For it says: "Favor is deceitful and beauty is vain, but a woman that feareth the Lord, she shall be praised."

There is even no appeal to verse 11: "The heart of her husband doth safely trust in her," as though this were said in praise of her marital faithfulness; for this word has nothing to do with it, and only means, that the head of the house is altogether confident, that his wife shall take good care of him. It states this literally and in so many words: "The heart of her husband doth safely trust in her, that he shall lack no good, i.e., not anything that he needs."

Overspiritual people will find this very prosaic; but such is Holy Scripture.

Does not Holy Scripture say of a minister or elder, that he who doth not know how to rule his own house, is worse than an infidel; which of course means to say, that such an one injures the church of Christ more still than an infidel.

But actually the fundamental thought in both Old and New Testaments here too is one.

The *real* minister or elder must first rule his own house and then the house of God.

So the *real* housewife is evident first in this, and most in this, that she shows herself capable of taking good care of her house and of ruling it well.

THE words themselves of the Proverb-poet indicate this.

That for which this genuine housewife is praised, consists of six things: first that she takes good care of her husband, second of her children, third of her maid-servants, fourth of the poor, fifth of her goods, and sixth of her house.

She cares for *her husband.*

This stands at the head in verses 11 and 12 as her first marriage obligation: "The heart of her husband doth safely trust in her, so that he shall lack no good thing. She doeth him good and not evil all the days of her life."

Then she cares for *her children.*

Read it in verses 26 and 28: "She openeth her mouth with wisdom; and in her tongue is the law of kindness. Her children arise up, and call her blessed."

In the third place she cares for *her maidens.*

This you see in verse 15, where it reads. "She riseth also while it is yet night, and giveth meat to her household, and a portion to her maidens."

In the fourth place she cares for *the poor.*

"She stretches out her hand to the poor; yea, she stretches forth her hands to the needy" (v. 20).

This is her care for her *live* goods.

And this care for her live goods is so brilliantly crowned, that her husband and her children receive honor in the gate of the city; and that every one in the gates praises her by reason of the works of her hands.

BUT this does not satisfy her.

The largest place in Proverbs 31 is devoted to her care for her *goods* and her *house.*

Especially for her goods.

In the house there must be provisions, there must be supplies, and abundance of all sorts of goods.

And this genuine housewife did not harbor the idea, that her husband must earn everything, and that she needs but live on his money; but she herself was diligent, she worked in the hours which she saved to prepare wares for sale, and these she did so well, that they fetched high prices, and thus brought in gains, even to the extent that she was able to lay by and buy herself a field.

She spins and embroiders and makes ornaments.

Read it in verses 13 and 14: "She seeketh wool, and flax, and worketh willingly with her hands; she is like the merchant's ships; she bringeth her food from afar."

After that again in vs. 19 and 22: "She layeth her hand to the spindle, and her hands hold the distaff. She maketh herself coverings of tapestry; her clothing is silk and purple."

And these products of her hands she *sells.* See it in vs. 17 and 18 and 24: "She girdeth her loins with strength, and strengtheneth her arms. She perceiveth that her merchandise is good; her candle goeth not out by night. She maketh fine linen, and selleth it; and delivereth girdles unto the merchant."

And with that merchandise of what she herself spun and embroidered she is so prosperous, that she lays by a small fortune.

So says v. 16: "She considereth a field, and buyeth it; with the fruit of her hands she planteth a vineyard."

AND what finally concerns her care in narrower sense for *house* and *household,* in this too she does excellent work.

She wastes no time in sleep, but works evenings longer than it is day, and in the morning she is the first out of bed.

As it tells in v. 18: "Her candle goeth not out by night"; and in v. 15: "She riseth also while it is yet night."

Neither does she leave the care of her house to her servants, but she herself giveth meat to her household. Read it in v. 15: "She giveth meat to her household, and a portion to her maidens."

She is most careful too as to her own personal appearance: "Her clothing is fine linen and purple. Strength and honor are her clothing," which means, that she wears articles of good quality, and knows how to do this with taste and good form.

She has an eye to the whole house, the halls, the garrets and the cellars. She is always busy. "She looketh well to the ways of her household, and eateth not the bread of idleness."

Yea, to add this to it also, she cares not only for her goods and for her household, but also for the house itself.

As it says in v. 21: "She is not afraid of the snow for her household; for all her household is clothed with scarlet," something that is to be understood of Eastern houses like this, that when there was no paper yet, the walls were hung with tapestries; and this was done with double thicknesses in winter, that the indoors might be the warmer.

All this the Proverb-poet adds together as marks of an housewife that feareth the Lord, and who for the sake of the fear of the Lord responds to her high calling as mistress of the house.

LEMUEL does not draw this picture of a woman of the middle class or of a woman of the lower ranks of society, but of a woman of years in the high walks of life. For it says that *King* Lemuel thus drew the image of a woman for his son.

This was not yet the Christian woman, but a Jewish woman, who lived in the fear of the Lord.

And he who in the days of the Reformation takes the Christian woman at her best, knows in how serious and substantial a way the real housewife acquitted herself of her task as wife to her husband, as mother to her children, and as mistress of the house to her servants.

So was, and sometimes still is, the real housewife, to whom God grants, according to v. 25: "*to rejoice in time to come.*"

That not every woman can be like this, is granted.

Not every woman has this physical strength and welfare at her command. Not every woman is endowed with such strength of mind, wisdom of insight, and admirable power of will.

And He Who knows the talents of every one, here too shall pass a righteous judgment.

It must also be granted, that with present-day factories and stores, a woman is now no more able by her spindle and embroideries to lay by competencies.

With the change of times this too is altered.

But when the genuine housewife in old times so cared for her husband, children and servants, and then had time left by spinning and embroidering to earn enough money to buy fields, how much greater should be the care for husband, children, servants and houses now, when the "real housewife" is under no more necessity to embroider for trade, and is able to give all her time to her household!

You realize, that the task and calling of caring for the interests of the home is so much the more urgent.

And in these days so many fall short in this, who, alas, thereby stand behind even this Jewish housewife.

And when by reason of this the reading of Proverbs 31 sends the blush to the cheeks of many of our women, is there then no cause for laying hold of oneself in the fear of the Lord, and of doing what it says in v. 17: "She girdeth her loins with strength, and strengtheneth her arms"?

XV

If Your Soul Were in My Soul's Stead

MUTUAL DEVOTION

Do not quarrel about it. Every one of us must carry his own burden, must carry his own cross. And this burden of suffering is measured out to you not according to your faith, far less according to your merit, but almost exclusively according to the sovereign counsel of God.

It is not denied, therefore, that patient discharge of duty produces results that make for happiness of life; and that throwing oneself away in sinful pursuits in the end makes the reckless one pay dear. But this contrast, without more, does not explain the very unequal division of life's happiness, nor the every time surprising inequality between the cross laid on one and that laid on another.

Once, in the day of judgment, as our sense of right spells out to us and as God's Word prophesies the same to us, this inequality which is so offensive to us shall be straightened out, when all that have died or are yet alive, shall appear before the judgment seat of Christ, and shall carry away according as they have done in life, whether it be good or evil.

But in expectation of that great and illustrious day, here in this earthly dispensation with respect to the mystery of suffering it remains a criss-crossing of two altogether divergent lines.

On one side *the line of Sinai,* i.e., the line of provisional retribution *here and now,* as when he who will not behave, goes under in the social struggle, while he who orders his way aright, makes notable advances.

And on the other side *the line of Golgotha,* i.e., the mystery of suffering, which foretells the cross to the righteous and makes worldly godlessness to triumph over the Man of Sorrows.

Yea, even in nature you see these lines go athwart one the other.

On one side a God, Who makes His sun to rise over evil and good, and rain to come down upon righteous and unrighteous. And on the other side a neglected field, that makes its owner suffer hunger, over against a vine or olive-orchard, which makes the diligent farmer dwell in peace and prosperity under his own vine and fig tree.

Always these two.

On the right a rule of retribution, which weds suffering to sin; but toward the left a rule, that mocks every idea of retribution, and erected for the Only One Who, born of a woman, was spotlessly pure, a tree of shame and on that accursed tree still held Him up to scorn.

And this antithesis is not explained from the blindness of human unrighteousness, for God hands Job over to Satan; and now sickness and death, which so often darken the path of the righteous by somber shadows, still come not from human failure or caprice, but from the sovereign counsel of the Eternal.

WHEN you ask, whether it is given us, already here, by the light of the Word, to solve that bitter struggle, which has weighed heavily upon the faithful of all ages, it certainly behooves us to confess, that we know more than the friends of Job, and more than the Preacher of Jerusalem. For Gethsemane and Golgotha, which then were yet to *come,* now lie *behind* us. But then every one of us is ready at once to offer the remark, that at Golgotha *worship* is so much easier than understanding.

So much only is clear, that the solution of the struggle between the *rule of Sinai,* which makes the godless, and the *rule of Golgotha,* which makes the righteous suffer, is to be looked for in a third rule, which interprets the mystery of love, and which speaks of a suffering by one *in the stead* of the other; of a going under and sinking away in *vicarious* suffering; of a coming of *the soul of one into the place of the soul of the other.*

For though at first hearing this sounds oracular, and though Job, who was the first to suggest it, speaks of it vaguely (16, 4), we ourselves well know this golden rule from our own soul's experience.

We have known, we have lived through, the sacred moments, when the sorrow of another weighed so painfully upon our own soul, that sometimes we were depressed and bowed down under it more than the sufferer himself.

And also, they are not strange, but from memory familiar, those blessed sensations, when it seemed to us, as though the sorrow dropped from our shoulders, because real sympathy on the part of another caught our sorrow of soul from beneath.

Both times it was vicarious.

Once when you removed the cross from the shoulder of others, to carry it yourself in their stead, to their relief. And again when some one took it from your shoulder, and by fellowship of love and thanks to the communion of saints, carried it in your stead.

It is true, this was not yet the highest. Not yet the full application of the golden rule of vicarious love.

That shone only and alone on Golgotha.

But Simon of Cyrene was there, who took the cross from Jesus, and carried it after Him, and dragged it to the cross-hill *in His stead.*

IF *your soul were in my soul's stead,* is of course unisonous with the opposite: If *my* soul were in *your* stead.

This operation of love goes over and back.

It is mutual.

From one to the other, and from the other to one.

But always with the mysterious effect, that the burden of the cross is transferred, and that with one the burden is lightened, and with the other it is made heavier.

Thus, you will say, this operation of love serves no purpose.

What good is it, when A suffers, that B assumes that suffering, to relieve A? Should not by this same rule A take his suffering back again from B, so that in the end he has his own cross back again? Yea, more yet, is it not love's claim, that you hide your suffering, so as to keep the other from entering into your sorrow?

And indeed, this would be so, if both times this suffering were borne *in the same way.*

And when you perceive, that it comes to this, you do better when you keep it to yourself, and hide it from the knowledge of your best friend, in the outpouring of your soul to make known your complaint to your God and your Lord alone.

But when it becomes a suffering of *love,* because you "put your soul in the stead of his soul," no, then that transfer, that exchange of cross, that vicarious suffering of love serves a purpose.

For see, the man, who bore the sorrow, because God's counsel brought it upon him, was burdened by it, threatened to succumb under it, and was going down in it. But when by the urge of love you take that same cross from him, it works the opposite effect with you, through love that same cross elevates you, enriches you inwardly, and allows you moments of blessed, soul-felt happiness.

For yours is at once the reward of your suffering, when you see that by you the sorrow of the other has been softened.

MORE familiarly we call this: *ability to imagine ourselves in the condition of the other.*

Surely, much love can operate in this, and hard will be the judgment of the man, who knew so little save his own self, and thereby was never able to understand others in their suffering.

But yet: to imagine yourself in the other man's condition, is something far more general and superficial.

It is *more general,* for to think oneself in the condition of the other is of use in almost every relation of life.

No father or mother can be a good trainer, unless

they are able to put themselves in the place of their children. No teacher can teach, unless he can enter into the condition of his pupil. No preacher can preach, unless he enters sympathetically into the condition of his hearers. No nurse can care for the sick, unless she can enter into the condition of her patient.

"To think oneself in the condition of others" is the general rule of all effective and fruit-bearing treatment of other people.

But the rule, which governs the mystery of suffering, aims far higher, because it does not remain on the surface, but enters into the reality.

When I hear of a terrible shipwreck, I can imagine myself in the midst of the dreadful scenes, which before the ship sank away into the watery depths were enacted on the sinking wreck; but this is pure *representation;* and even where I am moved by it, it is no deeper emotion than is stirred by reading Shakespeare's *Hamlet.*

But here it is far more, and something altogether different.

Not thinking oneself *in* and imagining the condition *of* another, but taking one's stand in his place; entering into what he is going through; taking the cross from him, and carrying it in his place and in his stead.

THIS is what, in fullest sense, and with perfect releasing effect has actually taken place on Golgotha alone.

There He bore the *punishment* that brings us *peace.* The curse, that lay on us, He took away from us and bore it Himself.

And of course, so to take the cross away from the

brother, is to us, children in love, as we are, not granted. For this you would have to be, as Jesus, altogether holy.

But walk in *the shadow* of love, thank God, yea, that we can do. Not by artificial intent, but as real love poured out in our heart by the Holy Ghost.

Then soul enters into soul. Then we do not regard ourselves but forget ourselves, so that we enter into the hidden sanctuary of the other person's sorrow, and at the altar of his grief, which then smokes with such leaden-gray clouds, we kneel by the side of him, bear him up from underneath, and take the weight of his sorrow upon ourselves.

Better still, for even that would be too much. Oh, the strength of our love is so small. But He Whose Divine beauty glistens most brightly in the sympathy of compassion, brings our soul, more deeply than we ourselves know, into the sorrow of the brother, and in the stream of this holy sympathy brings the overwhelmed heart of the brother toward us.

This then does not last long; and we can neither retain nor lengthen this sacred moment.

But it has been there, this one indivisible moment, when, in the place of our brother, our soul *suffered* what he battled against, and his was the balm of comfort.

XVI

The Men Which Knew of It

NO SECRET

In Israel the relation between husband and wife was *exemplary*. Exemplary in so extraordinary a way, that now, after two thousand years, the *type of Jewish wedlock* still operates among the scattered children of Jacob, yea, is sometimes still so beautiful and attractive, in the high esteem of robust and paternal authority, in the honor of wife and mother, and in the affectionate union of "husband and wife and children" almost to the perfection of an articulated whole.

What we still see of this in our own surrounding, is a fruit of what God's Word wrought in Israel.

He made known his ways unto Moses, his acts unto the children of Israel (Ps. 103, 7). *He hath not dealt so with any nation: and as for his judgments, they have not known them* (Ps. 147, 20).

Yet from of old the example of heathen women has worked evil in the life of Jewish women.

This was strongly evident, when, after the fall of Jerusalem, a number of Jewish families went into Egypt and took Jeremiah with them.

For then Jeremiah discovered, that many Jewish women on the quiet wandered off to the luxuriously appointed temples of the Heathen, and, with the strange women offered offerings to the idol, which they called: *the Queen of heaven.*

For this Jeremiah rebuked them and called them to repentance.

But the unholy association with those worldly women had already in a short time bewildered the spirit of these Jewish women in such wise, that boldly and recklessly they said to Jeremiah: "We will not hearken unto thee, but we will certainly do whatsoever thing goeth forth out of our own mouth, and burn incense unto the Queen of heaven" (Jer. 44, 16, 17).

This was provoking enough by itself, but there was evidence of still greater apostasy, when, as though to taunt Jeremiah, they added: "Would you think, that we offered incense to the Queen of heaven, without our husbands being in the secret?" (v. 19).

For this showed, that though the women committed this sin alone by themselves, yet their husbands, though they took no part in this, and held themselves as though they knew nothing of it, had truly been persuaded by their wives to contribute money toward it. For of course such outings to the heathen temples were expensive, both by reason of the costly garments they had to wear, to be in style with others, and the liberal offerings they had to bring.

Thus the women sinned grievously, but their husbands shared their guilt, for, says Jeremiah in v. 15, they were "*men who knew of it,*" knew that their wives despised God and bent their knee to the Queen of heaven.

By itself there was nothing strange in this.

From our sinful nature it springs, and in many

ways we all practice this principle of reserve, "to cover one's eyes with his hand," to be blind to much that takes place in one's own house, to hold oneself "as though he knows nothing of it," and to act "as though it has not come to his notice."

To some extent, it may be said, there is some good in this.

The "be not overrighteous" has a relative right. He who puts a restraint upon everything tires people and weakens the mainspring of admonition. He who always inhibits, in the end is no more heard. A clock that always ticks, strikes at last the hour and the half hour, without any one noticing it.

And the outcome shows, that in the end family affairs are best managed, when as a rule the rein is somewhat loose, and is tightened only when a matter is worth while, and then if needs be with the assistance of the lash.

But what is here told of the men and women in Tahpanhes is something altogether different.

What here took place was a creeping in stealthily among the women of an altogether sinful practice, but in such a way that their husbands were in the secret, and though they held themselves aloof, knew all about it.

Here was an evil, which the man, as soon as he knew of it, should immediately and inexorably have stopped, and which he suffered to go on, yea, contributed money toward it, to prevent disagreement at home, and not to come to a footing of war with his wife.

Here the wife bare rule, and the husband, who by God's appointment was responsible, did as though he knew nothing of it, and, in opposition to God's law, allowed himself to be subjected to the sinful law of heathen practice by his wife.

THIS is a subversion of the order which God has appointed for family life.

The man *is* the head and so must remain.

He is responsible to God for the spirit in which his family lives at home and reveals itself outside.

He is not to rule in the sense that in his own house he is to set up some sort of a little kingdom for himself, but he should so rule his family, that in his house all resistance against the *Kingship of God* is broken.

A family does not come of itself, God is the Author of it and created husband and wife and children for it. And therefore He has the right to declare what is best for the family, and to appoint His ordinances with respect to it. And in God's name and in God's stead the husband and father has been appointed watchman, to see to it, that these ordinances of God come to their own.

In that appointment roots his authority; therein alone; and by reason of this, he must resist every violation of his authority, neither should he neglect the use of this authority, but must apply it to this one great end.

All other rule of his family lacks higher consecration.

Only so does it take hold of the conscience.

And he who does not do this, renders himself guilty before God, while he makes a mockery of his responsibility to the Knower of hearts.

Whether his word is heeded, is another question. This they did not do in Israel according to Jeremiah's word. The brutality of wife and children can sometimes go so far, that even as those women to Jeremiah, they say to husband and father, in response to his admonition: "We will not hearken unto thee, but do our own pleasure."

Provided the man takes care not to throw away his authority, his conscience is clear, and the doubly guilty wife, with her tempted children, will bear double guilt before God.

MONEY here is of serious significance.

These Jewish women of Tahpanhes confessed this themselves, when they asked Jeremiah: "Do you think that we could allow ourselves this luxury, *without our men?*" (v. 19).

Not in Israel, but with us a wife can have money, and in the marriage contract have claims inserted, to assure her independence, and in that case the husband is responsible, whether he did well, to marry on this condition, but, once married, what his wife spends in such a way is beyond his province of authority.

As a rule this is *not* so.

As a rule the wife has no other money, than what her husband hands out to her, and therefore he remains responsible for what his wife expends.

The urge after worldliness, the tendency to vanity, the trait to do what women do who do not fear the Lord, can almost in no case be gratified except by *money*.

So it was at Tahpanhes, so it is still with us.

Therefore the man who says: "I give my wife money, and what she does with it is her lookout," must once give account to God for this light-hearted play.

Truly, to the wife, as she should be, and for so far as she walks in the fear of God, largest confidence and greatest liberty of action must be accorded.

But when the husband learns that things go wrong, and he knows that money is spent in sinful ways, he may not act as though he knows nothing of it.

For then, as regards his wife, the blood of her soul shall once be demanded at his hands.

THIS holds true also where no money comes into play, and it concerns evil practices, either in the training of children, or in dealing with servants, or in association with outsiders, or in expenditure of strength, of time and of life.

There is nothing in the home-life, regarding which there is no will of God.

God created nothing and called nothing into being, but gave an ordinance concerning it. An ordinance for the use of every power, for the spending of each day, for maintaining the purity of every relation. And certainly not the least power of the Christian life of our fathers consisted in this, that they recognized the obligation of the husband, to see to it, that *in all this* the Lord our God was duly honored.

Surely he must be priest in his own house, to lead in prayer, and to invoke the reconciliation of his God with respect to the affairs of his home.

But this cannot be all. It is also written: "*The lips of the priest should keep knowledge*" (Mal. 2, 7), which here definitely refers to the knowledge of God's law.

As it reads elsewhere: "The *law* shall not perish from the priest" (Jer. 18, 18) or as is said to Israel: "Ask now the priests concerning *the law*" (Hag. 2, 11).

So to stand in his house, belongs to the *priesthood* of the husband and father in his family.

A living preaching of the Law of the Lord must he be in the Christian family. If you will, the *public conscience* of all, who in his family are committed to his care.

And therefore it is a choking, a strangling, a searing of the conscience, when the husband makes common cause with his wife in evil, and well knows of it, but acts as though he sees nothing.

This is moral cowardice.

This is to throw away his honor as man, and his priesthood before God. A sinning against his own soul, and against the soul of his wife.

Of course this also applies the other way. A wife also must watch over the soul of her husband.

But yet this relation is altogether different.

Even a child is not free from the soul of his parents; and he who as child in a spiritual sense can be something to father and mother, and is not, is guilty. But this does not undo the fact that the responsibility of a father for his child bears an altogether different character from that of a child for his father.

That of the father for his child is official.

And so is the responsibility of the husband for the wife.

Here is a *special* duty, a duty of a particular sort and order, imposed of God upon the husband.

XVII

If Then I Be a Father, Where Is My Honor?

THE FATHER

To *serve* God and to *honor* Him, is by no means the same.

He who *serves* is in that service a *servant,* who fulfills his servantship by strict obedience and discharge of all his duties.

Hence in the service of the Lord our God this servantship stands in the foreground. To be a "Servant of the Most Highest" is an honorary title, and "servant of God" stands so high, that it is common to all angels and men, and to the Mediator between God and men. Even the Mediator is called "the suffering servant of God."

But true piety goes further than *service,* and the name of *Religion* points not to *the service,* but to *the honor* of God. And so in our circles we speak of the Christian *Religion;* but in the general understanding of the people this noble name has found no entrance.

The great mass of people know of nothing else nor of anything higher, than to *serve* God; something that ordinarily is reduced to the doing of one's duty, so that all religion is lost in the so-called *practice of virtue.*

And, however excellent discharge of duty and practice of virtue may be, when as ripe fruits they are picked from the plant of faith, yet, by themselves, apart from that plant, they can never make good the lack of real religion.

Surely, it is your duty to keep the commandment, but on condition, that you *honor* Him, Who gave you that commandment.

Every father of you, who has obedient children, who never do wrong and never make any trouble, but who never company with him, never honor, nor show him filial affection, might envy the other, whose children are not always exemplary for goodness and sweetness, but who dote on their father and carry him on their heart and are attached to him with their best love.

And not this antithesis, but this rule applies also to the Lord our God.

Altogether good people, but who have no desire after the hidden walk with God, are an offense to Him and an insult to His love.

And therefore calls and complains the Lord so touchingly and tenderly by Malachi (1, 6): "If then I am a Father, where is *mine honor?*"

WHAT this honor of God is, appears, when you consider two things, first *reverent praise,* and secondly, *attachment of soul.*

"Praise is comely for the upright" (Ps. 33, 1), says the Scripture. To *praise* it urges man and angel. "Praise the Lord, sing forth the honor of his name!" (Ps. 66, 2), is the call that is sounded in all the holy Testament. To make the name of God ever greater is the blessed accord, that is enticed from human tongue and angel voice.

In unhealthy mysticism, they who are overspiritually minded object to this, and put the question, whether before God anything counts except the impulses of the heart, and what that outward praise and Halleluiah Song can mean to Him; but this standpoint is false and is contrary to the creation-ordinance that created us soul *and body.*

Of course, praise in the lips *without* praise in the heart degrades the human psalm to the song of the lark. In the praise of the lips the heart must flow out. But the heart must never imagine that the "calves of the lips" have no significance before God.

As among men the tribute of praise to those who attain high and honorable posts is demanded, so the Lord your God demands of you, that you praise Him, that you confess Him, that you honor Him, that you thank Him, that you worship Him.

It is impious familiarity, which does not become you, when you deem, that your love for God excuses you from reverent worship.

Read it in Revelation, how even in the heaven of heavens, where love is perfect, the offering upon the altar of the Holy One is unalterably composed of love and *adoring praise.*

BUT you are right in this: in that outward worship the honor of your Father Who is in heaven does not come to its own.

If then I am a Father, asks the Almighty, *where is mine honor?* So in the honor which you offer unto God, the child-element also must come to its own, by warming the worship, that by itself is cold, and by making it glow with the *soulful affection of filial love.*

Also in this honor of God there operates a *centripital* and a *centrifugal* force.

A sense of deep reverence and respect, which would make you exclaim: "Depart from me, O Lord, for I am a sinful man." A trembling before His Word and a sacred fear before His Holy Majesty.

But also a deep-felt sense of clinging affection. A drawing of heart after the Eternal. Inability to rest before His holy fellowship is found. A thirsting after God, as the hart thirsts after the watersprings. A going out with all your soul after His hidden walk.

This is the second part of the honor that is due unto God *as* Father, and *because* He is Father.

The claim of the Father-heart, that is well-pleased and accepts the love of His *child*, and where in its sum-total it constitutes the outflowing love of His people.

A love in which we always fall short; which on earth shall ever remain a small beginning of what it must be; and which by reason of its insufficiency ever and again puts to shame those who spiritually are more deeply initiated.

When these two, this reverent worship of prayer and praise, and that soulful attachment of love, inwork one upon the other, then, and only then, *is worship and love mingled as offering*, and our Father Who is in heaven receives something, however imperfect, of His honor.

In addition to these two parts there is still another, even the *reflective*, which equally closely touches the honor of God as Father.

God the Lord has put into human fatherhood a *reflection* of His own Divine Fatherhood.

He could have ordained human procreation in another way, so that no man would ever have become a father.

But He did not ordain it so. By His ordinance regarding the propagation of our race, God made man a father. And even now, for as many as there are, whom God granted to beget a child, it is our God *Who made them father.*

Then in such an one He mirrors the image of His own Divine Fatherhood, and wills and demands, that in this reflected fatherhood we shall honor His *original* Fatherhood.

Therefore must a child honor his father.

Not to preserve domestic order. Not because his father supports him. Not because father is the older. But because in honoring father, we honor our Father Who is in heaven.

When I tear off the epaulets from an official, I do no injury to him, but to the king, who attached these epaulets to his shoulders, as a sign of his office. So also, when a child withholds honor and homage from his father, he does sinful man no harm, but he assails God, Who shadowed forth His Divine Fatherhood upon him.

To honor your father and your mother, is to honor God in them.

And he who professes piety, and breaks the fifth commandment, robs God with the left hand, of what with the right he offered upon His altar.

He who is an earthly father, sees in that part of God's honor an obligation for himself of highest seriousness.

You can mirror God's Fatherhood in your own fatherhood before your children in a beautiful and striking way, but you can also do it in an unsightly and false way.

Then arise those bitter conditions, that you do not entice honor and love from your children, but rouse antagonism in them, strife between dislike of your person and the honor which they owe you as their father.

The holy apostle calls this: provoking one's children. To demand: you must honor me, and meanwhile give them occasion to despise you, or at least to have no respect for you.

Something which never sets the child free from obligation to the fifth commandment. This, like all other Divine commandments, remains unshakable as a rock. But for your child it becomes a grievous temptation to sin. A temptation that goes out from you, to work its ruin.

Whoever therefore is father or mother, must in this respect also give God honor, that in their own person they bear *with honor* the reflection of the Fatherhood of God.

That in everything they prove themselves worthy of respect before their children, and make themselves a blessing to their children in the grave work of training and educating them, not merely to safeguard themselves against self-degradation, nor yet merely to teach their children order and discipline, but above all and first of all, in this matter of the home-life to let the Lord our God come to His honor as Father.

Here, too, in God the starting point and in God the final goal.

From, through and to Him likewise the honor of the fifth commandment.

XVIII

Can a Woman Forget Her Sucking Child?

THE MOTHER

WITH a beauty that never pales, the prince of poets celebrated in song the tie, that binds the mother to her child, which she bore in sorrow, fed with milk at her breast, and had carried for so long under her heart, as that which "unites *the blood.*"

The estimate was correct. The love of mother for the child she bore does not spring from a tendency of soul, but from the blood, and therefore love in wedlock stands higher, because, "stronger is the tie of the couple, that, hand in hand, joined not to separate," for they love each other from inclination.

You need but to compare the world of our human life with the world of animals, to see at once the truth of this antithesis.

If the love of mother for her child were indeed the outflow of an higher inclination of soul and of self-denial, you would have to find this beautiful trait among people, but not among animals.

Yet the *opposite* is the case.

You find this love of her who was permitted to give life for what came to life frequently more strong with animals than with human beings.

Birds and domestic animals vie with one another to make exhibition of this, and already in early youth we read all sorts of interesting stories of little animal mothers, that sacrificed themselves for their young.

Yea, more still, even Holy Scripture has so high an estimate of this animal love, that in terms of it our Savior expresses His own love for His people, as when He compares this His love with that of a mother-hen, that covers her chickens with her wings, while on the other hand in Isaiah 49, 15, our God assumes at least the possibility of the human mother, that can forget her sucking child.

For it reads: "Can a woman forget her sucking child, that she would not have compassion on the son of her womb?" And then there follows: "Yea, they may forget, yet I will not forget thee."

Somber prophecy of what did happen, when it came to the destruction of Jerusalem. For then, according to the dreadful historic narrative, in the insanity of hunger, mothers in Jerusalem killed their own sucklings, to feed themselves with their flesh.

WOULD you therefore count mother love for her child a small matter, and as something of minor importance?

You know that in more than one land, such as in France, and elsewhere, especially among upper classes, this love is ever more lightly counted. She who became mother soon abandons her child to the care of nurse and wet-nurse, and with many a mother all the concern with such a young child consists in this, that mornings and evenings she makes a short call at the nursery, or at times receives the beautifully dressed infant and makes a show of it in her luxurious drawing-room.

Even this some mothers deem too much. In France already two or three months after the birth there are many who send the little one far from home with a nurse to the country, that nothing may interfere with their pursuit of pleasure and enjoyment.

So in Paris, little mothers among animals do not act, but so frequently do they who become mothers among women.

Yea, there are those who purposely allow the milk in their breast that God gave them for their child, to dry up and disappear.

Thus in every sense there is reason, not to undervalue the love of mother for her child, but rather to hold it high among us, lest with us also the practice gains foothold, which elsewhere is established to the shame of the name of mankind.

For the love of mother for her child is very like the love of an animal for her young, but it is also different.

With an animal love operates *exclusively* by instinct, is nothing but an impulse of nature, and shows itself therefore always in the same form and in the same way.

But so it is not with human mothers.

With our mothers this love for the child is a mixed phenomenon. It certainly springs from the blood. For no small part as instinct also common to her. But yet with the mother it is bound and subjected to the control of her moral life.

Not the animal, but she, can abandon her child to others or neglect it. And also, not the animal, but she, can carry that love up higher, ennoble and sanctify it.

Here applies therefore the gift of distinction.

As regards the love of such a mother for her child, you have to distinguish between two component parts, on one side what God instilled into her mother-nature, and on the other side what she did with this.

For what is instilled in her by God, the honor is not hers, but His. This is the nature of all mothers, and common to all including domestic animals and birds.

By itself there is nothing noble in this, bears no moral character, and is absolutely no evidence of self-denial.

A young woman, who thus far lived exclusively for herself and vanity, and now having become mother, at once forgets her vanity, is interested in and by her child, and for months together nurses her child, lives for her child, plays with the child and enjoys herself, may thereby become accustomed to self-denial and weaned from vanity; but by all this strong mother-love she offers no proof yet in the least of moral devotion.

What she does, the mother-hen in her way does too.

In this therefore God is great, not she, and He alone is glorified, Who increated this beautiful trait in the mother as in the animal. A trait, which commonly is even more strongly evident among primitive peoples, than among civilized nations, in the country more mightily than in our refined cities.

BUT what the animal lacks, the human mother possesses, namely: by reason of her moral nature, she can either direct this love and sanctify it, or go contrary to it and sin it away.

The latter she can do in either one of two ways:

She can silence the voice of nature and commit her child to the care of nurse or governess; or she can let her love for her child degenerate into infatuation for her child, misuse her child as a doll, and by her passionate attachment to the fruit of her womb already from the first beginning spoil her child.

It can also be otherwise, and God be praised, among those who confess the Lord it frequently is otherwise.

A mother can also elevate and ennoble, what in her nature is common with the animal. With moral insight and tact she can take this trait of nature as starting point, to love her child *in the faith.* For God's sake and from an inner sense of duty she can devote herself to her children. And putting aside all maternal vanity and passion, she can so direct and train her child already in those first beginnings of life, as bears evidence of the rule of higher aim.

Then the mother sees in her infant not merely the fruit of her womb, but far more a little creature which by His wondrous power has been called into being, and by Him, the Father of spirits, has wondrously been embroidered in her womb.

Then in that young infant she sees not merely a bundle of soft and tender flesh, but a little human being, in which hides *a soul;* perchance one of God's elect, and therefore loved of God as the apple of His eye.

Then there is prayer for that infant before she sees it with her eye. Already during her carriage she avoids everything that can be of injury to her child. She struggles through her birththroes holding herself fast to the God of her life, that if possible, she might bring forth her little one. After the birth there is thanksgiving and making great God's glorious name. As soon as circumstances permit she seeks Baptism for her darling. The urge of her soul and the desire of her heart is, that her child may bear the seal of the Covenant. And she prays, not merely that God will spare her darling, but rather, that He may impart wisdom unto her, to show her child that real, that substantial, that glorious love, whereby from the very beginning she may convey not merely impressions, but *good* impressions to her little one.

And so real mother-love far excels the love of the mother-hen for her chickens.

There is indeed a common point of departure, but what the mother-hen lacks, the human mother shows that she possesses, even an higher, a nobler, a holier love, which what nature merely began, in and through grace makes perfect.

AND when finally it is asked, whether in Christian circles this higher, this nobler, this sanctified love bears rule, then there is truly cause for thanksgiving, but no less for complaint, and the reason of this backwardness for no small part is found with the mother of years, who gives her daughters in marriage, without having prepared them sufficiently for their task of life to come.

This is mostly left to take care of itself. It is thought that after marriage with the child true mother-love will come of itself. Training, direction, warning is here at least thought superfluous.

And then this very thing avenges itself.

The young mother is then presently so altogether

infatuated and charmed by her first mother-wealth, that she can think of nothing else, and almost will-less abandons herself to the impulse and passion of mother-love, and excludes from this her faith and her high calling.

This, too, will become different and better.

When presently Holy Baptism will resume its place of honor in our midst, from this holy Sacrament the spiritual call will go forth, which will impart to mother-love in our midst another, a higher, a holier character.

Not to say: "My child that I have borne," but the testimony: "A little creature of God, that I have received from Him, and that must be consecrated to Him," shall obtain the higher keynote.

And God, Whose is the blessing of children, shall become great again in the mother-heart.

XIX

Children Are an Heritage of the Lord

THE BLESSING OF CHILDREN

CHILDLESSNESS is a disappointment to the married woman, which grieves and in some measure even brings shame.

Later on this troubled feeling grows less, when more and more it becomes clear, that such is the will of the Lord; and years go on; and no one considers it any longer unnatural to find her without child; and other occupations are sought and found; and God Himself has reconciled her to her childless estate.

But in the first years first this deferment of hope, and presently the staying away of everything that can prophesy the fulfillment of that hope, is hard.

Many a youthful woman's heart has suffered bitterly under it. And sometimes after five or more years this bitter grief is taken away; but not always. There are many, for whom this sorrow of soul keeps on, and who all their life are bowed down under it.

In that one bitter word of childlessness there is such depth of sorrow.

Almost at once that uneasy feeling regarding the plant on which fruit is sought, but no fruit is found, and what of such a plant has once been said: Why cumbereth it the ground?

Then the void with respect to her own heart and womanly sense. To have a child of one's own, "flesh of her flesh and bone of her bone," is a luxury which naturally constitutes the dream of the young married woman.

There the heart went out to. There expectation adapted itself to. What had the impressionable mind not pictured to itself with regard to it. And then the disappointment. Every time again that biding and waiting. And always yet nothing but death within.

Then there is added to this, that the disappointment of her own heart painfully doubles itself in the disappointment of her husband.

A man who marries has no other expectation, than that after a year or more a descendant, a continuation of his own family, a child of his own blood shall be born, a child from her whom he loves, and whose love in that child shall be braided together with his own.

And now month after month passes on, and every time it is evident that such is not the case, and that his hope also is first deferred, and presently dismissed.

And though from love the husband hides this sore grief from his wife, yet she feels, and realizes, that he would be so happy to have it otherwise. And more still than by her own lack she is put to shame by the void in *his* happiness.

And as a climax of woe there are *the others.*

Young women, married almost at the same time she was, and who one after the other received the blessing of children from God; and every time it is reported again of one of her friends who had been confined, the old wound smarts anew.

And those other women-friends oftentimes make it yet more painful, by talking about her every time again, and inquire after and of her, whether she is not in expectation.

This is laughed off with a friendly reply. But the wound is opened anew, and the woeful pain of disappointment is suffered afresh.

THIS sadness of disappointed hope, as it expresses itself with the childlessness of a young married woman, is a witness, that has worth.

The voice of nature speaks therein, which is no other than the voice of Him, Who thus created this womanly nature.

It shows, that to receive a child is a blessing of God; one of those richest blessings, which He thought out for a woman; something that is hers to make her happiness perfect.

Without child she has not reached her destiny; and only when she may press her infant to her heart and may nurse it with her own mother-milk, she feels so deeply, that in this respect at least her destiny is reached.

If in this age more and more a demoniac power gains entrance, which seeks to avert the coming of a child by sinful practices, as though children were a curse, from which escape is justifiable, that bitter feeling of disappointment with a childless marriage, remains in the name of the Lord a protest against this demoniac tendency and a seal to the word of the Psalmist, that children are an heritage of the Lord.

But this protest also goes out toward another side.

There are many young women, who at first were so ardent in their desire after a child, but who, when God increases the number of their little ones, begin to be afraid of what at first is hailed with joy, and with the discovery of new pregnancy are filled with fright and dismay.

There can be a just cause for this.

There can be such a degree of bodily weakness, that new pregnancy brings danger with it. Business can be so bad, that the increase of her family fills her with concern. It can also be, that she does not feel capable to meet the ever-increasing demands, as her already grown-up children need her direction and help.

And much of this can be reverenced.

But there is also a complaint about that "being pregnant again" among women, with whom these causes do not exist. With whom it is simply a matter of weariness of the wealth of children. They were bent upon having the joy a child brings. But that want has now been met. And therefore it must end.

For that having children is still something else than a satisfaction of one's own desire. That there also is a duty in it, a calling on the part of God, such women do not realize.

"CHILDREN *are an heritage of the Lord,"* sings the Psalmist, altogether from the fundamental note of Revelation, which always presents childlessness as a bitter lot, and numerous little ones as a blessing of the Lord.

Heritage here means, that it is God, who *gives* us our children, because He *creates* them.

What you obtain by heritage, is something that comes to you from some one else; that of yourself you never would have had; in which his work and his power bore fruit; and of which the fruit is now given you.

Even a "portion of inheritance" not in the sense, as though it were an inheritance, that lawfully came to you, and to which you could lay some righteous claim; but such an heritage, as from an altogether sovereign disposition on the part of the testator is given to whom he wills.

The saying: *An heritage of the Lord,* thus implies two things: First that the child you receive is fruit of the *creative power of God;* and second, that it is given you from *sovereign free grace.*

Yea more still, because it does not say: Children are an *heritage of God;* but since it reads: Children are an *heritage of the Lord,* i.e. an heritage that comes to you from Jehovah, the God of *the Covenant,* this saying at the same time indicates the tie, which binds you and your children together and encloses you together in the Covenant of grace.

So that "heritage of the Lord" hangs together with the promise of: "You and your seed," and points not merely to the child-joy and child-blessing of this life, but also to the high and glorious calling, that a woman on earth may be mother of God's elect, and from her reins may bear not merely for this world and for the grave, but also for heaven.

MOCKERY is made of this, indeed, in light-hearted ways, and he who with his many children has difficulty to make ends meet, is easily enticed to say recklessly: "A fine kind of a blessing, so many children, when you scarcely have bread for them", but such words say nothing.

In part such complaints are explainable, because the duty which we have to make good to our children, is one of such long duration, one so continuous, and one embracing so much. And not infrequently sickness and adversity and perverseness in the behavior of our children, can make the performance of this long-drawn-out duty very burdensome.

But explicable or not, all such sayings are unholy. He who so speaks or complains, forsakes his faith and stands at the wrong viewpoint.

You are not in the world to follow your own desire or inclination, but to serve the Lord your God in the work He has given you to do.

What that work is, is His, and not yours to decide, and though he calls you to be nothing more than a drawer of water and hewer of wood, if He calls you to it, you must also in this your Divine calling be faithful and happy.

But when this same God calls you, to spend your gifts and your powers in the care and training unto eternal life of living beings, of human children, of beings created after His image, of the highest there is on earth, and therefore of beings whom He has elected, eternally to glorify His Name, then a Divine calling is thereby laid upon you, which far excels in excellency all other trouble and labor.

Nothing on earth is superior to man. Far above all gold and diamonds a human infant glistens, in worth and significance, because God created it after His image. And when God the Lord commits to your care not merely one child, but several children, and gives them to you as *your* children, and thereby builds up your house and generation, who then shall complain, who not glory, and feel himself honored of His God?

YOU only receive these children for a short time.

They are little beings with an eternal destiny. From these your children there shall presently unfold a new generation, and after that a third generation, and so on. And personally, too, these little ones are such wondrous creatures of your God, that, while everything passes away, your children are immortal, and have an eternity before them.

Of the thousand times thousand years of their existence, they stay with you and thus under your care, but for a little while. Sometimes they leave your house before they have fulfilled six times three or less years. And when they stay longer, it is always yet, oh, so short, compared with the eternity that awaits them.

And now they are given to you, in the time of their life, in which they are most susceptible and receptive of impressions. The clay is still soft, and easily takes the form which you impress upon it. And for these years they are committed to you, that you should give them a bend toward good, prepare them for the struggle that awaits them in the world, and give them sense and taste for that glorious, that ideal, that spiritual world, which is with God.

Is not this task beautiful? Is not this calling heart uplifting and inspiring? And it is not your heaviness and dullness of spirit, that, amidst the multiplicities of life, makes the beauty of this calling to be lost in the weariness of your cares?

And therefore God's Word is so encouraging and good for you. For when in your faithlessness and infidelity you sometimes complain: "Oh, those children," it always tells you again in the Name of your God: Do not complain, but give thanks, for your children are for you *an heritage of the Lord,* if you but have the obedience of faith in your children also, to see the costly, sovereign gift of God's grace.

XX

Curiously Wrought

THE EXPECTATION

OUR fathers loved to hark back to their own personal creation.

They came to this naturally by their going back to their fall in Adam; something of which superficial Christendom, that now prevails, simply knows nothing.

What, they ask us, did Adam's fall to me? "In sooth, I have enough to do with my own sins, than that I should trouble myself about the sin of a man, who has already been dead many thousands of years. Not the fall of Adam, but my *own fall* keeps my soul from rest. And the prayer that thrills my heart, is by no means how Adam was saved, but how I can be saved, and my sinful heart be delivered from guilt and sin."

The superficiality of this merely seemingly serious language is evident.

He who speaks thus, presents himself, as one who had suddenly been placed here on the earth, with no single tie to relate him to his former generation. All such Christians speak as individuals who stand alone by themselves, and understand nothing of the tie that binds them to our entire human race.

And, of course, then you are bound to come to a false conclusion.

For, you are *born*. Born from a father and a mother. From that father and mother you have been born *in sin.* Your moral life in part is still dominated by their moral life.

As it is now with you, it was before with them.

They too stood vitally related to *their* father and mother. And so it ever goes on. Back from generation to generation. Ages and tens of ages together. And when finally you ask: "Did this never cease?" the answer runs: "Yes, once and with one man it did cease, and that man was Adam," simply because Adam had no father and no mother, and with him alone there was no mention of having been conceived and born in sin. Of course from this Christ is excluded.

When one class of Christians speak of their personal guilt only, and another class of their *guilt in Adam,* the latter is no play of words, but profound and serious truth.

One acts as though he had no past back of his birth, while the other knows that he was already included in the loins of Adam.

THIS going back to Adam leads of itself to taking one step further, and thoughtfully to enter into the wondrous work of our own *creation.*

At that other standpoint one does not ask after this, and deems that our whole Christian religion consists in the confession of the Savior and in seeking fellowship with the Holy Ghost.

So the second and third Person of the Holy Trinity comes to His honor, but the first Person is passed by, and the glorious confession: "*I believe in God the Father Almighty, Creator of heaven and earth,*" is, at the recital of the Twelve Articles of the Faith, said after others, but one does not enter into it with lively concern and so renders it non-active.

Not that in general the work of Creation is denied. Sometimes even with enthusiasm the glory of God in the realm of nature is set forth. But the personal life of faith keeps no count with it. And when one speaks of his Christian religion, it is as though that first of the Twelve Articles of Faith does not belong to it.

And with respect to this the attitude of the "men of God" in Old and New Covenant was altogether different.

When John begins his Gospel, he begins with the majestic narrative, how and by Whom all things were *created.* With Matthew we learn, how Jesus spake of revealing secrets, which had been hidden from before *the foundation of the world.* In Revelation the Lamb appears, as ordained from *before the Creation.* And Paul every time puts not only the Creation in the foreground and points to the mystery, which had been hidden through all ages, but is now revealed, but also, takes special pains to lay bare the root of your personal salvation in and beneath the depth of Creation by directing you to an *elective* grace, which preceded all creation.

And when you come to the Old Testament, this going back to the Creation here bears even a still more severely *personal* character.

Does not David go back to the days of his own infancy, when he sings: "Thou didst make me hope, when I was upon my mother's breasts." Does he not celebrate in song what lay *back* of that child life at mother's breast: "I was cast upon thee from the womb" (Ps. 22, 9, 10). Does he not go back further still in Ps. 139, and does he not enter still more deeply into his own conception and birth and creation, when he says: "Thou hast covered me in my mother's womb. I will praise thee; for I am fearfully and wonderfully made. Marvelous are thy works. And that my soul knoweth right well. My substance was not hid from thee, when I was made in secret, and curiously wrought. Thine eyes did see my substance, yet being imperfect, and in thy book all my members were written, which in continuance were fashioned, when as yet there was none of them."

Succinctly and strongly expressed, without a trace of that prudishness, wherewith among some people all talk about human birth is cut off as less delicate.

And what you also observe, is, that by that going back to *the* Creation and to his *personal* creation, David as of itself comes up to foreordination.

Faith in *election* and faith in the *creation* hang inexorably together, and by nothing so much as by letting go one's hold on the Creation is the faith in God's election undermined.

FROM whence am I? How did I originate? Where lie the first origins of my life, before I was yet brought into this world?

Such looking at the riddle of your own life, of your existence, comes early or late to every one, who knows the urge, to withdraw himself from the distractions of life into quiet meditation.

He who takes his existence seriously, can not escape from the overwhelming power of these our whole existence dominating questions.

And is it not strange, that one finds people, who when it comes to an inheritance, or merely to be able to boast of high descent, with all accuracy examine their family registers, of three and four centuries back, to lay bare the fountain of their noble blood, but who never come to it, more yet than after these human origins, which so often occasion pride and vanity, to ask after the origin of *their soul,* and after their descent from the hand of their *Creator?*

The tie that binds us to God, must run along two lines: the one vertical, the other horizontal. That is to say, from our soul the one line goes up on high, to seek our God in His glory. But the other goes along the level of the ages, from us out to the generations, that have been before us, and arrives, where lies God's work of Creation and where full of majesty that Divine work of Creation comes forth from His Foreordination.

Once you were not. Then you came to be. You also are a creature of God, thus created by your God. From His hand you have come forth. The fountain of human life, from which as a drop you have come forth into the full stream, only operates by His Divine power and by the disposition of His holy will.

And therefore what David said, you must confess regarding yourself.

Not only that the Lord "has seen your substance being yet imperfect," but also that in your mother's womb with his own hand He has "curiously wrought you."

Yea, more still, that before He thus formed you, also your stature, your character, your mark stood written in His book, before at His high command all these things went forth, before you as child were born, and on this earth originated as man.

WHETHER the royal harpist sang this song of his birth before his God on his birthday, cannot be known. But it may well be said, that no Psalm can more deeply interest you on your own birthday. And that no day invites us more naturally than our birthday to this going back to our origin as man.

Surely, thinking back upon your past is profitable, and the going through once more in your imagination of the years, which you have lived, can make your praise of the mercifulnesses of your God very abundant and your estimate of yourself very humble.

Such a going through of our own life's history on such a day is in place.

But you do well not to confine it to this chapter of history.

This history of your own life is a page of God's Providence, but that Providence over you is only explicable from your *creation* and from what lies *back* of your creation.

Let every child of God therefore on such a day of commemoration enter also into that depth, until, by way of his own creation and of his own foreordination, he comes to that Divine good-pleasure, in which his life took origin.

And if you object and say, that on such a day of commemoration there is too much diversion and too much goes on, that renders even a few moments for serious thought almost impossible, then let me ask, whether a birthday is rightly spent without a quiet restful outpouring of your soul before the Eternal.

Among the Lord's people the *birthday* must bear another character than among the people of the world.

In the world that day is spent with family members and friends, and knows no other enrichment of life than the festal board and presents.

But he who may know himself as a child of that Father Who is in heaven, can on that day also not get along without that God of all mercies.

And though it is very possible, that that day itself was almost altogether filled with festive activities, and in the tension of festal joy every chance for quiet thought was cut off, there is a *preceding* day and a day *that follows,* and within the course of these three days the going back to one's origin from God should be known by every one of God's children.

XXI

How He Would Have Him Called

GIVING OF NAME

THE newborn child is by no means alone in getting a name. On the contrary there is a need, to call everything, that we severally desire to indicate, by a name of its own.

God the Lord Himself set the pace in calling inanimate things also by a name. "And God," so we read in the majestic document of creation, "called the light *day*, and the darkness He called *night*." In the same way God the Lord *named* the name of every part and element of the world, of the *firmament*, of the *dry* land and of the *seas*.

And when man, created after the Divine image, appeared on earth, his first thought at the sight of Eve, was how to name her (Gen. 2, 23); likewise God brought the beasts of the field to Adam, *to see what he would call them* (Gen. 2, 19).

To call everything around us by a name, has become a second nature to us, a necessity of our spirit. Every land bears a name, and every district and city and hamlet, and in city and village, every street and byway and alley. Even houses are numbered, but of old every house, even as now every estate, had a name of its own, and in our centers of commerce with our storehouses the case is the same.

Inexhaustible indeed is the flood of names, wherewith man has covered the world. There is no river and no stream nor pond, no bay or narrows, no cape or mountain, no coast or strand, in brief, no spot of ground of the whole earth, but man has named it by a name. By a name also every sort of plant and animal.

And this is not the end, for also in those sorts of animals we give our own animal again a separate name. There is no dog, but has a name of his own; no horse in his stall that is not called by a name of his own; and they who go out to milk the cow call her from afar by name.

In navy-yards this goes even so far, that at the launching of the ship, she is ceremoniously named. Even at the naming of a ship sometimes prayer is offered. Fortunately not in the Dutch language, but in English and French, in a questionable way there is frequent mention of *christening* a ship.

YET it is at once evident, that all this sort of naming is nothing but the far background, that lies behind the naming of the *name* in highest sense, and that in all name-giving this highest is only reached, when man kneels down, and prophecy is fulfilled, which God proclaimed by Ethan (Ps. 89, 26): "He shall call me: *Thou art my Father, my God and the Rock of my Salvation.*"

This is the *highest* naming. Thus resounds the name that is above every name. In the worship of the Only-One all giving of names celebrates its absolute triumph.

Between that lower and this highest name-giving stands the naming of the human child. Taken from the earth, and yet created after God's image.

It is for this reason that the naming of a child is a

piece of history; that Holy Scripture comes back to it so often; and that God himself has so frequently deigned, to change human names into new names. Think of Abraham and Israel. And stronger yet, that as promise it is sure for every child of God, that once he shall "receive a white stone, and on that stone a new name, which God shall give him, and which no one knows but God and he."

Thus every child that is born should really have a name of its own, a name which no one else bore; and every one elected unto salvation should before and in Baptism receive a name, that would express what once eternally he shall be in the kingdom of heaven, and what the particular and appointed calling is, which to eternity is laid up for him.

Of the stars Isaiah the prophet says, that God calleth them all by name by the greatness of His might for that He is strong in power. Those names, those real, actual names of the stars are unknown to us; those God alone knows; and we help ourselves with mechanical names and speak of Mars and Mercuries, of Jupiter and Saturn.

So the matter stands with respect to our children, in case they go into life. Their real name is not told us. That God alone knows, and only in eternity shall it be discovered to them.

If we could look into their being, we would know their real name; but now that we do not know this, we help ourselves with respect to our children with imperfect auxiliary names, and give them names from Scripture or family names, if not names, in which, as though they were dogs or horses, our whim is at play.

One knows that at the end of the last century especially this whimsical desire to choose fanciful names was very strong. Only think of the very common name of *Egalite*, i.e., *Equality*, wherewith then thousands and tens of thousands in France, and also in our own country, were named.

So when God gives us a little child, and we come to giving it a name, we should first of all sense our impotence.

We see that little child, that newly-born infant, in the cradle, or on the bed in mother's arms; but it is and remains a perfect mystery to us.

We do not understand that infant. It is a closed book to us. We can read nothing in that child as yet either of his disposition or of his character.

Also before such a newborn infant our impotence is so entire.

And yet the babe must receive a *name*. He must be named in his Baptism, he must bear a name, if you would make report of him to the clerk of vital statistics. Without name no infant is thinkable.

Then to find a name, that shall be prophetic, is a task of such entire hopelessness, that as a rule weeks before it is born, a name is mutually agreed upon.

And it almost never happens, that before the child is finally given that name, it is gravely considered whether that name is suitable to *this* child.

In Zachariah's home this went so far, that of itself the family gave John the name of "Zachariah." The first son must be named after the father. Such was the custom, it spake for itself. And only when Elizabeth raised the objection, and Zachariah's counsel was called in, did the child receive the prophetic, the of-God-ordained name of John (Luke 1, 62).

AND such is still the custom.

In every family certain names have become indigenous. From the two families of husband and wife these two series of names converge in the younger generation of the new household.

Right of custom has even here ordered a certain rule, and there are people, among whom this rule is strictly kept, that really every name of a child, that is to be born, is agreed upon in advance.

Such is the family rule, and so must his name be and not otherwise.

Herein lies something human, something that by reason of the coherence of our generation must be respected.

A dog, a horse, or a ship is just named. According to whim or fancy. Accidentally, and without further thought.

But with children the connection with former generations must be honored. Every child that is born, is no oneling, but a bearer of the blood, and thus also of the traditions of parents and grandparents.

People stand related with people. We belong together. Together we form one great and broadly ramified society. And that relation, that connection is expressed, by giving the name of father and grandfather, of mother and grandmother, to children and grandchildren.

In every family an emulation should be alive, gradually to elevate one's generation along spiritual lines; to lift it up to higher levels; to make it richer through and for God; and it is this stimulus to attain nobility of soul that comes to us from our ancestors, and which by this permanency of family names must operate in us.

SOMETIMES we diverge from this, and ask some one outside of the family, to be godfather to the child; or we give the child the name of a man of reputation, whose memory, after his death, is sacred to us.

In early Christian times this was done systematically. When from among the heathen one came to Holy Baptism, he had to give up his old name, and accept a Christian name. Such had been the custom in Israel with Proselyte Baptism. A heathen who went over to Judaism, had to leave father and mother and abandon his past after the flesh, to pass over into the spiritual Israel, and there receive a new father, and from that father a new name.

This became the custom among Christians. He who became a Christian left his heathen affiliations and bid his heathen name good-by, to pass over into the spiritual affiliations of Christ's people; among Christians to receive a new father, who was called godfather; and whose name he took.

With children, however, born of Christian parents this of course could not be practiced. They were born in the Covenant of grace, and as members of Christ's church they were baptized. So they received at once their permanent name, which name could not be heathen, but had to be a Christian name. Even in the days of the martyrs Baptism was denied by the Church, when it was proposed to call the child by a heathen name. This was not permitted. It was a denial of the Lord.

But a loved name from outside of the family was allowed to be taken wherewith as with a new element and with new spiritual power to enrich the life of one's generation. For by that name the spiritual significance of him, after whom such a child was named, was woven into the family traditions.

So it behooves us, in naming our children, to act consciously. With clear insight into our impotence, to call our children by that name, which they have with God; but also with clear insight, what the giving of such a family name or the calling after a revered name from elsewhere, means.

A name means so much. When in serious moments you call one by his name, by that name you bore down into the deepest being of his soul. When in bitter strife of soul one calls himself by his own name, the impression of it upon his soul's perception is so mighty.

Therefore one should really have but one name, and naming a child by three, four and more names, does not prevent, that only one of these lives, and that the other as dead names stand alongside of it as mere figurants.

But one should take the name one bears seriously. And the foolish urge, which is common especially among young girls, to maim her name and so to abbreviate it, that a striking sound is heard, and with that piquant nickname to make a show, is evidence enough that in her heart and upon her lips higher seriousness has not succeeded to banish vain self-complacency.

XXII

His Brother Abel

BROTHERS AND SISTERS

THE relation of brother to brother is the first, which after that of husband to wife, has originated among men.

After having heard of Adam and Eve, we hear of Cain and Abel, even with the dreadful outcome, that the one brother murders the other.

This last is not accidental, and points to the grave danger, that lurks in the brotherly relation.

Cain killed Abel, not because Abel had put anything in his way, but because as brother he stood in his way.

Cain was first alone, and when Abel came to stand alongside of him, the significant question arose, how to live with a second of like position, after higher ordinance on a footing of peace and love.

Adam and Eve did not stand as two equals alongside of and over against each other. In Adam there was superiority above Eve, and above all Adam and Eve complemented each other. She was "over against him as a helpmeet."

But such was not the case with Cain and Abel. These two were of one sort, both were *men*. And they stood on the foot of equality; both indeed were sons in the same family.

What Adam and Eve called their own, they put together as in one fellowship and for nothing could one envy the other. But Cain and Abel had to make division.

Also Adam and Eve were destined, till their death to remain united in the marriage bond; but presently Cain and Abel would each go his own way.

Even now this standing in the way of a brother is sometimes strongly evident.

There is an only child of rich parents. Presently he becomes heir to a million. But see, years after a brother is born, and that little brother, if he lives, costs him half a million.

Or, there is a king, who has two sons. The younger can become king, *provided the older dies.* The death of his brother would bring him the crown, but in case his brother lives, he is nothing, at most he is prince, but . . . his brother's *subject.*

So you perceive at once, what germ, what seeds of envy and sanguinariness can nestle in the seemingly so simple relation of brother to brother; and that germ, those seeds lodged in Cain's heart, and so was shed the blood of Abel.

The blood of *righteous* Abel, since in his heart Abel repressed these germs of brother-sin and overcame, while Cain fed them, cherished and as poisonous weeds allowed them to spring up in his heart.

Parents who discern this, know their calling, in the training of their sons to look carefully to the germination of this poisonous weed.

Also by reason of other interests.

It can scarcely be denied that in children generally certain traits of father and mother repeat themselves.

One time the likeness may be more striking, the other time weaker, but rarely is the likeness altogether wanting. The proverb "like father like son" conveys the general understanding of this.

But, and to this we would point, that likeness is rarely entire in a single child; and a father of six sons, will readily discover in each of them one of the main traits of his own character dominate. One will repeat more the trait of his heart, the other the trait of his thinking mind, a third the trait of his executive ability.

And this among brothers is so frequently the bitter fruitful cause of dissension and estrangement.

This would not be so, if the main features in our own character always belonged together. But we know better. All too often these traits of our character wage bitter war in our own person, and only with difficulty and by heroic inward effort are they reconciled one with the other.

But when these same traits of our character, which are reconciled in us, embody themselves in our children severally, and thereby show themselves the more one-sidedly, it lies at hand, that among these sons the self-same war breaks out, which we have waged in our own heart, but now without the tie, which the unity of our own person strung between them.

Or again, father and mother can be very different as to character, and then it is possible, that in one son the character of father and in the other son the character of mother repeats itself.

But while this difference of character with man and wife found a counter-poise in their marriage-tie, between brothers this counter-poise is altogether wanting.

Their taste and tendency go out in an altogether different direction, and not infrequently father and mother then forget themselves so pitifully, that from sympathy for their own image, by showing preference and choosing sides they make the estrangement yet more critical.

AGAINST this natural poison, which, by sin, has been infused into the relation of brother to brother, a strong antidote had to be provided; and this God the Lord gave us both in *common* and in *particular* grace.

In *common* grace by the feeling of mutual relationship and by common need.

This feeling of mutual relationship expresses itself so strongly, that even in every other association of life, to express, that one stands closely related to the other, purposely and by preference the brother name is used.

This is done in the professions, by those of spiritual affiliation, and even by Freemasons.

This feeling, this perception God Himself has implanted in the heart, and the admonition: "Leave him not to himself, he is your brother," in time of need, rarely fails of its effect.

Sometimes from this feeling springs up noblest friendship between two brothers.

This brotherly regard is strengthened, in the realm of common grace, by common need.

Land must be tilled, breeding of cattle must be attended to, and Cain has a taste for agriculture, Abel has more the nature of a shepherd. So one complements the other, and common need can unite both.

Far more sacred meanwhile is the counter-poise, which *particular* grace offers.

Christ Himself has sanctified the brother-bond.

He has deigned to adopt God's elect as His brethren.

And in connection with this blooms that sacred brotherhood in all that are born of God.

Born from one Father, and therefore all brothers together in the fellowship of the Only-Begotten.

And it is this brotherhood, of which a sacred glow shines out upon the brotherhood among sons in the same family.

IN our Christian families, therefore, the relation between brothers and brothers must be nobler and more choice, than is thinkable outside of the Christian domain.

Yet one must not depend for this all too greatly upon the natural course of things.

Father and mother, who were privileged to sanctify their sons in one Baptism, have to see to it in training them, that they draw the brotherhood closer between their sons.

It should not suffice them, that in their household it becomes no Cain and Abel's game. The brother-bond must also cast off positive fruit. There must not merely be no envy, but love must be cultivated. And that not only after the sons have grown up, and the characters have formed themselves; but this work of reconciliation and of brothering and of union must begin in their earliest youth. Already at their games.

That sisters also can exert a sanctifying influence on

this, shows many a blessed experience even in our days.

But yet the sons themselves, as soon as they awake to fuller consciousness, must look to this very seriously.

They too should know, what dangerous sparks they carry about in their own heart; and their prayer and their intent must be, to prevent every outburst of the evil fire.

XXIII

Am I My Brother's Keeper?

BROTHERLY LOVE

If ever there was what might be called a "winged word," to Cain belongs the drab honor, of having brought such an age-defying word across his lips.

Almost all the history of the world lies between him and us, and still it seems as though his evil exclamation: "Am I my brother's keeper?" translated in many hundreds of languages, ever yet grows in significance, and still more cutting than ever forces an entrance for itself into the inner chamber of our heart.

In that heartless, shocking exclamation Cain was so offensively honest.

Sin was yet too short a time on earth; it had just come up; it had not yet had time to make itself unrecognizable in its *deceptive* garb.

As it sprang up in the poisoned heart, so poisonously did it come to the outside in the word.

Applied to one's neighbor, sin was the disturbance of love, the breaking of the tie, the tearing up of all spiritual coherence.

Abel was there, and Cain was there, and these were two individuals loosely placed alongside of one another. As the mountains of Ebal and Gerizim lay each by itself over against the other, so stood these two men, in the mind of Cain, as two powers over against each other.

Abel did not need to be concerned *about him*. Why then should he in turn be concerned about Abel? Were he to do away with Abel, the chances would stand better for him, Cain. And so he slew the man, who stood over against him. And after that murder being asked, where Abel was, Cain carries the evil heart upon his tongue, and recklessly and brutally he puts the counter-inquiry: "Am I my brother's keeper?"

This question implies radically and plainly the denial, that we belong together; the denial of the love that must bind us together; the stopping of the mouth to the voice of the *one* blood, that calls in all that is called man; the unraveling of our whole race upon earth; the triumph of egoism.

And since this struggle of egoism, provoked by Satan, against the love that God pours out in our hearts, returns every day, in every age, and goes on between man and wife, between parents and children, among friends and relatives, between rich and poor, between him who offers wages and draws them, in brief in all the broad field of social life . . . therefore Cain's exclamation has lasted through the ages, therefore either as defense or as accusation this exclamation has been repeated among people at all times, and even now, as egoism ever lifts its head more boldly, that "Am I my brother's keeper?" becomes more and more the motto, that divides the main streams of our time.

On one hand egoism, with its cool calculation, not regarding the brother and aiming only at oneself, and seeing nothing else in man, as slave of wages, except a machine that grew of itself, which is used, and after use is thrown aside.

But also on the other hand the social power of love, which unites and weaves together; which deems no human suffering foreign to itself; seeks the brother to devote oneself to him; and which in man never forgetting God's creature, is ever mindful of the holy ordinance of God, that we should be a guardian angel to our brother, a responsible protector, a *brother* in all the rich meaning of the word.

WITH this struggle, however, this strange feature is encountered, that in this brother-protection there is continually and in all sorts of ways mention of the *more far away brother*, while the brother *near by* is scarcely noticed.

Originally and in the strict sense your brother is only he, who with you is born from the selfsame father and mother.

From the beginning the brotherbond is a *domestic* bond.

Your real, your near by, your full brothers do not live apart from you in the world, but with you under the same roof-tree, sitting down with you at the same table, sharing the same life with you.

And see, while every one is full of zeal about searching out his brothers among the heathen by missions, and honoring his brothers among his compatriots, and assisting his brothers among the working classes, and comforting his brothers among unfortunates and sufferers, it is as rare as a white raven, when, even in preaching, you hear the children of the same family admonished and urged to the practice of brother- and sister-love among themselves.

This is deemed superfluous. This needs no more to be said. This sort of brother-love the family cherishes of itself: It plants itself along by self-sowing. To press this matter were a preachment of what every one already knows.

And while as bitter fruit of this silence this love among brothers and sisters frequently leaves, oh, so much to be desired, there is abundant talk of a general, far-reaching, all embracing brother-love, with never a thought, that though it reaches very far, at the same time it becomes more and more estranged from itself, till what in origin and essence *brother-love* is, almost no one any longer understands.

Is not this the wrong way?

Between *brothers after the blood* occurs in Cain and Abel the quarrel of fatal egoism. The saying: "Am I my brother's keeper?" is meant of a brother after the flesh. Only taken in the relation of blood is the expression: *brother*, real. In every other realm it is merely metaphoric.

God Himself established the home; and in that home the life that is lived together, there to give rise to the brother-bond, there to have brothers live together, there to cherish brother-love.

In such a household sin first attacked brother-love in its main artery, and the blood of Abel, whom Cain, his brother, murdered, still calls from the ground unto God.

And while thus, not in sound and word, but really and truly brother-love has been instituted of God Himself as a power *in the home*, in order, when it turns into strife of brothers, from the home to bring curse and judgment upon the world, in our imagined wisdom we are full of talk about all sorts and all degrees of brother-love, and meanwhile at the home-hearth, where it ought to be fostered and cherished, not to forget, but scarcely ever to reckon with it.

Yet here also God's ordinances suffer no resistance.

In a land, with a people, where family-life flourishes, and in that flourishing domestic life the tie also between brothers and sisters strongly draws, from this friendly home-life, a binding power of love will go forth upon all society.

While on the contrary, in a land and with a people, where home-life languishes, and brothers and sisters suffer life together as a burden, in order as soon as possible to part and to estrange from one another, there also in society at large the bond of love will lose all blessing-dispensing operation, and the whole social system will be dominated by cold egoism.

THAT at least all such parents, as have brought their children to Holy Baptism, might understand the seriousness of their calling, to cherish among their children, from the very beginning, in the early stages of self-consciousness, that love of blood, that brotherly attachment and affection.

Not after the evil rule "every one for himself and God for all," but according to the voice of blood, in which speaks God's holy ordinance, that even the young child may perceive, that he exists and lives *with* others, *for* others, and also for the sake of others.

For though it is true that even when training is deficient blood still draws, and that with serious sickness, or in case of loss by death, even in most neglected families this natural brother-love is still wonderfully evident.

Yet over against this stands the fact, that actual life continuously menaces that brother-love; that all sorts of interests continuously put brothers and sisters against one another; and that from these seemingly insignificant domestic quarrels between brothers and sisters an impression goes out upon character, which presently bears fruit in envy of heart, in bitter, evil words, sometimes in actual ill-treatment.

Also among brothers and sisters the proverb holds true, that it is not all gold that glitters. And though followers of Christ may pride themselves on a richer home-life, yet he deceives himself by accepting semblance and blindfolds himself to reality, who imagines, that in our Christian households the spirit of Cain never entered and brother-anger was never known.

AND therefore put aside the idea, that brother-love is a planting, that cherishes itself, and can spare your tender interest.

On the contrary, this tender plant is menaced by many evil insects and poisonous mold; it frequently lacks life-quickening light and cherishing summer-warmth; it threatens so often to wither in summer-drought or to grow numb from cold—that it cannot blossom, except it is watched, directed, purified and protected by a solicitude, that never denies itself.

That solicitude is parental duty toward children, but also duty of children among themselves, especially of the older to the younger, of sisters toward their brothers.

Not least this last.

For does not experience teach, that in the same family the tie among sisters is far stronger than the tie which ought to unite the brothers?

Comparatively speaking one hears so much more frequently of *brother-anger* than the whisper of *sister-anger*.

This is because sisters are shielded by the home-life, walk less ways of their own, and thereby are less rivals of each other, while their brothers soon go out into the world, and are by nature more disposed to choose paths of their own.

For that reason mutual sister-love, and their love toward their brothers exerts an influence of such inestimable advantage to brother-love in the family.

That in this respect also our young daughters might understand their calling.

Of God's church we sing: "Behold, how good and how pleasant it is for brethren to dwell together in unity" (Ps. 133).

But that it might be *spiritually* true, and God grant that spiritually it might ever become more true, before all things else, the claim remains inviolate, that family-life, from which the spiritual image is taken, should exhibit such dwelling together of the sons of the self-same family.

XXIV

Rebuke Before All

DISCIPLINE

Wrong must be rebuked, but in that rebuke itself new wrong, even sin is possible, when it is administered from an unholy motive or in an unrighteous, unpsychological way.

With a judge at court this is not so evident, because he is bound by penal law, must take in consideration all sorts of forms, and passes verdict mostly long after the wrong has been committed.

But at home with wife and children and servants, and in the shop or office with those who draw wages, the danger of rebuking a fault in a wrong way is far from imaginary.

Think of the fathers and mothers, who with all sorts of misdemeanors of their child let everything pass, and sometimes even take pleasure in his misconduct, and so far forget themselves at times as to encourage the wrong. But woe betide that selfsame child, when he does something that personally crosses father or annoys mother by disarrangement in household order. Then not infrequently father or mother instantly lose all patience, speak angrily to the child by reason of a far *less* significant wrong, and rebuke him in a way that goes beyond all bounds.

Of course he who rebukes so capriciously and arbitrarily, does not rebuke for the sake of God's will, neither for the maintenance of His ordinances, rebukes not even to improve the child, but merely to show that he is master and from personal resentment and anger.

With all such rebuke he in turn lays himself open to rebuke, for in most cases the sin in his uncontrolled temper is worse than the wrong for which he corrected the child.

Between mistress and maid, master and manservant one frequently witnesses the same thing.

One lets all sorts of things pass, that really ought to be reproved and rebuked; and then all at once by reason of a relative trifle there are high words, because one is irritated, and cannot control his temper.

This manner of rebuke is not merely injudicious and shows lack of knowledge of human nature, but what is worse, it opposes the ordinances of God, because of himself no one has ever the right to rebuke, no one possesses this right save by the authority of God, and therefore no one should ever rebuke another save for the sake of God, and this renders every rebuke from ill-temper and in anger *sin*.

IN another way also all sorts of wrong steals in with rebuke.

As with the question, whether you should rebuke before others, or in private.

For with respect to this, you are offended again and again at the wrongfulness of the manner of rebuke. At one time because there was rebuked publicly what you felt should have been done privately. And at another time because on the quiet, without any one knowing anything about it, a rebuke was administered, that in all justice should have been done before all.

In this too the Word of God mingles itself, for the holy apostle writes to Timothy: "*Them that sin rebuke before all, that others also may fear.*"

This is different language from what now we hear whispered abroad.

For in the circles, in which the spirit of the age strikes the key-note, it has almost become the fixed rule, that all rebuke must be administered in private, and opposition is more and more pronounced against all public rebuke.

So it is said, that by doing this on the quiet, you spare the *feeling* of the offender, that you inflict less pain upon his sense of honor, that you do not humiliate him in the eyes of others, that you gain his confidence thereby, and, in brief, have a better chance, to influence him for good.

In private the offender will be more ready to acknowledge his guilt, he will be more open-hearted, more honest, while in the presence of others he will try to justify himself, and easily incline to brutal falsehood.

The presence of others readily stimulates resistance, and invites defiance.

And the result of it is, that rebuke before others leads to seeming subjection, but fosters anger in the heart.

So one speaks in a fairly general way, and undoubtedly there is truth in this.

Only it can not go on *always,* for the Scripture speaks very definitely of cases to which the rule applies: "Them that sin rebuke before all, that others also may fear" (1 Tim. 5, 20).

THAT in this connection the holy apostle Paul merely refers to Ministers of the Word and Elders who erred, has nothing to do here.

The rule here put is of *general* tendency, and that rule tells you, that rebuke before all can be duty Divinely laid upon us.

So in the home this means, that you rebuke when all the members of the family are present at the table, or after the meal with the reading of God's Word.

And now the emphasis naturally falls upon that *sinning*. "To sin" is a stronger expression than to be naughty. Sin bears a more serious character. "Sin" refers to a wrong, in which violation of God's ordinances took place.

To lie, deceive, steal, meanness, brutality, with taunts to irritate, to mock what is holy, etc., all these are evil phenomena, that fall under "sin."

When, for instance, a child or servant rises at half past six instead of six o'clock, if told to rise at that hour, this tardiness is wrong and bad, but no sin, and only comes to be "sin" when this child or this servant despises authority, purposely disregards the given command, and on being corrected assumes an attitude, as though he were free to obey or disobey.

Generally, however, people turn this rule about. Such not doing what one is told to do is considered a great wrong, while the despisal of authority is scarcely noticed. They are angry when *their own commandment* is not kept, but transgression of *God's commandment* leaves them indifferent.

To this is added, that "sin" here referred to by the apostle, assumes that the other members of the household *know about it.*

When a child or servant has done something wrong, but of which the other members of the household know nothing, then according to Matt. 18, 15, all rebuke before others is excluded; at least when in private the guilty one comes to acknowledgment and contrition.

But when sin is become public, at least public in the household, so that the members of the household all know about it, and if the offense bears that serious character, which lies in "sin," then, says the holy apostle, you may not end the matter in private, but must *rebuke before all.*

Then it is not a question, whether the guilty one would like it otherwise, whether he will find it disagreeable, or whether you would rather do it in private, neither whether perchance it might irritate the guilty one, and perhaps harden him, but you must rebuke before all the others, because God's Word demands it.

Even the exception, that this is impossible with grown-up sons and daughters, will not do.

For what St. Paul says, he says even with respect to office-bearers who went wrong. And for the sufficient reason, that when an Elder, or an older brother or sister in the family, disturb the domestic order of God's ordinances, they weaken moral perception in a far worse sense, than one younger and less thoughtful, can do.

For upon the impression and upon the results of such a sin upon the other members of the household, the holy apostle founds his rule of discipline. For he adds: *That others also may fear.*

Every sin that becomes known in the family, be it falsehood, deception, opposition to authority, brutality or what not, threatens to weaken the moral elasticity of all the others.

Evil examples draw so strongly. A bad child so readily corrupts the moral character of all his little brothers and sisters. A bad element among the servants so frequently poisons the whole kitchen. One bad farm-hand almost regularly infects the whole estate.

He in the household who "sins" does not merely render himself personally wrong and guilty, but attacks at the same time the moral power of reverence and regard for God's law, on which every virtuous household must remain afloat.

And therefore such sin cannot be dealt with in private. What has touched all, and menaces to work evil upon all, must also be rebuked before all, that so the *moral order* in living together may be restored again in the sight of all.

God's authority over the family in part is put aside by such sin, and therefore in the presence of all and in the hearing of all the authority of God must regain its right of say in the domestic circle.

At the same time the good of this is, that one does not mete out punishment at the moment; that first one becomes calm; puts aside all feeling of personal resentment; shows nothing but *holy* wrath; and now with the majesty of parental authority which God has laid upon us, so rebukes that both the conscience of the guilty and the conscience of all others may be touched.

This does not say, of course, that one may not deal beforehand with the guilty one in private, to bring him to confession and contrition. It may sometimes even be advisable, by admonition and prayer, to prepare him for the rebuke before all.

This public rebuke also must be avoided, when the matter is not known abroad or is of too trivial a character.

But when in the home, in the office, in the shop, or wherever else, real sin has been committed and in such a way that *all know about it,* rebuke must be administered before all.

God's Word binds us.

XXV

Sheep in the Midst of Wolves

TRAINING

WHEN it comes to the training of their children, some Christian parents put themselves above the Lord Jesus.

Christ has certainly declared, that between His followers and the world there is a difference as of sheep and wolves; but they seem to know *better,* and think that *their* children and the children of the *world* are all of one sort.

So they see not the least danger ahead, when their baptized and Christ-consecrated children associate and are on intimate footing with children of their years, from families, where Christ is not known. And when the choice stands between children of a somewhat lower social rank from Christian homes and children of their own more highly social rank, but who stand outside of the faith, all too frequently they give the preference to that more highly social association for their children.

Worse yet, when a school must be selected, for their children, be it a lower or a higher grade school, even then many parents are *wiser* than the Lord Jesus, and do not believe, that here, too, there is mention of sheep and wolves.

In general, they are in favor of Christian education. Of course by itself this is better. And everything else being equal they would give their preference to a Christian school.

But when everything else is *not* equal; and as a

Christian school either requires more expense, or does not offer like privileges, or is not of one's own social rank, it is dismissed from further thought, and the child is sent *among wolves,* as Jesus would say; but as, to improve upon Jesus, they say: among *society people.*

BUT, you will say, Jesus did the same.

He did not keep his disciples apart. For He Himself declared it, in the very word to which appeal is made: "Behold, I send you forth as sheep in the midst of wolves" (Matt. 10, 16).

And this is so; only with this difference, that Jesus sent them among wolves, *when they were ready.*

Nowhere in Holy Scripture do you read, that when He chose Peter and Andrew, John and James and others as His disciples, the Lord Jesus first sent them to the schools of the Scribes or to the then University in Jerusalem.

These men had first been at school with John the Baptist. Truly no "respectable" school. In the wilderness, with a man clothed with camel's hair, and all sorts of sinners and publicans as pupils. A strikingly *peculiar* school.

And then Jesus had formed a school for Himself, and in two classes, if you will, had taught the twelve and the seventy each by themselves.

And so greatly concerned is He, lest His disciples should come under wrong influences, that, when He meets the masters of other schools, He almost always carries on the conversation Himself, and shields His disciples.

So the Lord Jesus, who evidently thought altogether differently about it from such parents, has trained His disciples quite *apart from* and *outside of* the influence of the official schools.

And only then; when this had been done; when their education was sufficiently finished and they were prepared; only then did Jesus appoint them, to begin their official ministry, and sent them out into the world, saying: "Behold, I send you forth as sheep in the midst of wolves."

AND of course this then is necessary.

When our children are matured and ripened, they must go out into the world; then there is no more room for delay. Jesus Himself prayed in John 17: "I pray Thee, Father, *not* that thou shouldest take them out of the world, but that *in* the world thou shouldest keep them from the evil."

To fight *for* Christ *against* the world is the calling in life also for our children. Thereby alone shall they once obtain the crown. And of course you cannot fight the world while you keep yourself apart. For this you must go out into the world. And as a sheep of the fold risk yourself among wolves.

So *you* must do, and so *your child* must do. But not until he is prepared, until he is matured, until he is well armed and equipped.

But such parents do not mean it in this way at all. They do not say: "My son is mature at an early age and burns with such zeal for Christ, that he is ready now to go out among wolves to fight for his Savior."

No, nothing of this.

If such zeal for the Lord Jesus had been fostered by them in their sons, they would be the first to send their children to a school, where the Christ is held in honor.

But they have not fostered this zeal from infancy. This zeal is *not* kindled in their child. For this reason their children find the wolves so nice and pleasant. And say: "Father, let us rather go out among the wolves. Such strong, noble animals. With those sheep things are so tame."

And then such parents answer: "Well, my boy, I do not want to compel you. If it can make your life more pleasant, go out among the wolves. But let them not bite you. Look out."

SUCH is the condition.

A condition which is only possible, when one accords his own insight a *higher* place than Jesus' utterance, and does not really believe what Jesus says. When in general one believes in Jesus, but does not give himself captive to His word.

There is, it is granted, *some* truth in it. There are wolves among them. But first they are not all such. And then there are wolves and wolves. And these men at least are not such very wild, devouring wolves. Among them there are wolves that are even lovable.

And after having so weakened oneself by all sorts of shallow, superficial representations, one proceeds to reason further about as follows: "My child has always been present when the Bible was read. I have always set him a good example. Really inimical he is not. And, moreover, so long as he is not converted, it makes no difference, whether I send him to a Christian school or not; if he truly is a child of God, his Savior will protect him even among wolves."

Oh, our heart is deceitful above all things, and desperately wicked: who can know it? (Jer. 17, 9).

And this is called, loving one's child. Such are parents that have made the Baptism vows. And every evening you may find such parents on their knees, praying, that God will keep their child.

But of what it is: *to tempt God*, such worshipers seem to have no faint idea.

One thing, however, may be asked of them, and that is, whether, after such a loveless weakness with respect to their children, they think that they can find ground for such praying in any internal address of the Holy Ghost?

CONSIDER indeed, what is implied in that sharp antithesis, which Jesus makes between sheep and wolves.

Does Jesus mean to say thereby, that his followers, without exception, are all so gentle and so dear; and that on the other hand the people of the world are as malicious as a wild animal?

Not in the least. With such self-complacency and with such self-conceited looking-down upon the people of the world, Jesus' saying has nothing to do.

You have seen in the meadow, how violently sometimes a sheep can butt and be anything but lovable.

But *this* is the point: A wolf is strong in defense

of his own domain, and this makes the people of the world so much stronger *in the world* than you; so that you are no match for them; so that your child stands *defenseless* over against them; and certainly is *lost* when he comes among them.

This first. And in the second place, the people of the world are fanatical in their zeal for the world, and are bent upon inspiring your child, who now still resists, with the spirit of the world. They cannot rest, until your child is become part of the world. For this reason Jesus calls them *wolves.* They want to make your child like unto themselves, identify him with themselves, and thus spiritually *devour* him.

And in the face of them we and our children stand as defenseless *sheep,* but as lambs of the flock of our Lord.

Not as an hart or an ox, which a wolf attacks also, but very definitely as "sheep."

Why so?

Simply because an hart defends himself till he drops, but a sheep, when the wolf comes, *flees to his shepherd.*

And so the lesson is this.

First keep your children with Jesus and under the shadow of His wings educate them until they are ready.

And when they are ready, send them out into the world, let them out among wolves, but as sheep, i.e., as young people, *whose shield is the Lord.*

XXVI

As a Lamb in a Large Place

GOING OUT

"LIBERTY" is the magic word of our age.

No tie, no limitation, no confining or encircling of your person nor of your life.

Our self, our individual being, our own insight and our own will, presently our own inclination and desire, must be all our law.

And where one still continues to be called "Christian," or even in a more serious sense still wants to be a confessor of Christ, and therefore does not say: "Let us break their bands asunder, and cast their cords from us" (Ps. 2, 3), and far less in the *"ni Dieu ni maitre"* (no God and no master) takes up the cry of the revolution, yet as Christian one dares to demand *the large place* for the "lambs of Christ."

On conscience, more than on God's Word, one will depend. One's own insight and one's own inspiration is of higher validity than the confessional standards of the Church. And not the spiritual *being-bound* in the Body of Christ but *liberty,* that moves itself about the pivot of one's own conviction, must have the promise of eternal life.

Such is the fanaticism with respect to a false idea of liberty, which is devoid of all harmony and deprived of all counter-poise. And such is no less the fanaticism with respect to our own individual excellency, which from the circles of the revolution has gradually gained admittance also in the circle of confessors of the Christ.

By a talented writer like Vinet, unintentionally on his part, this untrue movement has found its seductive interpretation.

Without knowing it and equally unintentionally John Darby has given to this revolutionary Christendom a form and an expression of its own.

The thesis heralded even among us, that the age of confessional churches was past, and that henceforth Christendom would float upon *the mysticism of the heart,* has given admission to this unchristian purport in wide circles.

And if in these our times, one would describe this critical phenomenon by a short word from Holy Scripture, there could ever yet no better expression be found, than what we read in Hosea 4, 16.

For insooth, what at this false viewpoint even a Christian desires to be, is nothing else nor better than: *a lamb in a large place.*

THE lamb does not belong in a large place.

The place of the lamb is *in the sheepfold,* or, when it goes grazing, with the flock, under the eye of the shepherd.

The lamb must not go for pasture, where it chooses, but must confine itself to the narrow range, appointed by the shepherd.

Large places are for wild animals, that wander from forest to forest, and by night come forth from among the trees, that, according to the picturesque expression of Psalm 104, they may "seek their meat from God."

And when the lamb, that belongs in the sheepfold and with the flock, but *not* in the large place, hankers after that large place, and possessed of longing, wanders off to that large place, it is exposed to a thousand dangers, and feels itself pursued and restless, and, unless the faithful shepherd finds and carries it back, it becomes a prey to the wolf that lies in waiting.

What Jesus says of the good shepherd, who for a moment leaves his ninety and nine, to fetch back to the flock the one sheep that strayed, is precisely the same image, that is drawn by Hosea of the "lamb in the large place."

The "lamb in the large place" is the image of man, of the youth, of the child of God, that cannot bear the bands, that before all things else wants to be free, and that deems in the large place to be able to watch over himself.

The "lamb in the large place" is the prodigal son, who wandered off in the world, and in that wide, wide world ended with sitting down weeping in the midst of the husks of swine.

"IN a large place" to walk about to one's heart's content, such is the sinful trait, which at the awakened and awakening life naturally exhibits itself in our human nature.

Not in the house, but in the street.

Not under parental oversight, but free man in the world.

Not bound by ordinances and usages of life, but play with life after one's own inclination and whim.

Such and not otherwise is the trait, that awakes in the heart of every youth, when he approaches the stature of a man.

Out from the sheepfold, away from the flock, to a large place, begins with being the thirst of every heart.

The more one is out in a large place, the freer and the more unconstrained, the happier one is, and the more highly honored by his equals.

This is not every one's good fortune. There are those, who, by sheer necessity of life and by the arduous day-task, or by a weak constitution, are held back from this vacuous, dangerous large place.

But there are others, who persistently carried their point, who unarmed and unhindered entered into the large place, and boasted, that at length they were as free as fish in water or as birds in air.

And when in the end accounts are examined, what has become of all these young men, or young women, who managed to get out into the large place?

Insooth, a few strong, vigorous natures have in the open field held themselves aloof from the wolf.

There are those, whom in His grace God took hold of in the open field, and brought them back to His sheepfold.

But, who can count them, the perished ones and those forever lost, who have paid the price of their wanderings about in the large place, in the loss of honor and virtue, of the plenitude of their strength, and of the promise of their future?

LET no one deem, that the evil trait, as lambs to wander off in the open spaces, mortifies with the years of youth.

Rather, be it in modified form, this evil trait continues to follow us after until our death. And every time again, even among God's best children, you meet with self-willed natures, that love spiritual wanderings, and deem that, when they have withdrawn themselves from the discipline of God's majesty, things will be better.

So to all appearances they live their spiritual life on their own responsibility. They have their own code of morals, which at one time arrests them at some point of law, and then again allows so much to pass by unheeded.

So they wander along in all sorts of paths of eccentric teachings or of excessive spiritual fanaticism.

No connection of the past, no tie of church or creed has any more hold on them. They are they that have been *set at liberty*, and therefore *free* Christians, and without compunction surrender themselves to the lust of their spiritual eye.

So they wander round and about, pitching their tent now in the woods and again in the barren wilderness. And in the wolf they no longer see an enemy. But against the dog of the shepherd is concentrated all their hatred.

Or, with them the spiritual is nothing but semblance, and under this pious mask they seek, worse yet, the lust of their heart, if not the evil lust of their flesh.

They still hear the voice of the shepherd calling: "Turn back!" but they will not turn back, and choose their own paths, and their heart beats faster within them, if they may but roam and wander about in large places according to their own caprice.

And so they get farther and farther away from God, they become more and more unused to Him, and the narrowness of the sheepfold begins more and more to offend them.

Till at length everything can pass, while at an evil hour something of the *wolf-nature* is entered into the nature of the wandering lamb, that has altogether gone astray.

AND worst of all is, that God the Lord not merely allows such wandering off, but sometimes lets it come upon us as a punishment, and brings it over us as a judgment under which we must succumb.

By Hosea says the Lord of Israel: "*I will feed* them as a lamb in a large place." That is: I will harden their heart. I will make them wander off from the flock. I will make them lose the path to the sheepfold. And it will be *My* holy judgment, that at length they wander about and go astray as a lamb in a large place of the unprotected field.

When God's first child, Adam the father of us all, sins away his Eden, God drives him out from Paradise, and exiles him to the broad places of the world, where thorns and thistles are prepared for him.

And so the Lord still does.

When it concerns a child of God's grace, of course, it is always with the purpose, and unalterably with the result, that the lamb in the large place at length begins to feel his need and death, and becomes conscious again of home-sickness after the sheepfold, and by the faithful Shepherd is brought back again to the flock, that God's angels might rejoice, and God's grace in His child might triumph.

But woe to him, who ever allowed himself to think: "Why should I not wander off? I am still God's child. In the end I will be all right," and under this deceitful pretense strangled reproach in his heart, stopped the ear to the voice of the Shepherd, and recklessly persevered in his roaming.

And therefore—since now again the lambs that wander about in large places are so many—by this brief word let the call go out to all who wandered off: "Abandon your false liberty-urge and turn back!"

"The place for the lamb, that has been purchased by the most precious blood, is not in the large place, but in the arms and at the heart of his Savior."

XXVII

Forget Not Hospitality

HOSPITALITY

IN His faithful Father-care, that extends to the whole of our human life, God the Lord has not deemed it beneath His Divine Majesty, in His holy Word to express Himself even with respect to *hospitality*.

To God's child nothing happens outside of holy ordinances, and he who fears God, will, even in this matter of hospitality, allow himself to be led not by impulse and whim, but by the ordinances of God.

At once be it observed, that now the holy duty of hospitality demands less from us than in the days of patriarchs and apostles.

In patriarchical times, when they who had been called of the Lord still dwelt in tents, the holy duty of hospitality required, that at the close of day one call in, refresh and lodge every traveler, that passed by his tent.

This had to be so and could not be otherwise, because a human being created after God's image must not be left like an animal to spend the night in the open.

Without this sacred duty of hospitality a traveler in those days would have perished from thirst or by night have become a prey to wild animals.

Such hospitality which was incumbent upon every one to offer was then indispensable to intercourse among people and to the maintenance of human society.

In the appearance at Mamre Jehovah Himself has sanctified this bounden duty in the tent of Abraham.

And when Eliphas tried to accuse Job of one of the most dreadful sins, on account of which God's wrath had come upon him, it was not least in this, that perchance he had dismissed some poor, weary traveler from his door, and had received in his tent the man of position and power (Job 22).

And when the Lord's people were settled in Canaan, tents of canvas and skins gave place to houses of stone and wood, but the duty of hospitality remained the same.

Even in the days when Jesus was on earth, His twelve disciples went through all the land, and took up their abode with people who were unknown to them.

Yea, our Savior goes so far, that in His striking sermon regarding the last judgment, He puts inhospitality in the foreground as reason of condemnation, saying: "I was hungry, and thirsty and a stranger, and ye took me not in, neither gave me to eat nor to drink."

And thus it was altogether natural, that the apostles of the Lord repeatedly bound the duty of hospitality upon the heart of the redeemed of the Lord.

Paul, when he wrote to the Romans (12, 13): "Be given to hospitality," and presently to the Hebrews (13, 16): "And to communicate forget not."

And likewise Peter (1, 4, 9), when he saw how hospitality began to be a burden to some, emphatically commanded them: "Use hospitality one to another, *without grudging.*"

Of this sacred duty God's Word demands, that you quit yourself according to the Lord's will.

"Inasmuch as ye have done this unto one of the

least of my brethren," spake your Savior, "ye have done it unto me" (Matt. 25, 40).

The world dares to say: "Uninvited guests one puts outside the door," but in God's Word it is counted you as sin, when, though you help the stranger along, with anger in your heart, you do it grudgingly.

Not only your friends and acquaintances, who can requite you again, but the humble and needy Jesus wants you to invite to your table.

Hospitality must be shown, not because the company of the stranger gives you pleasure, nor because presently in turn he will receive you, but because man, created after God's image, is not to be left to himself, and the brother in Christ must not be neglected.

This is still the case in out-of-the-way places, in villages where there is no inn. This duty still holds good in newly settled places in America, where one travels from homestead to homestead. In our East Indies the single European who lives in a *dessah,* is obliged to open his house to every white man that comes along. Even in some of our villages it repeatedly happens, that one does not dare to refuse a peddler a place of rest at least in the hay-mound.

Yet in all this there is but a faint reflection of what the sacred duty of hospitality once was.

Life and social life of men is so greatly changed, and with it the obligation which hospitality imposes on us.

IN two respects, especially, this change is very great.

First, in that now there are on every hand good

opportunities to spend the night for money, and then of course you should not burden strangers. Or, where there is opportunity, but one lacks the money, provision can be made, at the cost of the community, or privately by Christian charity.

But what above all brought about so great a change, is the rise of the generation of vagabonds and landlopers, in many cases tramps bent upon thievery, who abuse hospitality to perpetrate mischief.

These are they, who have desecrated hospitality, and have made its ancient practice almost impossible.

Hence the new form, which hospitality gradually assumed, by provision of shelter for wanderers, and by opening of all sorts of institutions and homes, where strangers are entertained.

Hospitality in the ancient sense now merely exists among relatives, friends and acquaintances, and, provided they have letters of introduction, among brethren in Christ.

YET the apostolic admonition, to be given to hospitality, has even in our days in nowise lost its force.

Does not every one in his own circle know these two kinds of households, one of which lock their doors upon themselves, and the others that are known for generous hospitality?

On one hand a father or mother, who never concern themselves about the homeless and the helpless, and on the other hand men and women, who are constantly alert to help the desolate and the wandering.

Here is a household where a Christian brother, who

has lost the way, never knocks in vain, and next door to it a household, in which they know no further care than for themselves and their own.

Again on one hand households, where the note of hospitality ever sounds a welcome, and others, that retire within themselves, and care not for what moves outside of their narrow circle.

Generous and friendly one, reserved and almost repellent the other.

On one side a self-sufficiency, that affects you coldly and uncomfortably, sometimes exhaling the odor of selfishness, and on the other a captivating, cordial and enticing approach, that warms your heart by the warmth of the heart, that goes out toward you.

Between these two lies all the broad difference, whether the spirit of hospitality is upon us, or whether we do not count with this holy ordinance of our God.

Truly, the rights of individual home-life come first.

There is first marriage, the household, husband, wife, children, servants. This is the starting point. There must first be a household, before it can offer generous and hospitable shelter to those who stand without.

There is order in the ordinances of God, and after this order the household comes first, and after that in the household the stranger.

And bitter have been the results, when one had always strangers about, and always spent oneself on strangers, until at length one could no longer get along without them, and had no social life without them, even at the price of neglecting one's own wife and children.

A family-life, that seeks to develop a rich social life within its own bosom, is indispensable for the formation of heart and character. Only in such families flourishes tenderly Christian faith and Christian love. Yea, in such a family only does the stranger feel himself truly happy.

Only, this flourishing of happiness in one's own home must not degenerate into incapacity for general fellowship, into cold indifference to what goes on outside, into withdrawal of oneself from society and into making little islands of life, without a bridge that links them.

Where such becomes the case the spirit of narrow-heartedness creeps in, which overestimates everything that belongs to one's own home and hearth, which with disgust and envy spies out what others do and not do, and surliness that repels rather than generosity that invites and attracts is made the rule of life.

Especially among Christians with holy seriousness such an evil spirit must be excluded.

This exclusive, repulsive and self-sufficient spirit is the direct opposite of the spirit of hospitality, and curses God's holy ordinance.

Sin separates and closes up the heart, but the Spirit of the Lord opens the heart wide, and makes the warm glow of uniting, of *brotherly* love go out toward you.

XXVIII

None of Thy Kindred

FAMILY

YOUR home naturally opens itself to two classes of people. There are two kinds of folks, who mingle in your narrower environment. There are two groups of persons, which, though they do not belong to your immediate family, are inseparable from the family-life; first your *kindred* and in the second place your *intimate friends.*

Such the Scripture calls these two groups, and when Captain Cornelius, who was in garrison with the legion *Italia* at Cæsarea, as the first convert won from the heathen world, received the holy apostle Peter from Joppa in his house, to get instruction in the Gospel of Jesus, it was not with wife and children alone, that he welcomed the apostle, but in company of many others, consisting of "his *kinsmen* and *near friends*" (Acts 10, 24).

By two links your household is connected with the broader life outside. The one of kinsmen and blood-relatives, and the other formed by sympathy of spirits.

Your kinsmen you *find,* your close friends you *choose.* But both circles are woven in with the circle of your own life. Something which is at once evident, in that you have other "acquaintances" and to some extent other "friends," but with whose family you are not intimate, while on the other hand with your kinsmen and close friends it is the rule, that of itself *their* children associate with *your* children, and the common intercourse of the households establishes something more than a personal, something different from an individual, if you please a sort of household-relation.

Yet, although these "kinsmen" and "close friends" mingle not infrequently on a footing of equal confidence with your family, the relation of the two to you and to your household is an altogether different one.

The tie of "kindred" was laid without your cooperation, that of intimate friendship alone by the *choice of the heart.*

Thereby the tie of kinship lies more in our *natural*, the tie of close friendship more in our *spiritual* sphere of life.

Result of this is, that, so long as life in your circle moves along a lower level, kinship is more strongly emphasized, while, the higher the spiritual life becomes, the more highly the more particular friendship is esteemed.

Almost every one has uncles and aunts, cousins, nephews, and nieces, even he who himself is nothing; but to have intimate friends, one must himself be something; something that attracts; something from which a spiritual tie can be woven.

From biographies of great men, you rarely learn anything of their uncles and aunts, cousins, nephews and nieces, but all the more of their *spiritual* kingships, of their bosom-friends, of the Jonathans who were permitted to associate with their Davids.

And among those who as God's children stand higher the case is the same. They honor indeed the ties of kinship, but they have their closest ties with the brethren in the Kingdom.

According to rank *kinship* precedes, but, weighed spiritually, "special friendship" wins.

In the face of this would you assert, that the tie of kinship *is from God*, and your friendship's tie *from yourself?*

Then you make a separation which is false, and you oppose the teaching of Scripture as well as the experience of life.

For shall not he, who is rich in both, thank his God for a sympathetic kinship, and for finely attuned friendship, and honor Him as the Fountain of all good, from whence came to him this tie of blood, as well as the relation of the heart of a friend?

And as regards Scripture, is it not implied already in the paradise-word: "A man shall leave father and mother and cleave unto his wife," that the tie of *blood* may not discard the tie according to *choice*, yea, that, where the two clash, the tie of blood must recede?

Is not the call that went out to Abraham: "Get thee out from thy country, and from thy kindred," the parole whereby spiritual calling, spiritual environment of life, and so also the spiritual tie, is put above the natural?

And when Jesus says, that he that doeth the will of His Father Who is in heaven, is to Him a brother and a sister; and elsewhere tells us that he who cannot leave father or mother or child for His sake, is not worthy of Him,—does not this same Divine ordinance express itself herein, that both, the natural and spiritual ties, have rights, but that, as often as difficulty arises, the lower tie of nature must lower the flag before the higher spiritual tie?

When the infant John was born, both came out at the same time.

First the tie of kinship, which spake from the family when they said: "There is none of thy kindred that is called by this name John" (Luke 1, 61). And then the spiritual tie, when Zachariah wrote: Apart from all kinship, with an eye to his spiritual calling, his name must be John.

Not Zachariah, but *John* would be his name!

IN our Christian households at times this twofold tie occasions difficulty and conflict, when we have a family behind and a family around us, who do *not* seek with us the service of the Lord.

If in your house you serve the Lord, and if His service stands equally high in the households of your kindred, the tie of kinship is not weakened by the spiritual tie, but rather strengthened.

But if from a not-believing family by wonders of grace you yourself have been drawn to the service of the Lord, then there is not the same tone of life in *your* house and in *theirs*. Involuntarily a certain coolness arises. And the spiritual antithesis between you and them of itself introduces a certain *tension* in the mutual attitude.

This gives rise to a twofold tendency, which both can go too far.

On one side the tendency, insomuch as spiritually one stands over against the other, to discount the tie of kinship. And on the other side the tendency, for the sake of the family-ties, not to let the spiritual be heard.

The latter then goes at length so far, that, being among one's own, for dear peace' sake, one shamelessly denies his Savior. While the former can lead to such inexcusable hardness, that in the end one counts for nothing even the tie of one's own mother or child.

Against both these sins you have to watch.

The tie of kinship has been laid by God. And therefore you have to honor it, so long and for so far as you can possibly do this, without in anything denying your Savior. But this same tie of kinship is by God Himself Who laid it, made absolutely *subordinate* to the tie that binds you to Jesus, and therefore you sin against your Savior, when in associating with your family the family-tie gets the better of your heroic love for Him.

WHICH way you have to take, depends therefore upon the attitude, which your family assumes towards *your faith.*

This attitude can be of threefold kind. With self-conceit and mockery one can look down upon your faith; one can treat it with cold respect; or with interest one can envy you.

When you notice that your faith creates interest among your kindred, the way of itself is open before you. Then you let your light shine, that at length they, too, may glorify your Father Who is in heaven. Then you join yourself closely to them, and try to make yourself an instrument of salvation to them or to their children.

If, on the other hand, they show no interest, because they have no part in your confession, even though they may profess respect for Jesus, the glorious propaganda of your faith among your kindred is truly difficult. Yet there is no cause of breach. And it must become more and more the sacred art, without too free an approach, to make it evident in an unobtrusive way, that He Who is in you is stronger than he who is in them, and at the proper time the proper word of confession can be spoken.

But when your kindred take their stand over against your conviction and confession; when they drive their spirit in opposition to the spirit of your household; and conceitedly look down upon you as backward obscurantists and fanatics; and, in your presence or even in that of your children allow themselves expressions that are offensive to your devout feeling and insulting to your Savior,—then you *must* contest the tie of kinship its right, and without giving offense, carefully see to it, that no corruptive influences go out from your kinsmen upon your children and upon your own heart.

THIS becomes particularly painful, when joy or sadness in the family brings you together with those kinsmen who are your spiritual opponents, on such occasions as weddings and funerals, at which in all sorts of ways the higher questions of life come to order.

No one may then say, that, *because it concerns your family*, at such happy or sorrowful solemnities, for the time being you are to lay aside your conviction. "Let the dead bury their dead," said Jesus, "you, preach the kingdom of God." And therefore he who for the sake of family takes part at funeral or wedding after modernistic ceremonial, commits sin. For though you have no right, on such occasions to make your confession the rule of procedure, or place it in the foreground, neither have you the right, for the sake of the family-tie, to assume the appearance or the attitude for one moment, as though for that time being your tie to Jesus is consigned to non-activity.

A redeemed one of the Lord, who knows that it will come to this, however close the family-tie may be, stays away from such solemnities.

Nowhere and at no time may the tie of kinship enter claims against the tie that binds you to your God.

And then . . . think of your children.

Or are they not to be pointed out by name, baptized children from Christian homes, who, estranged from the faith, are now abroad in the paths of unbelief, because no one took it to heart, that, while young and inexperienced, with dear uncles and aunts and cousins, they came unobservedly under worldly, Christ denying influences?

This went on over the signature of the family-tie! One should not and could not keep his children away from their relatives! And one did not notice nor see, how by this very thing he kept his child away from his God.

He who loves his child and consecrated it to God, will be on guard, to avert *every* wrong influence from his darling, knowing how easily the young are lured astray.

Wrong influence is never more strongly seductive, than when it comes from one's kindred.

XXIX

Account of Income and Outgo

MEANS OF MANAGEMENT

HOWEVER spiritual the note, that from God's heavens is sounded in the everlasting Gospel, it never went so high, but that in Holy Scripture the very prosaic "account of income and outgo" also could come to its own (Phil. 4, 15, Dutch Version).

Altogether different from what you find with visionary people.

With them it is said that writing books of *poetry* and *keeping account* of one's finance cannot go together.

To keep book, to write down everything, to plan in advance and in the end examine results, is deemed proper for ordinary souls, which do not rise above the prose of life. But it will not do for freer spirits, for men of larger talent, for those who drink the cup of poetry, and while they do not eat the bread of the mighty, yet eat the bread of ideals.

To count and keep book, is fit for the grocer. It is the flat art of the miser. But he who has wings and learned their use, and who on mountain-tops has breathed other air than that of the dull marshes, feels heartily averse to dealing with stiff figures and keeping troublesome accounts.

No, he who lives in higher spheres despises ledgers and takes no part in bookkeeping. Or, if he does keep book, he outwits the evil spirit of figures, by making entries as he likes and somehow making totals agree. But real bookkeeping, *precise,* according to right and truth, accurate and painstaking bookkeeping, such an higher spirit does not.

He leaves this to others. He leaves this to his inferiors. He spends, so long as he has money in the bank or in the house. When it is gone, he begs or borrows, and pays back or not, as suits his convenience. Or he does not borrow, but buys on credit, and lives on the money of his creditors, and when they dare to dun him, for what is coming to them, calls them cruel.

In this way from of old lived the men of art, students at the academy, thinkers and philosophers, men of the sword and of the pen.

Not infrequently women in these circles took part in this guilty slovenliness of life.

And they who also at times, and *this is the worst,* took part in this, were mystically minded Christians, who deemed earthly cares too unspiritual to concern their soul about.

History even relates of *spiritual leaders,* who fell into this same error.

THIS sin also is rebuked by the Word of God, and punished afterward by much financial *loss,* if not by financial *ruin,* which of the slovenly handling of money is oftentimes an unavoidable result.

God's Word teaches us to attach value to money, not because gold glitters with such yellow brightness, not because money buys almost everything, but because it is a talent, entrusted to us of God, primordially *His* property, put into our hands but *for a time,* obliging us, not to use it in *our service,* but in *His* service, once to give to Him an account thereof.

This is the first foundation, on which a Christian's financial structure must rest.

In addition to this is the second, that God's Word demands accurate, strict *honesty,* and condemns all dishonesty as despicable sin. He to whom it belongs is *master of the money,* and Holy Scripture calls *theft* every act of yours, by which you prevent money from going back to its master. Prompt payment on the day, punctual return of what is borrowed, never postponement of payment of wages or of what has been guaranteed. On these three depends the right of your *expenditure.* And in addition to this, equally sternly demanded, with respect to your account of income the other commandment, that under no circumstances at any time anything may flow into your bank or purse that has been gained by lottery, by unrighteous dealings, or by dishonest practices.

As a third foundation comes this, that, according to the demand of God's Word, you shall manage and direct your expenses, not as you desire, but according to God's will. Not for sinful use, but for what is expedient. Divided with respect to the present and to days that are to be, even when wife and child are here, and you are gone. Also, that with your account of income and outgo, as with everything else, you shall "love God *first* and then yourself and your neighbor"; and thus *not* say: *first* for all earthly needs, and if anything is left a bagatelle for the cause of God. No, *first* the gift for the cause of your Lord, and after that for your own needs. Think of the poor widow, she gave all *her living,* and thereby won the approval of the Lord.

Finally, to these three foundations there is added still this fourth, that Scripture demands *order and rule* in all things, and for this reason claims, from every one who has money at his disposal, that the account of income and outgo be at all times so accurately in order, that, should you die this very day, everything would be found accurately recorded and in perfect correspondence.

The fathers in our Reformed churches have always insisted in practical matters, that is it not spiritual, but *over*spiritual and therefore *un*spiritual, when in his accounts of income and outgo one does slovenly work.

It should not be the *soul* for God and the *purse* for self.

Soul and purse must both be God's.

So punctiliousness, preciseness, tenderness of conscience demands it.

SCRIPTURE designs least of all to be hard. She defies you, to find tenderer compassion for shortage in income, than she offers.

To see expenses increase, by sickness or accident or dearness of food, and then to learn that income does not suffice, yea, in times when there is no work to be had, is for those who must themselves live and carry the care for others, a bitterness of soul; and which can not be borne when you feel your faith give way, your faith in Him Who has numbered the hairs of your head, and in the love which He wakens in the brother-heart.

With respect to such trying conditions you never

find in God's Word one hard expression. On the contrary words of tenderest compassion.

What Scripture condemns is every life lived at random; every expenditure in advance of money that has not yet materialized; prodigality in expectation of inheritances still to come; use of capital laid up against the rainy day; the so-called stopping up of one hole with another; recklessly spending without forethought or care; wasting money as long as it lasts, that, when it is gone, one may live on the good graces of another.

And what is no less condemned, and in which so many err, is spending *more* than one receives, not because one cannot live on it, but because he says he cannot live on it according to his *imagined rank* or his imaginary needs.

House, clothes and food are indispensable, and when the income does not suffice for this, seeking help incurs neither loss nor shame. Then indeed you may call in help. Then according to God's will you *must* be helped.

But to what is above and beyond this, when God does not give it you, does not put it at your disposal, does not send it to your house, you are not entitled.

You cannot fit your income to your outgo, you must direct your outgo according to your income, and he who did this punctiliously and strictly from his youth up, has never come to want, and has never felt himself poor.

One must cut one's coat according to one's cloth.

A MERCHANT must practice regular bookkeeping, because human law demands it. But every Christian also must keep book, because the law of his God lays it upon him, and that presently the name of his God be not slandered on account of his dilatoriness.

So must the man do as head of his family, and the wife in her housekeeping, and the servant in the kitchen, and every child of his small earnings.

Always keeping count, and never allow carelessness.

You have to put this into practice yourself, and instill it into your children, so that with the coming generation the flabbiness of life go no further, and still more pitiful victims be sacrificed.

For do not forget, that that very light-hearted dealing with account of income and outgo, has already brought many a family first trouble and sorrow, and ruin in the end.

AND what you should not forget either, is, that in the last instance all account and responsibility are one.

Therefore our Confession and our Catechism have so much to say about the account we have with our God.

Spiritual flabbiness has made a mockery of the idea, that with God you should mention payment, since His love is far too exalted and His compassion far too infinite, than to apply the flat idea of *payment* to your relation to the Holy One. But does not Scripture itself speak of a *ransom?*

And these two hang together. He who makes light of this accounting and paying among men, as a rule does not take his account with God seriously. He wants indeed to be pious and mystical and holy, but God's *righteousness* has no hold on him. And what it is to be *justified* by faith he does not understand. But by this very emphasis, which our fathers put upon that *justification*, they have strengthened the *right*, have deepened the *sense of right* among men, and have advanced *righteousness*.

And therefore, do not deem that account of income and outgo a light matter. For whether you come to tenderness and compunction of conscience, to standing just before your God, to the payment for you of the ransom that saves you eternally, or to the account of your income and outgo among men,—is at heart all governed by only one all-decisive question, namely: Whether you are your own lord and master, or whether *you stand under God*, and as such have to reverence *His* ordinances, and owe *Him* an account.

He who is truly pious, keeps account of his money in the first place *for God*.

XXX

She Girdeth Her Loins with Strength

MANAGEMENT OF THE HOUSEHOLD

No, there is not alone *sickness* or *health*. There is still a *third* something. Something, that lies in between "health" and "sickness," and that sometimes already at an early age, follows us after as decline of strength; *weakness*.

"Nerves" it is called with one, "poverty of blood" with a second, with a third "exhaustion." But, by whatever it is caused, or to whatever cause it is attributed, the result is one. There lacks strength where strength ought to be. And the anxious feeling of not *being able* where one wants to do, comes back every morning, and to the exhausted man or woman continues as a plague until evening.

Especially woman, and not least married woman, *suffers* under this plague.

She became mother. What in Gen. 3 God laid upon Eve, that she should bring forth with sorrow, is also fulfilled in her. Thereby her constitution not overstrong already, suffered the more. And now the activities of life became too much for her. It went more and more above her strength. And while she tried to row against the stream, she became more and more worn out, till at length the weary head became so heavy, and the arm she would stretch out, fell almost helpless in her lap.

And though in this measure it is, thank God, the case with but a few, it is an almost *universal* phenomenon, that our housewives and housemothers, who are at the head of a somewhat busy household, frequently have no more strength of head and limbs for their difficult task of life, and that they themselves first, but also the family, and especially the children, suffer under this.

This distressing condition is even frequently aggravated by the fact that her daughters also lack freshness of vigor. So that, instead of supporting their weak mother, they themselves rather lean upon her.

And when the sons of the house also look pale, and need tonics, and instead of giving the impression of healthful virile strength, already at an early age begin to show shadows alongside of the unevennesses of the face; and also the man of the house complains; and as a climax of trial the very servants almost make you say, that as regards weakness of health they are part of the family, in the end it becomes too much for "mother," as on her rests the heaviest part of the burden of family cares, and many a housewife is at length carried out to the grave, because her busy household, in addition to her weak constitution, it is not too hard to say, had literally killed her.

To the danger that threatens the housewife from this side, the Proverb-poet also had an open eye, and therefore of the virtuous housewife he writes, that: "*She girdeth her loins with strength, and strengtheneth her arms*" (31, 17).

Just what the Psalmist sang of Jehovah; sang of the Lord of hosts, when he jubilated, that our God had clothed Himself with majesty and strength, and presently focused it all in this one note of joy: *He hath girded Himself.*

And because the Lord Himself "girdeth His loins," therefore it is He also, Who is able to stand by His beloved in their weakness, even as, in the very words of Solomon, in Ps. 89, 21, it is said to David: "With whom my hand shall be established; *mine arm also shall strengthen him.*"

To gird the loins, is the perception, the feeling, the sensation of increase of strength, till you say to yourself: *Now I am able again.* And *to strengthen the arms* is to bring this restored strength into the arms, not now to be idle but to apply this regained strength after the Lord's ordinance.

This virtuous housewife herself girds the loins, not merely when with advancing years she becomes conscious of failing strength, but while as the picture of health she still directs the affairs of her household.

Of course this is figurative speech, and has nothing to do with putting on of a corset to feel oneself more firmly attired.

This girding is not done with a girdle which externally is fastened around the waist, but with a girdle of *will-power* and *self-control* and *prudent exertion,* which is woven in the inner chambers of the heart upon one's knees before God.

An imagery, which tells you, that this woman did not let herself will-lessly drift with the stream, did not let go of herself and did not succumb under her task, but consciously controlled the task, took hold of herself, exerted herself, and regulated the expenditure of her strength. Also that she took care in time, that when the lamp had burned many hours, fresh oil kept the flame burning, before it would die out.

NOT *complain* and *sigh,* but *pray* and *give thanks,* and with courage in the eye face the life of each new day, is the precious effect upon the busy housemother of *quiet trustful faith.*

For faith is to live, not from what one sees before one's eyes, but from what one does *not see.* Hence after the rule, that not the *body* the soul, but the *soul* must govern the body, and that in cautious wisdom of the *understanding* and in steel-strength *of will* the weak woman has been equipped of God with two mighty weapons, wherewith to do battle against weakness.

Reports of healings by prayer are abroad again, especially in America. And the fact can not be denied, that by spiritual operations of faith, among Protestants as well as among Roman Catholics, remember Lourdes, healings have taken place, that make you think of miracles.

And yet these healings are nothing but the effect of will-power inspired by faith, concentrated upon one single point, which will-power, with higher strength, reacts against the appearance, that over against the body the soul stands impotent.

With cases of weakness one generally summons a physician, and who would despise the blessing of medicine. But it is a subversion of the Divinely appointed order, when the soul in you imagines that it stands impotent over against the body.

By all sorts of sins, also by unbelief, to a dreadful

degree you can weaken your body and especially your nerves. But also by faith and an holier sense you can to so uncommon a degree strengthen this same body and these same nerves.

This is *girding your loins with strength.*

And the young married woman, who begins this early; who, with the increase of her family, uninterruptedly goes on with this, and never for a moment allows her family to run away with her, but calm and "strong in prayer" prepares herself for her task, will obtain the glorious experience, that in the midst of the distractions of a busy family-life godliness has a blessing also for her physical powers.

She who has neglected this and for years has brought her will into bondage to her nerves, and thus in old age reaps the bitter fruit of this, is of course not able to restore this wasted power by a single act of will.

But even then, it still holds true, that girding the loins with strength, by serious, prayerful exertion of faith, is the only means, to come away from under it, Even in such almost hopeless conditions, faith *never* refuses its strength-restoring operation.

Does this mean to say, that now the weak housemother may withdraw herself in the mystery, and neglect the outward means of support?

Of course not, for then it were purely the operation of the feeling and no healthy working faith.

No, faith knows *how* to apply means.

It knows that God Himself has not merely foreordained salvation for His elect, but at the same time and in that same counsel has ordered the *means of grace,* to bring about the salvation.

With mystery it must begin, but it must not stop therewith.

Faith fosters *wisdom,* which is something altogether different from school learning found in books.

You can so plan your household and so direct it, as to show lack of wisdom. But you can also do all this in such a way, that wisdom *shines out* from it.

There can be exhausting activity and confusion and disorder. But there can also be good rules, fixed procedure, steady direction and thereby beneficent order.

And in the measure in which this prevails in your household shall the use of your strength be either a wasting of the same, or a harnessing and effective application thereof.

YOUR strength is a gift of God, a *talent* entrusted to you.

This strength, this talent, must not remain what it is. It must be put to usury. Gains must be won by it. It must increase. And before God you must be able to say: "Three talents hast Thou given me, see Lord, three other talents have I gained therewith." And though as regards strength, you received but one talent yet this one talent must not be buried, but must be *doubled.*

But whether it is only just received, or whether it is already doubled by faithful discharge of duty, you must be sparing in the use of it.

It must not be *played with.* It must not be *wasted.* Self-control must direct all your doings.

There is division of time. There is division of the daily task. There is division of what you charge others to do. And not the woman who rushes along with things all day long and wears herself out, but the woman who, calmly seated in her armchair, plans the daily run of the household and tactfully directs its course, serves her God in her carefulness and radiates blessing in all her environment.

Even the matter of sleep, which increases strength, and regular meals, which feed the body, are to the believing woman parts of serious and regular performance of duty. She knows that the lamp, which receives no oil, gives out, and the hearth that is not continuously replenished. And therefore also sleep and feeding are no play with her, but a part of performance of duty and of obedience to her God.

To surrender a part of her housekeeping cares, that the whole slip not out of her hand, may at times be a demand of faith.

Nothing by way of material aid is to be despised, provided it renders her service, and she does not lean on it.

Upon God alone she must lean, and upon that *spiritual strength* of soul which God has granted her.

She alone who believes, not *sentimentally*, but *practically*, shall in this also be more than conqueror.

So in this struggle let the girdle of *faith* be the mystery of your strength.

XXXI

A Portion to Her Maids

OUR SERVANTS

OF how important a significance "servants" are in our social economy, you never learn better than when you hear "housewives" discuss among themselves domestic affairs.

The husband is momentarily dealt with, the children a little more at length, but the maids are given the lion's share of attention. And when a maid has only just come, she is often spoken of with disproportional praise, but soon after in a way, which is in between complaint and indignation.

This is natural, and it would not be fair to our housemothers, if we were to hold this up against them as proof of their readiness to take offense.

The fact of the matter is: the conflict that goes on in every department of life between the more privileged and less favored among us, is introduced into your own home by your servants and forces you as housemother personally to come in contact with it.

The man, too, comes in contact with it, but always from a certain distance. In his factory, in his store, in his field, but not so directly in his own house, and therefore only now and then, and not from morning till night.

For our housemothers this is different.

They receive their maids in their own house. They are in close touch with them. They must endure it that their maids intrude themselves into everything. With every difference of idea, with every neglect, with every transgression, the housemothers are bound to straighten matters out and maintain order. And such not from a distance, not through any intermediary, but directly they themselves in person face to face.

This difficulty, already great where only one maid is kept, is much aggravated where they come in touch with the jealousies and minor disputes of the maids among themselves.

More painful still this difficulty becomes where the children of the household have reached adolescence, and presume upon all manner of authority over the servants.

And it becomes most painful of all, when the family purse is but poorly filled, and ever and again house-motherly economy must be defended in the face of the not wasteful, but yet careless hand of the servants.

The number of devout, faithful housemothers, who for years have faced this difficulty with their servants, and what sacrifices of rest, and of their own convenience, yea, sometimes of their own food, they have made, to keep up the honor of the house, and yet avert the sin of running into debt, is known alone to Him, Who has overheard the painful sighings of their heart.

THE relation therefore between housewives and servants should have been estimated at its truer worth, so as both in training and in preaching to have demanded more attention.

For do not forget, that these relations of service

bring the two struggling ranks of society most intimately into contact with one another.

From lower ranks young daughters go into the houses of the higher rank. There they find an entirely different life from what they have known at home; oftentimes a wealth of which they had no idea before. They come among people who as a rule stand at a higher level of development. And now they are called to *serve* these people.

In this service, they come to know these same people, who before they saw only in the street, in their private life, sometimes at very close range; and they see how higher development in turn goes hand in hand with particular sins.

Moreover, frequently they have sharp eyes and practiced ears. They see much, and they hear much. A new world opens before them, and in their visits at home all sorts of inquiries are made concerning this new world. And they readily tell their tales, so that our servants form a sort of living connection between those who keep servants, and the households from which one "goes out serving."

And then it is self-evident, that the constant intercourse between "housewives" and "servants" cannot be maintained, apart from mutual influence. Whether you want to or not, you always undergo certain influences from your servants, even if these are not so strong as those from you.

So it cannot be denied, that the good relationship between higher and lower classes of society can be advanced by nothing so effectively, as by an happy intercourse, an intercourse after God's ordinance, between our housemothers and their servants. But also that few causes bring about so much bitter animosity between class and class, as the strained relation so many housewives sustain toward their servants.

Do not forget, that these servants presently marry, become wives of "working men" and mothers of young children, and that it makes all the difference, whether this "wife" and mother helps avert the coming storm, or whether she encourages the outbreak of this storm of violent passion.

Also in the workingman's family the influence of woman is so great.

THE responsibility of every housewife, with respect to her "servants" can therefore not weigh heavily enough upon the conscience.

Here also is a moral obligation toward Him, Who grants one woman the right to be served, and imposes on the other the duty of serving. And of the way in which this duty has been discharged, *account* shall once be given.

What renders the understanding of the just relation of these "served" and "serving" women, so very difficult, is the lack of written law. It all goes by custom and habit and local usage. Hence the difficulty, of deciding in many a case, what is permitted and what is not permitted. For naturally they who serve, do not serve except upon an understanding, in which they want to feel themselves protected by certain valid statutes.

So long as this common law was fairly operative, everything went well. But in our days this common law is undergoing all sorts of modification. In America the relation between housewife and maid is already altogether modified. Even in Europe it is already far more favorable for house servants than in the East. And it is difficult to prophesy what these changing conditions will bring about before long.

Meanwhile our housemothers experience all the inconvenience of this uncertainty. And thereby pay the penalty for the sin of housemothers of a former generation, who in many ways took unfair advantage of the dependence and helplessness of their maids.

This leads to this constant "giving of warning to quit" from both sides.

This constant "changing" weakens the mutual relationship. The heart gets away from it. The real *human* is being lost from it. Nothing rests save machines for use.

And where the feeling of the heart does burst into flame, it is always with respect to the "portion" set apart for them.

A portion which the "housemaid" ever enlarges and the "housewife" ever desires to reduce.

So from both sides sin is committed. And the evil that so makes progress in our families, and from our families in society at large, becomes ever more menacing.

THE Proverb-poet says, that: "Whoso findeth a good wife, obtaineth favor of the Lord" (18, 22); and so it can be said of the housewife, that whoso hath found a faithful, good maidservant, should thank God for this token of His favor.

A faithful housemaid is worth her weight in gold, especially in a Christian home, and she who is able to train a young daughter to be a good housemaid, prepares a blessing for the family to which she comes.

And truly thanksgiving for the gift at the hand of God of a faithful servant, ascends from many a Christian home.

Our believing housemaids are even to be preferred so far above the daughters from neglected homes, that people of the world, who long have put their faith to a side, not infrequently are bent upon the maintenance of the faith in their kitchen.

There is still a blessing, which must not be perverted.

Yet this does not dismiss the question, whether as a rule our Christian housemothers and our Christian housemaids deal with one another in such a way, that the name of the Lord is praised, and whether a power of salvation goes out from good relationship between those who are more rich and those more poor.

In this respect our calling is so high. There can go out from our homes so much influence for good. But also, because of the Name of the Lord which we confess, by wrong relationships so great evil can be occasioned.

A tie, which people of the world know not of, binds us together. We are under human ordinances not merely as men, but also as one in Christ, our Savior, under the Divine ordinance of a love sealed in the blood of the holy Lamb of God.

Housemaids, who abuse this sacred tie, to withhold from housewives the Divinely appointed portion of faithfulness and honor, commit grievous sin. But the housemother also sins, who withholds from her housemaids the portion appointed by the selfsame God, of love and solicitous care, and of appreciation of their services.

Our fathers ordered things aright. They adopted their housemaids as members of the family. Our housemothers of the Reformation dealt with their housemaids on a footing of motherly intimacy. And still they had sufficient sense of duty, not to spoil them, or allow the ordinance of "serving" to lose its stress.

Even yet with our housemaids we come to one Table of the Lord. Even yet in most Christian families the praiseworthy custom prevails, that together we pray, and together read God's Word, and together sing His praise.

And surely this is a "portion," which is our housemaid's due (Prov. 31, 15).

But this is not enough.

This making of prayer together rather courts a judgment, when it stands over against a separated life on a strained footing of quarrelsomeness. And this fellowship in holy things, can only be such a savor, that is well-pleasing unto God, when it is the expression of a friendly, pleasant relationship which strengthens and feeds what is good in the same.

Not to take our maidservants out of their place. "To serve" remains their calling. And provided they do this as "serving not people, but the Lord," they will be blessed in the same.

But as it has pleased the Lord our God, to have us be His menservants and His maidservants, and yet with *fatherly* faithfulness to watch over us and to accept filial love from us, so should it be in our households.

Serving as maidservants, but at the same time benefited by "motherly" disposition, and responding to this portion of love with something of "filial faithfulness."

XXXII

Be Subject with Fear

DUTY OF THOSE WHO SERVE

THE apostolic warning to submission, addressed to menservants and maidservants, can no longer without more be applied to those who are in service.

The relation of master and manservant, was then different as a rule. There were those, who as freemen made agreement as to wages, but this was not common. In general one was served by male and female slaves.

Such male or female slaves were in their master's power. They were his property. However hard their master was in his treatment of them, they could not get away. Of giving up a servile position there was no mention. And as a citizen was subject to his king, so slaves owed submission to their master.

Only he who has this in mind, can understand what the apostles said to the men and maidservants of those days, "Servants, be subject to your masters with all fear; not only to the good and gentle, but also to the froward" (1 Pet. 2, 18).

The apostles knew full well, how hard it was for one who had been made a freeman in Christ, to remain slave with a heathen man or for a female slave with a heathen woman. They realized in full, how the inclination to exalt themselves rather above their masters or mistresses, would root in the heart of baptized male and female slaves.

Were they not children of God and called to be

saints, and could it be right before God, that in spite of this, perhaps all their life long, they should remain in hard, always humiliating slavery, not willed of God. And could it be counted evil of them, if they set themselves in opposition against so shameful and hurtful a condition?

And yet on this point the apostles have never hesitated. As we know from the striking example of Onesimus and Philemon, they have never willed nor tolerated, that because a slave had become the property of Christ, he should shake off the chains of social slavery.

Even he who in an evil hour had run away and escaped, was bound, willingly or unwillingly, to return to his master.

And for this reason the apostles warned the men- and maidservants, not merely to subjection, but also to submission.

Both male and female slaves were often bodily punished, and even this baptized men- and maidservants had to endure for Christ's sake.

For, it is ever demanded, not that they merely bend and yield, but much more that for conscience' sake, while such is the ordinance of God, faithfully and with a good heart, they shall serve their lords and masters.

From this, however, follows, that you neither can nor ought to apply this apostolic warning in its original meaning to your own servants or working people.

They who serve you, are neither male- nor female-slaves, but freeborn men and women, who have entered into some sort of an agreement with you, if you like, have made a contract with you, that they will do this or some other thing for you, and render you this or that service. And that as compensation, they will receive from you a wage, beforehand agreed upon, be it merely in money, be it in shelter, board and wage.

So you cannot say, that you are *"lord"* over your servants or employees, neither can you assert, that they are your *subjects.*

Such relations existed aforetimes, but not in our social conditions now.

Lordly rights you can no more exercise in a single particular over your servants. And the claim, that in the real sense of the word they shall be subject unto you, will absolutely no more do in our times.

By rights the only ground for your mutual relation is the agreement, which you have entered upon with your servants. A servant who does not live up to this agreement, violates good faith and as such stands guilty before God and you. But for this reason it can never be said, that as subjects they have fallen short in submission or have slighted your authority.

Especially among us, Christians, this should clearly and definitely be understood.

We must never claim a right, which is not ours.

We are no longer lords, and our servants are no longer slaves.

What dominates our mutual relation, is the relation of agreement, contract and accommodation, but always agreement and contract between freemen mutually.

AND yet, however definitely and unhesitatingly we say this, with equal clearness of consciousness we add, that in the apostolic warning there lies even now a tie on the part of God for our servants.

As a rule our servants refuse to acknowledge, that they are *in service,* and by preference speak of a "position."

In this they are partly right.

Over against men and women, alas, also among Christians not infrequently, who from the heights look down upon their dependents, and only partly acknowledge their personal liberty, there is some fairness in it, that the word "position" gets the emphasis.

Sometimes even children in the family assume an attitude of authority toward servants, which wounds and is irreconcilable with the honor of the name of Christian.

But from this it follows least of all, that therefore every idea of *service* can or must be abandoned.

Rather it should be emphasized, that that, wherein our servants are generally engaged, is *a position of service.*

In a family of any size there are all sorts of activities, which one cannot gauge accurately beforehand. In all manner of ways assistance is needed. In the course of a day all sorts of occasions arise, at which we need *service* from others.

For these services one takes servants into his house, and such on the self-evident condition, that willingly and faithfully they will render the services, which reasonably are demanded of them.

Though it be undeniably true, therefore, that our servants hold a position with us, yet the peculiarity of their position brings with it, that they do not merely perform a task previously agreed upon, but that they serve us; do, what they are told, and with discretion and fidelity continue in the doing of this daily task.

In this sense alone, it may and must be said, that they must be submissive in the fear of God.

Submissive, not by reason of a glorious right, which we as lords and ladies have to exercise over them. But submissive, because by coming into service with us, of their own free will they have bound themselves to this submission.

If you say, that they need not have done so, in the abstract is correct, but actually the matter stands differently.

The actual condition in our present-day life is such, that there is no other way open to many, except that of service. It is their appointed lot. And in this lot they have to reverence the counsel of their God.

The character of a service brings along, that very much must be entrusted to our servants; that so much depends upon their good care; and that it is almost impossible, to admit any one in his house on a footing of such unlimited confidence, in his more private life, and with his children, unless, apart from all agreement, and from all wage, an higher principle unites both the members of the family and the servants.

And it is this higher principle which the apostolic warning rightfully emphasizes, and which, by us Christians, whether we are served or serve, must be brought to honor.

Your contract and your stipulated wage govern the mutual relation according to right. But back of this external right lies the deep-going right of your God.

The right of your God, that in your servants you shall honor His freeborn creatures, His baptized ones, called unto eternal life, and that you shall repress and bring to nought all pride and highness, to which the flesh tempts you.

But also the right of your God, that you, who, under His government, have been placed in the position of service, shall to the end perform your given task, not for the sake of wages, nor yet from eye-service, but for the sake of the will of God, as in His holy service, and that not from necessity, but willingly, you shall seek your delight in your service itself.

XXXIII

Fragments That Remain

ECONOMY

WHAT think ye, when Christ multiplied the loaves and fishes, did He produce *too much bread* by mistake, so that fragments remained contrary to His intention, and that these fragments surprised Him?

This cannot be so.

What operated with this multiplication in and through Christ, was *Divine* almightiness. To do what here is done, falls outside the range of our human nature.

What God the Lord has put in our power is, to multiply grain by agriculture, in the course of months. But it is altogether outside of our power, immediately, and in one moment to multiply bread. And this Christ did, and this He could not do except Divine almightiness operated in Him. And this Divine almightiness can not work at random, because almightiness and omniscience in God the Lord are one.

Thus you clearly see, that at the miracle of the loaves the remnant of fragments was *no* mistake, that it took place intentionally, and thereby the twelve baskets of fragments became to us an instruction on the part of God, as to what we are to do *with what remains.*

The narrative in John shows indeed, that Christ Himself was interested in those remaining fragments.

In the hands of the apostles nothing was left over. They had distributed everything.

No, these were remnants left *by the masses.*

Hungry at first the multitudes had too much. Now they were satisfied and there were left-overs. There was more than they could conveniently consume.

What remained the multitude evidently had, if not thrown away, at least carelessly left on the ground.

For in what Christ said there was something of a rebuke.

He said: "Gather up the fragments that remain, that nothing be lost" (John 6, 12).

Christ would not have said this, if the people had taken the fragments with them, to eat them on the way home.

For then they would not have been *lost* but *used.*

What Christ said, suggests, therefore, that by the carelessness of the multitude these fragments would have been lost, and against this Jesus sets Himself as against *a sinful something.*

This must *not* be.

There must nothing *be lost.*

And that nothing be lost, the disciples, and through them the church of all ages, were commanded of the Lord, that always and everywhere the "fragments that remain" shall be gathered up.

THANKS to the instruction in the Word, our fathers, and no less our mothers, in former generations, have understood this well. And in true Christian families it is still the rule, to keep strict guard against this.

You see this in the expression: *'Tis a sin.* An expression, which from Christian homes was introduced into common use of language and there lost all meaning, but which originally, and on the lips of our devout forebears meant: You must not deal carelessly with what remains. For also food that is left over is created of God. And irreverent dealing with what God has made, is sin.

Hence it does not do to say: A poor man might have eaten this,—or: A famished dog might have had his life saved by it;—but rather: You have no right to neglect the fragments that remain, because God created them, they are God's belongings, and lightsomely to play with anything that God has created, is sin.

A child of God, at least if he is recipient of this great grace as a Christian of the Reformation, to obtain the purest knowledge of the will of his Father, brings everything into relation *with his God.*

This relation, in which he stands with his God, governs all of his life. And by reason of this, he stamps all recklessness or neglect of whatever it may be, with the name of *sin.*

This was *serious business* with our church fathers. They lived by it. So they understood it and not otherwise. All neglect was felt by them as *sin,* was confessed as *sin,* as *sin* to be atoned by the blood of Christ alone.

This the world still repeats. Again and again you hear it said among unbelieving people: "'Tis a sin, man, in such weather as this to put on your best clothes!"—and so this saying: *'Tis a sin,* is common on many lips.

But on such lips this saying: *'Tis a sin,* is nothing but a stop-gap, almost half an oath.

For, *sin* is always taken with reference to God. And he who makes use of anything that is valid only with respect to God, without intending to refer to God, or to think of God, gives himself to the habit of blasphemy.

In what remains the almightiness of the Creator, but also *His unbounden mercifulness* toward you and your house is to be reverenced.

In most families nothing ever remains over, everything is clean gone, and more would be used, if there were more.

If in your family, at your table, in your kitchen, and in your bread-box there is too much provision for one meal, it certainly implies this very great grace, that all your needs are met, that you may eat until you are satisfied, and that God's hand opened itself to you generously. But it also implies the obligation of responsibility with respect to what you do *with what is left over.*

With respect to the kitchen and table, the housemother is the person responsible to God.

She must be on the watch.

God will require it at her hand.

She must watch kitchen and table, and even when she leaves it to her daughters or servants, it is charged to her account.

Not the servant, and not the daughter, but she as housemother has been set over these things of God.

First of all with respect to this, that she has to see to it, that there being always more than is needed is no result of careless housekeeping.

Ordinarily she should be able to judge about *how much food* should be bought and prepared. And in this purchasing at random, and always buying too much, so that after every meal quantities of food are carried away again from the table, there is guilt of carelessness and of abuse of the Lord's goodness to her house.

ALSO what is done with the fragments that remain, is not a matter of indifference.

Even anxiety about left-overs may cloak the spirit of parsimoniousness.

A housemother who carefully gathers what was left over to-day, that she may serve it again to-morrow, is right in doing so, provided necessity compels her to do this, or the money so saved is laid aside for the cause of God or for the poor.

But when there is no need of thus saving food, or when money so saved does not go to the poor, the left-overs themselves should go to the poor, as in former days every well-to-do family, where there was always a greater abundance of food than could be used, had some poor family at hand, who took away what was left. And as though this were not enough they so directed matters, that more food was left over, just to be the more generous.

Birds also were cared for, at least in winter. Not from sentimental devotion to animals, but because they were creatures of God, which by God's appointment flutter and sing before us, and should not suffer want, when with us there is abundance.

So must the housemother care for her house, because God has set her over it, and addresses also her with the words: *Gather up* the fragments that remain, *that nothing be lost.*

All food that moulds or spoils in the house, cries against the housemother, bringing accusation against her before God.

MOREOVER, this word of Christ applies not merely to *food* and *drink.* It refers as well to *clothes,* to *furniture,* to *ornaments,* to the fragments of your time that are being lost, and no less to what is left over of your *money.*

Nothing is your own property. It all belongs to God, Who gives it you for use, and holds you responsible for what you do with it.

What Christ says: "Gather up the fragments, that nothing be lost," is the pure Christian principle, that stands over against the economic passion of the world.

"Save" is the watchword of our age, to gather treasures for yourself upon earth, to make yourself a proprietor, to bend your energies upon making money. Everything going on outside of God, keeping no count with God, directed to selfish ends, ending in the passion for material things, nursing the deadly spirit first of the grocer, then of the capitalist, i.e. the spirit that brings money to the man, and after that brings the man *under the money.*

God's child also is frugal, but from how much higher an impulse!

Not to raise himself up in wealth, but to honor God in His gifts. From those gifts of God to do well to the poor. To spend all good things entrusted to him in the Lord's service and to His glory.

XXXIV

Keep the Body Under

HIGH STANDARD OF LIFE

You are mistaken, when you seek the seat of indwelling sin in *your body*, and when you brand your *flesh* as the malefactor, upon whose head comes down all guilt.

He who says this, directly contradicts Jesus' saying, that not from the flesh, but *from the heart* proceed all sorts of evil things, because from the heart are the issues of life.

Laying all guilt upon the flesh, is an invention of Satan, who himself is nothing but *a spirit,* who does *not* have a body, and therefore, in case sin dwells *merely* in the flesh, goes out free. Such also is the cherished opinion on the part of those who suffer from all sorts of pride and those who have been hit by the arrow of envy and hatred, because their sin hides within the *spiritual* domain, and when the *flesh* is made the scapegoat, there is no fault in them.

But let not the more sensually disposed natures deem, that therefore sin lies in the spirit only, and that, in the weighing of sin, our *flesh,* i.e. our body really has no count. For this would be an equally strong denial of another word of Jesus, when He said: "The spirit is willing, but the flesh is weak" (Matt. 26, 41). Or also against what Paul says: "So then with the mind I myself serve the law of God, but with the flesh the law of sin" (Rom. 7, 25).

As Paul writes (Gal. 5, 17): "The flesh lusteth

against the Spirit, and the Spirit against the flesh; and these two are contrary the one to the other."

And so also: "They that are after the flesh, do mind the things *of the flesh;* but they that are after the Spirit the things of the Spirit" (Rom. 8, 5).

For this reason it is your Christian duty, to recognize your flesh, your body to be an enemy, whom you must fight. A power, that struggles with you, to see which is the stronger. But a power, which, as child of God, you can, must and shall overcome.

So the holy apostle presents the case.

He compares life here on earth with the sport-life of his time, or more accurately, he thinks of the Isthmian games, which used to be played in close proximity to Corinth.

At these games Paul had seen, how a bad wrestler struck out with the fist toward his opponent, but did not hit him, and thus beat the air. But also how a good wrestler hit his opponent, overcame him and got him under the knee, and now dragged him along as his prey.

And so, says St. Paul, I wrestle with my body.

I wrestle with my body, not by way of a game-fight; when I attack my body, I strike not amiss; not as beating the air, but with effect; and the outcome is, that I have my body under me, that I am master over my flesh, and as conqueror freely dispose of my body.

I can do all things through Christ, Who strengtheneth me.

How is this to be understood?

As man you exist after soul and body; but these

two are not equal. For, when soul and body are torn apart in death, the soul continues to exist apart from the body and to live and to enjoy, but the body without the soul is a corpse.

So your *ego*, your person does not throne in your body, but in your soul. Thus your body is nothing but an instrument, which God gave to your soul, through which to reveal itself and to have fellowship with the visible world and with your fellowmen.

No sooner is the working of your soul upon your body broken, than life about you falls away from you.

You see this in part already in sleep. Stronger still when one is chloroformed, and his leg can be amputated, without his knowing it. Also when one faints, and has no knowledge of himself.

Thus to this extent your soul is bound to your body and is dependent on it.

Suppose, one wants to commit sin, what sin is there, which he can carry out and perfect without the help of his body?

Surely, in his spiritual thought he can sin before God, without any one knowing anything of it, and the dreadful struggle between our *ego* and our God, which must end in the total denial of our most deeply hidden *self*, takes place altogether in the soul.

But apart from this one principle sin, what sin is there, that does not touch the body?

When unholy passions rise in you, thirst after money and pleasure, anger against the brother, and what not else, even all these hidden sins are unthinkable apart from the body. Or is it not through the body, that impure desires come into your mind? Through the body that you learn to know money and pleasure? And also through the body, that you know what another does to work you harm?

Also of sin, which does not express itself in outward act, it must be confessed, that, the one sin of our *ego* against God excepted, it were unthinkable in us, if the body were not there.

But far greater still becomes the significance of the body, as soon as it comes to *outgoing* sin, which refuses to remain hidden in the heart, but wants to go out, wills to reveal itself, and carry out and perfect the premeditated wrong.

Then it must be confessed in the severest and most literal sense, that there is no one single sin, which can express itself in action outwardly, otherwise than through the gate of your body from your heart.

When one is chloroformed, while the effect lasts, no one sin can be committed by him. And when one is in a faint, it is equally impossible.

But when the body is awake and active, so that the senses perceive, and the soul through our nerves has our body at its disposal, the gate is open, and sin rides out.

You are mistaken, when with sin you think merely of voluptuousness, drunkenness and debauchery.

He who is angry, exhibits his sin equally by means of the flesh. He shows it by the look of his *eye*, by the features of his *face*, by the language that passes his *lips*, by the serpent-hiss, that goes out from his throat, sometimes also by scornful or menacing gesticulations with *finger* or *hand*.

Passion equally shows itself through the body. You see the *veins* swell, the color become *red,* the whole *body come* into action, evil words go out *of the mouth,* and sometimes the *hand* or *fist* is lifted.

Backbiting and slander, written or told, are unthinkable apart from the body.

Heaviness, laziness, dilatoriness, wasting of time, it all depends upon the question whether you govern your body or your body you.

Self-conceit, vanity, desire to shine, pride, self-exaltation, cannot exhibit themselves, except by the carriage of the body, by the way in which you dress, show yourself, and treat others by words or motions.

And so along, you can literally name no single sin, but, for outward action, always needs the body.

Without the flesh sin can be active in your bosom, but cannot reveal itself.

BUT as it is with sin, it is also with your holier sense.

Whatever good and holy tendencies may waken in you, whatever lowly sense of humility may fill your heart, whatever urge of love may speak in you, of this also there is no revelation possible save *through your body.*

Without your body there is no fellowship of saints in the earth. Without your body no single utterance or exhibition of love in look, in word or deed. Without your body no single revelation of the life that grace poured out in you. Though there be light in you, it can not shine out through the windows of your body. What does not shine out through them, remains hidden.

For consider well, without your body you can hear nothing, read nothing, say nothing, show nothing by look or face, and can absolutely do nothing outwardly.

When in the future day of the Lord you will have your *glorified* body, all this will present no difficulty, because your body as it shall then be, will altogether be disposed to this outshining of spiritual light.

When in Paradise God created Adam, this cost Adam no trouble, because then too the balance was perfect.

But now this is not so.

Now your body is no more in this pure condition that with equal readiness it gives sin and holiness a passage through and out.

On the contrary, now your body gives sin an easy passage through, while all too frequently you must do violence to your body to effect a through passage to an utterance of higher life.

THE struggle born from this, is very bitter and long.

For of course, by nature your body is still corrupt and thus subject to all sorts of weakness. Thereby the body acquired certain habits of its own. From the body a certain action begins to go out upon the soul. And you meet with resistance every time you attempt to use your body for something holy and of God.

The question is, whether you oppose this, or whether you give in to the flesh.

In either case, there is always a struggle, and the question is, who overcomes in the same, whether you yield to your body, or your body to you.

And Paul truly complains: "O wretched man that I am, who shall deliver me from the body of this death"? (Rom. 7, 24). But this same Paul glories nevertheless: "I keep my body under, and bring it into subjection" (I Cor. 9, 27).

This does not mean, of course, that Paul *always*, and always *altogether* overcame. Wounds he too incurred with it. Marks of his struggle the apostle of the Lord also bore.

But it does mean, that he did not give up the battle. That in the struggle he gradually gained ground. And that by grace it was given him, that his body did not always run away with him, but that he ruled his body, as a rider his unwilling horse, which then indeed offers resistance and opposition, and sometimes makes a false motion, sometimes even throws him from his back, but without the rider giving in.

In the end it is always the child of God, that is master, and, because he continues such, triumphs.

XXXV

The Ways of Her House

CARE FOR THE HOUSE

Of the good housewife the Proverb-poet writes, that she does not eat "the bread of idleness, for that she ever looketh well to the ways of her household" (31, 27).

There was a time, when especially in our large cities, some housemothers thought, that this looking to the ways of her house, referred to her care of the marble hall-ways, and when she knew, that the spotless flooring glistened with whiteness, as she had overseen the work of her maid, the reading of Proverbs 31, 27 gave her quiet self-satisfaction at the thought: "Such a woman who looks to the ways of her house, I am too."

This took place, even very frequently, in days of petrified piety, when many a housewife became very angry at seeing the least bit of dirt on the polished floor, but had no concern about the *baptized* maid-servant, who had to clean it.

They were evil days, when the marginal readings of our Bible ceased to be read, and the beautiful interpretation of our fathers was forgotten: "The ways of the house here means, the whole course of *the household life,* so that the housewife keeps oversight over her *children,* over her *servants,* over the work that each has to do, and looks well to the *furniture,* and also to the *means* which her husband allows her."

This explanation was beautiful and rich, and at the

same time made it plain, why there is added to it: "*and the bread of idleness she does not eat.*"

This the woman does who prides herself on the spotlessness of her floors, and for the rest lets her household affairs go as they will.

But this doeth not the woman, who literally is busy from early morn till late at night, looking after all the interests of life in her house, to watch over and to direct them, and knows the ways of that life to its minutest particulars.

A PIOUS and scholarly expositor added to this: "A good housewife does not remain seated in her chair, as though from the domestic throne to give out orders and instructions, but with her own eye she looks to the ways of her house, i.e. she has her hand in everything, and rules her house not as an officer by orders, but much more as becomes a careful mother, in person."

This does not mean, of course, that she gives *no* rule and *no* definite instruction. For where these are wanting, life loses its course. There things go haphazardly and slipshod, and domestic life makes no progress. You see this plainly in those neglected households, where one always drudges and is never done, and where endless confusion rather makes the impression as though one was ever on the *move,* instead of quietly *dwelling* in one's house.

Both are necessary. There must be fixed order in the life of the house. And that order must continue because the housewife continually has her eye upon it and is with it. Only then can you say: *"She looks to the ways* of her house."

And when you apply this to everything the marginal reading sums up, and to the order in which this is summed up, you need not fear, that such a woman will eat the bread of *laziness.* Rather the question rises, how this delicate woman stands it?

CONSIDER, that the *order* in which the Annotator sums up her activities, is not: First the chambers, the furnitures, the money, and then the servants and the children. But reversely: first the children, then the servants, and only after that furnitures, money and chambers.

The children come first. They are the live goods. The pledges entrusted to you of God, who have been baptized into His holy Name. And a housewife, who leaves her children to the care of a nurse, to a "bonne" or governess, that she herself might go out more freely, can take better care of her furniture, and more uninterruptedly keep at work on her embroidery, will bear her judgment of God, because she has neglected her duty as mother.

And though in the days when the marginal readings were put in the Bible, there was no social question as yet, even then in the estimation of our fathers the servants came *before* the furniture, chambers and stairs.

Also servants are live goods, they are human beings, members of the church, baptized persons, and a housewife, who does not look to her servants, to care for them and to provide for their body *and soul,* shows that she does not understand what it means, that God has given her human beings in her service, that He has entrusted to her individuals that have a soul to lose.

Also what is added about "the means which her husband entrusts her with" is not considered by every housewife a matter of sufficient importance.

Also money is given of God. This also for His sake may not be carelessly handled. All money is *entrusted*, and therefore of *all* money we are accountable *to God.*

Two things only the Annotator forgot.

The housewife has also first to care for the *friends and guests of the house.*

Especially in a house with busy ways of life her task is thereby very comprehensive.

And in addition to this is the *husband.*

He too needs looking after. Not merely in clothing and food, but also in his way of life and formation of his character. And again, a housewife does not understand her calling, when she exerts no beneficial influence upon the formation and development of her husband's character.

AGAINST this pious interpretation of the task of the housemother the spirit of our age meanwhile more and more opposes itself.

A woman who thus almost loses herself in the ways of her house, is scornfully looked down upon as a "housesparrow." A woman should be vivacious, interesting, especially in social conversation. And, therefore, all this more ordinary life of the household, by way of a small barracks, must be finished by strict orders in the early morning-hour. For the rest it must be handed over to the servants, that the wife may have leisure to read, to play, or to go out, and to develop herself for a higher sphere of life.

According to God's Word the woman thereby *lowers* instead of raises herself.

Not as though the "housedrudge" is the Scriptural ideal. The sort of characterless women, who sink away in their household affairs and are nothing else than the copy of them, rather diametrically oppose the word of the Proverb-poet.

"To look well to the ways of her house" one must stand *above* it, occupy a higher viewpoint, and thus in spiritual contact live with that holier world, from which direction must come down with respect to the life of the household.

For a woman who fears God, the leading of the ways of her house is a matter of prayer.

For the "housedrudge" therefore we make no plea.

But when you ask what is of greater benefit to our people, and what advances the Kingdom of God more effectively, whether it is a woman's life that goes up in much reading, in much visiting, in much going out and for the rest in public "Christian activity"; or the life of a woman, that is bent upon being the warm and inspiring center of the domestic circle, upon devoting itself to bringing up the young and developing the older children, upon taking to heart the physical and spiritual well-being of the servants, and upon maintaining from house to house cordial friendly relationships between the families—who then hesitates to acknowledge, that the last by far the most interesting, creates the richest, the most noble womanly existence?

UNDOUBTEDLY life out of the house has certain conformableness to duty, but never otherwise than by receiving continually leading and direction from the center of the domestic life.

Everything out of the house that does not touch *your* heart, is abstract and barren. And according to God's ordinance your heart finds no other fireside, from which it can borrow its glow, than in the household thought-out of God, worked-out of God, created of God.

Where the household life is sound and healthy, you find people, old and young, who are healthy of heart.

And a people even as people never has more real strength, and as a nation can never take a higher standpoint, than when from the warm and inspiring home-life power and glow of enthusiasm stream out also in the veins of national life.

That so many serious-minded folk labor to stem this hand-over-hand increase of life out of the house in society, in coffee- or beer-house, is not because by itself there is evil in such a beer-house. But because by it the elasticity of the home-life suffers loss. And that loss affects injuriously the moral fiber of the rising generation.

As long as the household flourishes, everything is to be hoped. Where the home-life begins to weaken, the worst is to be feared, not merely with respect to your national future, but even for your church-life.

And therefore there depends so much more than one can say upon the housewife.

According as *she* takes her duty seriously or lightly, she actually has in hand the welfare of the family-life, and through the family-life the future of the church and fatherland. And of this she will give account to God.

Account to God for herself, but account also for her daughters, how she has trained them, as women, for the task that awaits them in life and what mind and spirit she has developed in the female personnel of the house.

In those daughters of the family, provided the mother leads them aright, the good tradition of a former generation can be revived again, and so pass on upon those that come after, to the good of church and fatherland, to the benefit of all that are alive, and to the praise of the Name of our God.

But there can also be fostered in those daughters an *un*homelike, an *anti*-homelike spirit, which as an hereditary cancer enters into our families. And then it will be God, Who will visit the sins of our duty-ignoring housewives by punishing them in the ways of their children.

XXXVI

Labor Not for the Meat That Perisheth

NOT LIVE BY BREAD ALONE

To *work*, each day God gives us; something that measures up to the length of that day; yea, in so real a sense to *accomplish* work, that when at night we retire, the result, the fruit, the outcome of the past day is stored up; is the Divine ordinance, not merely with respect to him who became a sinner, but to all mankind.

To labor, to be busy, to work is our high human calling.

For though it is true, that God the Lord, after the fall, has said: "In the sweat of thy face shalt thou eat bread" (Gen. 3, 19); yet in this saying the emphasis and stress fall on "the sweat of the face" and upon the "eating bread." With wonderful accuracy of expression the word: *labor or work* does not occur in this punitive judgment.

So to have to work, that it exhausts our strength and forces sweat from the body, and to have to do this to keep the mouth open, has come upon us by reason of sin.

But by itself work is so little an outflow of sin, that Christ rather glories in the fact: My Father *works hitherto and I work.*

To be able, to be permitted, and thus to be obliged to work, is the privilege that comes to man, because he is created after the Image of God. What Jesus said, was spoken far less after His Divine than after His *human* nature. He worked because like the Father He worked, as our Mediator, i.e. as the *man* Jesus Christ.

One speaks sometimes of a *right* that comes to man by reason of work; and surely in the sense here given, there is such a right.

Because the Lord your God is a God Who always works, and you are created after His likeness, the right, the high privilege of being permitted to work, is your due as a man.

This is what every Sabbath declares unto you anew in God's name.

In six days the Lord made heaven and earth, with all that in them is, and because the Lord your God so *worked,* therefore you must *labor* six days and do all your work, and only in connection with this does the Sabbath have a meaning as a day of rest, so that there be no other rest in your life, than in the life of your God.

They, who picture blessedness to themselves before the throne of God, as consisting in the fact, that all labor shall then be ended and all work be fallen away, that in a *dolce far niente,* i.e. in a blessed doing nothing, one might taste heavenly joy, neither know their God, nor His angels, nor life as it shall be in heaven.

For your God works *always.*

And the angels are *ministering* spirits.

And with a view to blessedness Christ says to His elect: "Over a few things hast thou been faithful, I will make thee ruler over many things" (Matt. 25, 23).

BUT this beautiful ordinance of creation sin also has broken up.

Not to work, has now obtained a charm. And sinner after sinner dies, of whom it must be confessed with sorrow, that really, all his life long, he accomplished as good as nothing.

Such as these God's Word points to the small, insignificant ants, and asks: "How long wilt thou sleep, O sluggard? When wilt thou arise out of thy sleep? Yet a little sleep, a little slumber, a little folding of the hands to sleep: So shall thy poverty come as one that travelleth, and thy want as an armed man" (Prov. 6, 9).

The sinner indeed knows well, that he receives his day from God, to labor, but in his heart he says: "I shall be wicked anyway, why then should I labor in vain" (Job 9, 6, Dutch version). Or when he has labored, in his selfishness he says: "He that laboureth laboureth for himself, for his mouth craveth it of him" (Prov. 16, 26), (boweth itself before him).

When there is no bread in the cupboard, and no money in hand, one cries and longs for work. But when hunger does not sting, and our portion is secure, idleness seems preferable, laziness to be human wealth, and even in the early Christian churches you see such do-nothings corrupt the life of believers in such wise, that the holy apostle is forced to make threat: "He who will not work, shall not eat" (2 Thess. 3, 10-12). And again: "Even when we were with you, this we commanded you, that if any would not work, neither should he eat. For we hear that there are some which walk among you, disorderly, working not at all, but are busybodies. Now them that are such we command and exhort by our Lord Jesus Christ, that with quietness they work, and eat their own bread."

Not in Paradise, neither before, nor after the fall, but by Christ Himself it is said: "Are there not twelve hours in the day, so then let us work, while it is day: the night cometh, when no man can work."

So the entire Scripture is opposed to being busy doing nothing, in which so many among us spend their days, rising and dressing themselves, walking hither and thither and chatting somewhat, eating something and drinking something, looking into the fire or through the window, and then lying down again, to return to their friend, a long loved sleep.

God in His Word knows, that work is a blessing, that idleness is the root of all evil, and therefore that Word always warns against idleness and indolence and urges one to work.

Even of the wealthy housewife in Proverbs 31 is it said: "She riseth also while it is yet night, and eateth not the bread of idleness."

CONVERTED or unconverted therefore makes here no difference, here or hereafter. Always to work is our glorious human calling, because we have been created after the Divine Likeness of Him, Who *always* works.

We must rest from our *sinful* works. On the Sabbath we may rest from our slavish labor, to be spiritually more richly engaged. After death we shall rest from our earthly labor; but always to work is and *remains* the calling, which in our patent of nobility as man we received from our God.

And the outcome shows, that a people, a family, a person, that works, is happy. But that indolence works ruin to a people, breaks up the family and unnerves your personal life.

And yet there is a considerable difference between him who is converted to Christ, and the other who still wanders about without his Savior.

First of course in that a converted man, who plays the sluggard and spends his days in idleness, is far more guilty before God.

But this is so self-evident, that it scarcely bears mention, even though many confessors of the Lord, will do well, to pay heed to this.

But there is still another difference, which is more significant. Namely, that the unconverted works for the meat which *perisheth*, and that the converted man at least *can* work for the meat which abideth unto *eternal* life.

The sinner as such works, and must work, to have bread, wherewith to sustain life.

He stands in the humiliation.

He knows that as to worth his body is subordinate to his soul; and yet, almost all his life is spent in the care to feed and maintain *the body*.

This is now done in terms of money, but that makes no difference. In almost every family almost all the money, that comes in, is spent on the body. To give the body shelter, to clothe and to maintain it.

So one works for wages, one works for money, wherewith to buy bread and clothing, and with millions and millions of our race it is still the rule of life: "In the sweat of thy face thou shalt eat bread."

This ordinance is God's ordinance over the sinner, and mankind does not escape it.

For what is said, that many people in the higher walks of life, do not labor for their living, is untrue in part. Labor with the mind is also labor. Far heavier labor even. And when at sea the storm arises, and amid the howlings of the wind the sailor must go in the rigging to take in sails, while the mate stands quietly on the bridge, no one will say, that the sailor works, but not the mate.

And as regards that small group of rich people, who live on their income and have bread and to spare, even though they do not work, God's judgment awaits them also, in case they have not understood their calling, of being even in the enjoyment of wealth the more zealously engaged in the interests of people and in the things of the Kingdom of God.

BUT for the converted man God the Lord removes this humiliation from labor.

He is become God's *child* again.

And as in the family the child renders assistance and co-labors, without thinking: "by doing this I earn my bread," but works simply because mother tells him to work and because assisting mother is a pleasure, so it has become for the Christian.

Care for his living he has none. What should he need to be troubled about, saying: What shall I eat, or wherewithal shall I be clothed? Do not the heathen the same? And when he sees the birds of the heavens, that they sow not, neither spin, and yet are fed of his

God, can he lose confidence in his Father Who is in heaven?

We do not say that such is the case with every Christian, but that such it ought to be.

As a child does not care for himself, but lets his father care for him, and now works for father, with spirit and love and in obedience, *because* he is his father,—so also does a child of God leave the care for his living to God, and meanwhile works all the hours of the day in the service of his God.

Hence what he works for is not wages, not money, not bread, but the *good pleasure of his God.*

He is at home with God. He is in God's service. And in his Divine calling he is all day long at work, because God has placed him in it, that therein he might please God.

So he works not to make his living, i.e., not for the meat which perisheth, but to enjoy the good pleasure and the favor of God, i.e., for the meat which endureth unto eternal life.

Thus is the humiliation overcome.

It is no more all of life spent in the care for the body. For even the most slavish and material labor is included in the service of God and therefore sanctified in Him.

Every morning, as a new day begins, his inquiry and prayer is: "Lord, what wilt thou have me to do?" And every evening, when the day's work is done, he brings the same as an offering to God, giving God the glory.

XXXVII

Of Her Living

CHARITY

A WHILE ago, a policeman fell into a murderer's hand, and his body was found floating in a lake. This man left a widow behind. And at once among the "well-intentioned" and "charitable" the sense awakened, that they should do something for the widow. So it was done. A brilliant festivity was organized. Admission was rated high. And after reduction of expenses, the proceeds were given to the widow.

A fine, delicate trait of the modern-times sense of charity. When by miscreants your husband is killed, ladies and gentlemen "amuse" themselves for a whole evening, and what comes of it is for you.

Of course they who take religion more seriously took no part in this. Through the Young Men's Christian Association they contributed a sum of money outright.

But for the rest the whole city took part. Not to take part was considered cruel. It was in behalf of the poor widow of the murdered policeman.

Of this no more needs be said. From our side warnings have always been sounded against those false forms of so-called "well-doing." He who gives must *give outright.* All concomitant artificial means are unworthy of Christian love.

But what such an offensive occasion lays upon you

is, that in your own circle upon giving, yea, upon giving from your own purse and by your own hand, you must let the light shine from Above.

Nothing so much as alms lends itself to show, self-misleading and misleading of others.

And yet, especially with respect to "giving," our Savior was so strict and inexorable.

What was not given for God's sake had no count. When the right hand knew of it, the left hand was condemned. To give from one's abundance was worthless. Only what was given from one's indigence, from one's living, shone in the treasure-chest of the Lord as fine gold of Ophir.

You remember the Jerusalem widow, in whose behalf no one made a benefit-feast, but *who herself gave* all she had in her house, two small farthings, money for which bread should have been bought, and which she spared her own mouth, to devote it to the Lord, her God.

Well, before and after this widow's offering, gold and silver was cast by the handfuls into the treasury-chest. But this did not prevent Jesus from saying in the hearing of all: These two farthings of this woman are more than all this gold and silver. For what the others cast in, was from their abundance, what this woman gave, she gave from her poverty (Luke 21, 3).

"GIVING" is a trait of beauty of soul, for which, when you may observe it among your people, in your own circle, in your own house and in your own heart, you should give thanks.

"Giving" by way of exception, to make a great show, was indigenous with the heathen, and to a certain extent is this to this day. But *giving* as we see it in our Christian circles, and more strikingly still in English, Scotch and American lands, is a fruit of *Christian faith.*

We stand far behind England's colossal gifts. But he who considers what especially not the well-to-do, but the people of small means among us give; give in church offerings; give to subscriptions; give to associations, for school and church; and then what is given at times privately, to help unfortunates, finds that it reaches a total, which is truly astonishing.

One cannot estimate such sums. *True* giving escapes statistics, and is bound to do so. But so much can be said, that all money devoted in other circles to pleasure and travel and excursions, is in these circles to the last cent brought to the altar of love. And that there are savings and privations, and garments worn somewhat threadbare, for the sake of the greater joy, of making somewhat more liberal contributions, or of giving to something, for which thus far no gift had been set apart.

There hides in this one of the vital powers of soul on the part of our lesser well-to-do people. It is a larger grace that is given them of God; and which strengthening and ennobling reacts upon all their life and existence.

THERE is *an art* in giving, which you must learn of God or never know it.

There is first the ordinary, general giving to be

rid of it. Laying up and accumulating so many thousands, and then also a ten dollars or more for the needs of all Christendom together.

One drop from the abundance. And therefore without moral value, because there is no saving, no privation, no restriction of luxury back of it.

That was giving *without* art. Giving for the sake of doing our part with others. Well meant, but with no inner address from the heart behind it.

One gave nothing for his church. No penny for Christian schools. A small contribution to three or four associations. And then a bit of loose money for the coming and going man.

But by "need" God has modified this, and introduced *art* therein.

Ten times as much more is estimated too little, to express the difference between what the ordinary man now contributes yearly, compared with what he used to give before.

He who took the trouble to count all the budgets, great and small, of all diaconites, churches, schools and associations, etc., which in our country keep head above water, and thereby in his thoughts kept apart *grosso modo* what comes from the pockets of the humbler classes, would ask himself with astonishment, how from such people counting so few rich among them, such colossal sums could have been raised.

And yet no one has less because of it. The general feeling has rather been heightened thereby than depressed. Of becoming poorer by giving, there has been no mention.

And if in connection with money you refer to the

wondrous mystery, which is implied in "the blessing of our God," confess freely, that here the blessing is seen.

Something of the oil in the vessel, from which continually went out and was not emptied.

SUCH giving as fruit of higher, holier art, was at the same time productive of indirect benefits.

Think of your *church* life.

It is almost universally recognized among the confessors of the Lord, that conditions in Reformed and Lutheran churches subsidized on the part of the State are unbearable. Nothing was more desired than to make an end to them. But . . . this meant standing on feet of one's own. Then the goldstream of the State freezes over and flows no more. Then everything must be paid by themselves. Who will be able to meet it? Who dares to face it?

That is the rock on which the churchly zeal of so many foundered.

But it was altogether different in those circles, in which the holy art of giving had been learned. There was no need there to ask, how the money was to come. There was known what the art of giving was capable of doing. And the happy outcome was, that through the art of giving one regained his liberty in Christ, while the other brothers from lack of power to give remained in the clutches of their chains.

So it is with respect to social interests.

There is no equality on earth, but Love can do all things, and is a power in this world, which smooths many unevennesses, and thereby dulls the sharpness of the same.

And here also this power of Love has shone out. Not the pride of the benefactor who dispenses charities from the heights, and thereby insults, but the love which gives for God's sake, and thus on the part of God distributes to those of lesser and humbler estate.

Of course giving of princely gifts is something altogether different, belonging to an altogether different order of things, and in our country one knows merely from hearsay, what is ordinary in America.

Gifts of a million dollars at once, or even of seven millions as a while ago was given by one man to the University of Chicago, we know nothing of. Only at times, such as recently, when we were taken by surprise by a large gift of many thousands. But for the rest the impulse of such large gifts, in life or at death, is not yet indigenous with us. Though we must not forget, that fortunes among us do not begin to measure up to accumulations elsewhere. Also that no little human vanity and jealousy find expression in such gifts.

Yet we do not relinquish hope, that among us also great capital shall come to the practice of this noble art. Of course according to the measure of our power, but still as exhibition of higher enthusiasm. There are so many institutions, which only in this way can be founded and maintained.

But whatever course this takes, it is certain, that after Jesus' standard, the bottom of the money-chest of mercy is yet by no means seen.

Already now we give ten times more than fifty years ago, but in the fifty years to come this already large sum may well be doubled or tripled.

If he who is just a little above the humbler class, could be persuaded to apply this system of giving, an incredibly large sum would thereby be rendered available.

And even then the point would not be reached at which finally Jesus would have us.

Jesus desires self-restriction in spending, so that giving may be enlarged. Jesus does not disapprove, but calls it praiseworthy, that the poorest take part in giving.

Take the two together, both that you come to the art of needing less for yourself, and of giving what you save thereby, for God's sake and for His cause, and that on every hand you widen the circle of givers, and guess yourself what this would imply.

The poor widow who gave her two mites out of her living, has age upon age been the means in God's hand, of making rich the church of God in the world; and surely the sum cannot be estimated, which the memory alone of this woman, by putting self to shame, has brought to the altar of Christian charity.

This woman gave her two farthings in the treasury, but by the mention of her on the Gospel-page millions and again millions to Christ's church.

And this propaganda goes on not only among the more poor. Relatively the members of your household also are not rich in money, and your children, who live on you, and have but a small sum of money weekly or annually at their disposal.

All these must learn to *give,* give from a need of

their own soul, give of what is saved and of what they have denied themselves, that later on, when God shall have entrusted more to them, they will of themselves give more abundantly.

So the treasuries of Christ's church are well-nigh numberless.

Provided she casts it upon her Lord, He, Whose the gold and the silver is, shall neither forsake her nor put her to shame.

This is the mystery of self-sufficiency in the love of Christ. It always demands more, but is also always ready to make still greater demands upon itself.

It is with this as with the vapors, that rise up to the heavens, presently in abundant rains to descend from thence again.

The need itself here brings provision.

XXXVIII

Hasty in Words

MUTUAL QUARRELING

EVERY gift of God brings its temptation. For it can either be *used* for God's glory, or *mis*used in the service of sin.

This applies surely not least to the wondrous gift of *language*, that high privilege whereby, among all creatures, man distinguishes himself.

For though in our times reports are abroad of a language of animals, and a man of learning has devoted three years of his life, to the study of the supposed language of apes, already now the folly of the undertaking has been exposed by the result.

True, animals make sounds, and these sounds vary, and from this difference of sounds something can be understood. When a dog growls, it means something altogether different than when he barks, whines or howls, and we understand well, what these different sounds of a dog mean. But all this has nothing in common with *language*.

We ourselves have such sounds, to express sensation, as when we laugh or cry, sigh or groan, scream or jubilate. But our speech, our language, the gift to express ourselves in *words* is something wholly by itself.

That you have a language you can speak, means, that you belong to a people, that for ages have exercised *thought*, for those thoughts and connection of those thoughts have found a *sound*, have cast that sound into *words,* and that, carrying this language in you and speaking it, by those words and by those sounds you are able to have communion of thoughts with your people.

Human language therefore stands so high and is so glorious a gift of God, that the Son of God Himself assumes the name of the *Word* of the Father. "In the beginning was *the Word* and *the Word* was with God and the Word was God."

It is by the *Word* that our God has made the heavens.

He bears all things *by the Word of His power.* And when even now some mighty event takes place in the world it is because a "Word of God" has gone out, which never returns to Him void, but doeth that whereunto He hath sent it.

So the difference is evident.

He who drifted and wandered off, seeks for our human language to find a point-of-connection in the sound of an orang-outang; while he who lives by the Holy Scripture, finds this connecting-point in the Son of God, Who is Himself the eternal *Word* of God.

This must be so.

For the mighty antithesis is and remains, whether you take man as having come up from the ape, or . . . *as created after the Image of God.*

For this reason human language stands so high, and human song, that melts word and melody into one, excels so far the song of nightingale and lark.

Only language, the *word,* is a power, which is ever

yet able to maintain the competition with the *money*-power.

That wondrous Word in our human language, which draws out the soul, and is able to enter deeply into the heart of the neighbor.

In poetry it works as by magic a world of thoughts around you, and is able to estimate and govern the world in which you dwell.

Our language is the vehicle of our seriousness and of our mirth. It breaks the tension of our sorrow and gives expression to our joy. It creates fellowship of soul with soul, gives birth to the sociability of life, it weaves a tie around man and man. And above all it is language, in which we express God's thoughts, make confession of His Holy Name, pray to the eternal, and lose ourselves in adoration and praise before His Majesty.

To the faithful in Israel this latter stood even so mightily in the foreground, that they shrank from the idea of losing in death their mouth and their language and their word and their song of praise, and therefore so frequently moaned: In the grave who shall give Thee thanks? (Ps. 6, 5).

YET language cannot spend itself exclusively in praise and thanksgiving.

Our human language is also given us for the practice of fellowship and love toward our neighbor, goodwill and seriousness among our fellow-men.

But thereby originates temptation.

There is indeed another temptation for our human word, the carnal temptation to swear and take the Name of our God in vain. A temptation so strong, that many people cannot utter a sentence without an oath forming a part of it. But *this* temptation we here pass by. We now speak only of the temptation which in our language is abroad among men.

This temptation also is of many sorts. The temptation to flatter, the temptation to lie, the temptation to taunt and so much more. But also the temptation to be *hasty in one's words*, and this especially God's Word avenges as we read in Proverbs 29, 20: "Seest thou a man that is hasty in his words? there is more hope of a fool than of him."

Against this temptation one should be warned, especially in everyday home-life.

In public, or in more or less strange places, among those with whom we are less familiar, one naturally more or less restrains himself. Here speech is bound to a more polite form. One thinks before one speaks. Sometimes one even complains, that at such times words are slow, rather than that they come too fast.

But in the common trend of family-life, among those with whom one feels at home and at ease, when no forms bind us, and words are freely spoken, the temptation is but all too great, that the word discards the bridle, goes beyond the limit, is too hasty, in passion, in petulant folly or in familiarity exceeding all bounds, to say bluntly, what should have remained unsaid, and thoughtlessly to let one's tongue run away with oneself.

THIS subverts the ordinance, which God gave with respect to language, your human word. His ordinance is, that first there should be the thought, and that this thought as the *soul* should *embody* itself in the word.

In your speech according to God's ordinance, your heart, your head must govern, and your word, your organ of speech must be servant and serve.

But as a matter of fact this order is frequently reversed. So you meet people, who are sometimes called *moulins à paroles,* i.e., word-mills. With whom the tongue speaks of itself, and always keeps on talking, and rattles; like a clock that always ticks. An endless stream of sounds and dripping of words, which makes you seasick and wears you out.

Then rules not the rider the horse, but the horse, here the rattling tongue, runs away with the rider, and what you hear is no longer the utterance of a warm heart or of a clear head, but a leaking gutter, that can not be stopped.

Now this seems, when it does not go too far, sometimes a great convenience. Then one is never confused, can say everything, and has what the world calls an easy *flux de bouche,* i.e., a rare outpouring of a flood of words.

The trouble in the domestic circle, that such continuous speech disturbs the peace and finally creates such weariness, is by no means yet the worst.

No, it is far worse, when such hasty speech inadvertently makes one lose all self-control and moderation in his words, till nothing more is spared, and one literally says everything, that comes to mind.

And in the domestic circle, in familiar intercourse this is the cause of so much bitterness and disturbance of spirits, of so much disputation and estrangement.

Then one word brings out another, the tongue of one sets that of the other free, the eloquence of the Evil One masters husband and wife and child and servant. The one tries to excel the other in rapidity of speech. Lack of patience cuts the other short. The one constantly interrupts the other. It becomes a raising of voice in against each other. Abusive language sends blood from the heart to the head. And the end of it is, that the Divine gift, which was given us for the utterance of praise and love, serves time and again at the table, in social intercourse and familiar fellowship, to disturb the domestic peace.

But this must not be so.

Our language, the glorious gift of speech, we have received of our God, and ours is the responsibility, how we use also this gift of our God.

AND therefore with the use of our *human word* God's Word warns us so solemnly before all things else to be on our guard against *hastiness* of speech.

Not of course, as though taunting, lying, flattering and cutting with the word were not far worse, but because all these other evils hang together with this one ordinance of our God, that language, that the word must be *servant,* that the word must serve, and *not* rule.

To keep silent, betrays so much higher grace, than speech. Speech is silver, says the Scripture, but silence is *gold.*

To hold one's tongue in leash, and when it is on the point of saying the evil word to *tame* it, is evidence of noble strength of soul. "Whoso keepeth his mouth and his tongue," says the Proverb-poet, "keepeth his soul from troubles" (21, 23).

And therefore see to it, also with your children, when the young twig is readily bent. Especially a child speaks quickly and thoughtlessly. And upon you rests the responsibility, when instead of having accustomed your child by your own more quiet seriousness to a more easy flow of words, you *over*hasty have added your part to his already so great hastiness of speech, by the unrest in words, which in your home-circle you have made to be a second nature to yourself.

XXXIX

Forget It Not

FORGETFULNESS

Is it *sin* to forget? Or, when something escaped us, are we done with it by saying: I forgot it.

One would almost grant the latter. For, when you have simply not thought about a matter; when remembrance of it did not come to you, and nothing whatever reminded you of it, how in the world then could you help it, and how can you be held accountable for it?

In by far most cases with neglect of domestic duty accompanied by the excuse, that forgetfulness was least of all intentional, pleasure is taken, even though as a rule the person, who suffered inconvenience thereby, ends by saying: *You should not have forgotten it.*

To this remark the conscience involuntarily responds *yea and amen,* even though one is conscious, that it cannot be altered. Something from which it is evident, that, at least with respect to tender and serious matters, one regrets his forgetfulness, thus feels and acknowledges that to forget is something wrong, and thus truly sees guilt in it, and, at least where it concerns a forgetting with respect to the Lord our God, truly recognizes, that in *forgetting* there is sin.

In God's Word forgetting is represented as sin. "If we have forgotten the name of our God," says Ps. 44, 21, "Shall not God search this out? He Who knoweth the secrets of the heart?"

What is more, again and again in Holy Scripture

the "*not* forgetting" is laid upon us as an indisputable *duty!* Something from which directly follows, that, "forgetting" undoubtedly is judged as a discarding of our sacred duty, and thus as *sin.*

For instance it is bound upon our heart, that we shall not forget the Lord our God, nor His Name, nor His Covenant. "Bless the Lord, O, my soul," it is said in Psalm 103, "and forget not all His benefits."

To all Israel the duty is put, to take care, that also the later generation shall not forget *the acts* of the Lord.

And, what here we emphasize is, that in Psalm 119 it is said repeatedly: "*Thy Word* I will not forget," "yet have I not forgotten *thy law,*" "Thy statutes do I not forget," "I do not forget Thy precepts," and so in v. 176: "I do not forget Thy commandments."

The same sense in which Moses, after having placed before Israel the ordinances of God, closes his address with the solemn warning: *Thou shalt not forget it* (Deut. 25, 19).

YET distinguish here well.

When by pressure of business or by interruption, you have unintentionally forgotten a duty that was laid upon you, in your neglect of duty at that moment there is in itself no sin.

Were we responsible only for our temporal acts at a given moment, however, it might be maintained, that forgetfulness is free from guilt.

But such is not the case.

We are by no means responsible merely for what at a given moment we do or do not do, but also very really for *the condition of our person,* from which such negligence springs.

Now forgetting by itself is a direct illness of our spirit, which is occasioned by our sinful state. Sin has not merely attacked our will and weakened it, but it has also darkened our understanding. And one of the most pitiful darkenings of our understanding consists in this, that the defectiveness of forgetting is come upon us.

Adam in the state of rightness could not forget. And when once, free from all sin, we shall dwell with the redeemed of God, forgetfulness will never be possible in us again.

Forgetting is a weakness, a defect, a disturbance in our human consciousness.

And insofar as we all stand guilty in Adam, we are also responsible for the sad fact, that forgetting so oftentimes betrays the brokenness and weakness of our consciousness.

BUT there is more.

Also the sinful weakness of forgetting stands under the healing influence of grace. And in common grace, which is the portion of all men, as well as in particular grace, which is bestowed upon all God's elect, a means is offered us, by which to remove this forgetfulness from ourselves and from our children, if not altogether, at least considerably to temper it.

Of course here we do not count with the gift of a specially strong memory, which it has pleased God to impart to some generations and persons.

He who would boast of this, and by reason of this gift would look down upon those less favored, would rob God, Who gave him this gift, of His honor.

But apart from this the fact is undeniable, that early training, even a good school education, can be a great means, to confine this slovenliness of forgetting within certain limits, and that a lively sense of duty also in later years has no small power, to resist this sinful forgetting.

The complaint is general, that pressing business and mobility of the turbulent life of our days, has perceptibly weakened the attention, i.e., ability to center one's mind upon a given matter. And this very lack of attention is a grave aid to forgetting.

Yet conversely it follows from this, that we can do not merely something, with respect to this ugly forgetting, but even a very great deal. And that the duty with all training, of our children as well as of ourselves, is with effort and perseverance to encourage the binding of our attention, to what we must not forget.

Thinking about something and *forgetting* of something has such a deep moral significance.

Just consider, how rarely we forget something that can benefit our own selves, heighten our reputation, or advance our influence. And again, how easily we forget all sorts of things, with respect to which love for God and for our neighbor must inspire us.

Back of that forgetting is really our selfishness and our lack of love.

Much love makes forgetting so much *less*. Orderly living, serious interpretation of one's task in life, deep fear of God works continuous prejudice to forgetting. And he who knows the secret of God's hidden walk, is least of all a stranger to that mindfulness-making operation of the Holy Ghost, which has so often kept us from this sinful forgetting.

See, there works a twofold power upon our memory, upon our remembrance. On one side a power which from without works in us, which makes the terror of our sin to haunt us, renders it impossible for us to forget a suffered wrong, and incites certain weighty moments of our life, continuously, as of itself, to loom up again in and before our spirit.

Under this we are *passive*.

But there is also a power of our own spirit, which inworks upon our memory and our remembrances. And it is this power, that renders us guilty, when we do not use it, and which helps us to overcome forgetting, if we apply it in the fear of the Lord.

BUT here also man has made straight things crooked and with respect to forgetting it also applies: What we should forget, we continuously remember, and what we should never forget, escapes us constantly.

What wrongs others have done us, should be forgotten, and these are continuously remembered and poison our mind. God's acts we forget, but what we ourselves have done continuously inspires our reins to pride. The love we enjoyed from others passes into forgetfulness. But what we ourselves did for others, in mind we continually charge up to their account. Our own trouble is constantly before our eyes, while other peoples' trouble scarcely ever moves us. Regarding comforts for the body and the things that can afford us pleasure, we have wondrous memories, while the interests of our soul in view of eternity continuously escape us. In brief, what with a noble character would hide itself in the background, sin in our memory puts every time again to the fore. And what always should fill us with seriousness, we must be reminded of again and again.

Oh, this forgetting, which in the main is passed over so light-heartedly, what sorrow does it not entail. A forgetting, like that of which Joseph became a victim in prison. A forgetting of the unfortunate in the land, who cry unto God. A forgetting of an act, which hung by a moment, but which brought irreparable loss. A forgetting of what we had promised, to have the deferred hope as a reproach work usury against us.

The bitter fruit of forgetting reaches so far. And why not acknowledge and confess, that among the Lord's people this far-reaching sin is even as lightly dealt with, as among the children of the world.

And yet the Lord our God does not let go of us, He, Who never forgets, and holds in everlasting remembrance the hope of His needy ones.

Forget it not, He continuously calls out to us, deeply inculcating in us our sacred obligation.

Forget not My benefits to you, forget not the grace I showed you, forget not My holy Covenant, but above all forget not the *high* and *holy* commandment I have given you.

Our forgetting helps Satan, and is cause that temptation to sin every time takes hold of us and temptation brings us to fall.

Then we are as Isaiah calls it: *Forgetters of the mountain of His holiness* (65, 11). We do not think of God's commandment, and His ordinances do not stand before us, as a mighty mountain, which of itself shows itself before our eye and by its position points out our way to us.

And therefore God calls out to those forgetters of His holiness: *Forget it not.*

That word He drives into our soul, to rouse to awakeness what was asleep in us.

By that word He brings it to pass that we remember Him again, that His commandments assume forms for us again, that His statutes become again our rejoicings.

And the fruit of this His love is, that less forgetting makes us climb the mountain of His holiness with firmer tread.

He does not forget us, that in us guilty forgetfulness might be broken.

XL

With Contentment

HOME HAPPINESS

"Go thy way," so says the Preacher (Eccl. 9, 7), "eat thy bread with joy, and drink thy wine with a merry heart; for God now accepteth thy works."

And this he says not once, but every time comes back to it again. "For a man hath no better thing under the sun, than to eat and to drink, and to be merry; for that shall abide with him of his labor all the days of his life, which God giveth him under the sun" (8, 15).

Many a pious man, who is spiritually disposed, takes offense at this utterance, among Moderns as well as among Orthodox, even though, from reverence for the Scripture, many Orthodox people would not openly confess it.

What Jesus said: "Seek ye first the Kingdom of God, and *all these things* shall be added unto you," addresses the heart, that seeks God; but not so this interpretation of life, which is sensual at heart, and which ends in eating and drinking.

And of course, if this were the sense and the purport of what the Preacher says, every child of God would have to oppose the Preacher, and the whole book would have to be put out of Scripture.

But such is not the sense of the Preacher.

He has in view something altogether different, something which, real Christians of all lands, can so well understand.

He had a knowledge of men, and his look went deep into the human heart. And he saw with others, and experienced with himself, that our heart does not incline to esteem properly, what our portion in life is, the lot appointed to us, the talent entrusted to us, but continually stretches out the hand after what is more, and higher and less ordinary.

He had observed what endless treasures of life's happiness, which had been given of God to the children of men, were thereby lost. And against this willful destruction of one's own happiness of life, he enters his protest, admonishing every one, that he should take pleasure in the ordinary, everyday life, and have an eye for the treasure of life's happiness, which that ordinary life contains.

Always to be at home, never to have any change, just ordinary living, is what every growing youth, and every young woman, oh, so easily looks down upon from the heights.

There is nothing to it, it bores, it makes one dull and doting.

No, this tameness of existence must be ended. What we want must be sought outside. In what is uncommon. In what is *extra*. In what is not of everyday recurrence.

Such is the call that is abroad. Till the booty found in the uncommon, disappoints more bitterly than the common. And in the end, weary of life, one has no more pleasure either in the everyday concerns, nor in what is uncommon.

One had bread and wanted pastry. And the end is, that both pastry and bread nauseate.

And against this altogether unhealthy interpretation of life the Preacher raises objection, and points out, that the real nerve of our happiness in life must be sought in what is common, in the ordinary, in things of everyday recurrence, in home-life, and that it is against the ordinance of God, and misappreciation of His love in everyday life when the bread-crumbs of domesticity vex us.

And therefore he says:

"Go thy way, eat thy bread with joy, and drink thy wine with a merry heart; for God now accepteth thy works. Let thy garments be always white; and let thy head lack no ointment. Live joyfully with the wife whom thou lovest all the days of the life of thy vanity, which God has given thee under the sun, all the days of thy vanity; for that is thy portion in this life, and in thy labor which thou takest under the sun. Whatsoever thy hand findeth to do, do it with thy might."

And to this all who understand aright the tie of *nature* and *grace* still respond, with an whole-hearted *Amen.*

EVERY other view of life is cruel, and offensively puts the appointment of God's Providence to shame.

For is it not fact, which suffers no denial, that millions and again millions of men and women have nothing else than this *ordinary life*, whose whole life consists of these very *ordinary* relationships and very *ordinary* occupations, and never come to anything extraordinary, yea, even cannot think of it.

And if now, truly, this ordinary, quiet, domestic, everyday life were so poor, so barren, so unrefreshing for our heart, and so empty of life's happiness, where then is the Providence of your God, by which just this, and no other, lot for ninety hundreds of His human children has been appointed and determined?

And when, by your abuse of this ordinary and quiet and very everyday life, you spoil the taste to enjoy it with others, are you then not cruel, offensively cruel, since you are utterly incapable of giving to these millions and millions another, an higher happiness in its place?

And when the Preacher tries to instill again a mind and a taste for this quiet and commonplace and domestic happiness, do you not recognize in him the Preacher of the Word of his God, who endeavors to disclose to you, what happiness of life God included in this ordinary existence?

"GODLINESS with satisfaction is great gain," wrote the apostle to Timothy (I, 6, 6, Dutch version).

Notice carefully the word "satisfaction." Even as the Dutch word for "taking satisfaction in a thing," it has the meaning in it of the word: *enough.* Not only in our language, but also in the original language of Holy Scripture.

He who has "enough," is satisfied, and tastes "pleasure."

And godliness brings you this "satisfaction," because it makes you believe, that God appointed you your lot in life, that your environment is of His making, that the work in which you engage, is the calling given you of Him, and thus that in this your existence, because God has so apportioned it unto you, there must be enough to satisfy your heart, provided you but know how to get it out of it.

He who always looks for something else than he has, wants another house than the one in which he lives, another environment than that wherein God has placed him, another garment than what he wears, another calling than that wherein he works, is conscious at last of a *dislike* in his heart against that house, that garment, that calling, that environment. He becomes peevish and irritable with respect to it. He is unable to appreciate all this, and utterly incapable of getting the relative good out of it. He draws poison from it, and cannot gather honey out of it, because he sees nothing but thistles round about him, and nowhere flowers.

But he who faces all this differently, thinks and knows: This is the life I have to live. These are the persons from among whom I must form my circle. This is the house in which I must be happy. This is the work in which I must find pleasure. . . . So he looks away from other and greater things, fixes his look upon what he has, and gradually comes to discover how great a treasure, and ever increasing a wealth there hides in that ordinary life, which God included in it but which he failed to observe.

WE, Christians of the Netherlands, understand this, because to us above all it was given to bring this costly gift of the quiet common home-life to a rarely high development.

In the height of our spiritual life, our Christian

people did not lend themselves to foreign or uncommon matters, but applied themselves to develop as richly as possible the home-life, the common calling, the everyday labor, the altogether ordinary life-circles, to cultivate taste and mind for it, and to abound in praise and thanksgiving for the uncommon treasure of both material and spiritual happiness, which is found in just ordinary human life.

Even foreigners have admired the life of our fathers, poets have celebrated it in song, and artists have lauded it in our national character, that Calvinism gave rise to that glorious, and to this day world-renowned school of painters, who most always brought upon canvas the ordinary life, and as by magic made its expressive of rich satisfaction and inward delight.

And that in connection with this the Preacher every time puts eating and drinking in the foreground, is no fault, but must be so.

For "eating and drinking" is the *family meal*, and that family meal, especially at midday, is in sooth the *crown of domestic life*. Then all come together. Together they enjoy each other's company. They are conscious of their oneness as a family. Together they enjoy the fruit of their common labor. Together they praise and give thanks, together they pray and supplicate. And strengthened by this delight shared in common, each returns to the rich task of the common life.

AND does this search after "satisfaction" in everyday life work injury to the growth of spiritual life?

Forsooth, when this inward "satisfaction" was the hall-mark of our national character, spiritual life among us was strongest.

This very sobriety of everyday life fosters piety and honor, and holds the young man in bit and bridle.

It distracts less, and encourages the soul to turn in more upon itself. By less diversion outside it *creates* time and cultivates taste for sound literature. It spreads a sheen of satisfaction over every member of the family. And in this quiet atmosphere provides what is required for a *life of prayer.*

We do not even admit, that that over-stimulated spiritual sense, which always seeks spiritual *extras,* and pursues piety outside, and enjoys nothing spiritually, except something special attends it, is of a higher cast.

On the contrary, this spirit of detachment is less pious. Spiritually it leads to over-stimulation, and renders the ordinary means, ordained of God for our edification, insufficient.

Spiritually too one then becomes nauseous of common bread, and always asks for what a proverb calls "crusty pastries."

Healthy at heart is only such a life, in which the *ordinary* is *enough* for us, and thereby all of life is made to be one rich satisfaction.

Then there is happiness and thanks well up in the heart. Then the usual mood of the heart is that of glorifying God. Then there is courage of life and strength of life to bear the cross, which each day lays upon us.

Then there come days indeed, that we go from home to the country or sea-side.

But always such, that, when presently we come

back, we feel, we realize again, that being on the wing was good for a few weeks, but that our real life, and therewith our real happiness in life is hid of God in just our ordinary home.

If only in the home we might but learn *to find* it.

XLI

Luxurious Living

KEEPING IN ONE'S STATION

DOES the Christian faith condemn all *luxury* as such? For an answer to this question, compare the ministry of Christ with that of John Baptist; and see how Jesus Himself pointed to the fact, that John refrained even from food and drink, and they said: He hath a devil; while the Son of man came *eating and drinking*, even in such a manner that they said (Matt. 11, 19): "Behold a man gluttonous and a winebibber."

At the marriage at Cana things are by no means provided on a contracted scale. And after the supply of wine is exhausted, Jesus by His wonder-power renews wine in the firkins.

Yea, even the spilling of a bottle of costly nard, to anoint His feet, Judas disapproved. But not Jesus. With some one else it would have been waste. But for Him, and at that moment, it was not.

You should not say, therefore, that they who prefer the method of the Baptist, oppose the Christ; since Scripture teaches that the Baptist did not oppose Jesus, but prepared the way for Him. Also great sobriety, even abstention can in all sorts of ways be right. Only, the idea that *all* luxury, for every one and in all circumstances is censurable and sinful, will not do as life's image of our Savior.

Jesus by no means antagonized *all* luxury as such;

rather has He honored the relative right of luxury by His own example.

Only, by wrong use, the balance can lean toward evil, and then the rich young man goes away weeping, the rich cannot enter the Kingdom of Heaven, and after death poor Lazarus sees the rich man in hell.

LUXURY is, oh, so relative.

What is abounding luxury to one, is sobriety to another. It all depends upon station and means. Solomon bathed himself day by day in the glitter of an Eastern court-luxury, far more so even than his father David, and who would censure this in a king? Or should not a prince maintain a far different station, and for the sake of the crown he wears, does not splendor and pomp behoove him?

A laborer in the country from his savings may make a feast on his festal day, which to him is uncommonly rich and abundant; but a well-to-do nobleman need not on this account be pleased with it as his daily fare.

God Himself has divided unequally the wealth of His creation. He clothed the birds in their feathery garb, and how simple is that of the sparrow and of the nightingale as compared with the splendor of the golden pheasant. Compare the dun dress of the ass with the striped coat of the tiger.

And so it is among men. Among people there is no equality and there can be none. Everything differs. People from people, station from station, and even in the same social station family from family. Means differ. Positions in life differ. And since the house, dress and style of living must be the expression of the position one holds and the calling which on the part of God he has to fulfill, there is bound to be a mighty difference in manners of life, so that to one is ordinary sobriety, what would be luxury to another, of which he never even thought.

What rich shepherd-princes the patriarchs Abraham, Isaac and Jacob were, and how utterly lacking in worldly goods were a Peter, an Andrew and a James, just fishermen on the shore of Nazareth.

So you see luxury has a twofold significance. The one good, the other bad. There is a good luxury, which belongs to one's station and position. But there is also an evil luxury, which is the result of bad stewardship of one's goods, fruit of the chase after sensual pleasure and desire after vanity.

This first-named luxury Scripture never condemns; the second always. And from this follows, that God's child shall not despise this first luxury, but will avoid the second as evil and sinful.

This detracts nothing however from the fact, that in their better days our fathers too maintained a style of their own for a higher walk in life, floored their houses with marble, wore very costly garments, and even spent sometimes large sums on ornaments.

And this should and even must be so, for pearls lie in the stream to be fished up, diamonds are not meant to remain hidden in the sand, wine does not gather in the grape to dry up on the vine, and the silkworm does not spin her silk to have it spoil on the mulberry-tree.

All things created of God have their use. And not only this, but also this of God intended standard of luxury is the bread of the workingman and of the artist. In a world of only monks there would be no trades or sales.

To the standard of luxury in the higher walks of life you can even add the luxury of festal days and occasions. When with God's ancient people it was the feast of tabernacles, every family lived far more luxuriously than at ordinary times. And the age-old custom of Christendom of going out on the Lord's Day in finer clothes, than on week-days, continues also among us, Christians of the nineteenth century, to maintain its noble tradition.

But this never condones sinful luxury, i.e., luxury above one's station, the luxury of sensual delight and unbridled self-indulgence, neither what the apostle calls the "daily luxury" of wantonness (2 Peter 2, 13, Dutch version).

That sometimes ambition stirs a man to climb the social ladder a round higher, is by itself no sin. Scripture cites again and again cases of men, who from lower walks of life have been elevated to higher stations. But this ambition must be noble. Not to abuse the rise in station as means for more luxurious living: but the nobler life itself in this higher rank must be the attraction, and the freer life merely the *result* of it.

He, on the other hand, who lives above his station,

shows that vanity and self-indulgence is to him the chief attraction, and that already in advance he reaches out toward this more luxurious life, before by diligence and effort he was able to work himself up to that higher place. He then undermines his own future and that of his family. A sin which sometimes goes so far, that one stints his children in necessary food, so that in rich apparel he might attract the greater attention in the street.

Neither let any one say: "As long as I have the means, I am free to buy what luxuries I please." For God did not provide these means for you and your family alone. He made you steward over these means, that among other things you should remember His church as well, His institutions, His poor, and if possible lay something by against the day of evil.

But luxury becomes far more evil still, even when means increase, when that which makes you pursue it, is the sinful motive to live a life of self-indulgence, in your pomp and vanity to please yourself, and to gratify the voluptuary desire that stimulates you.

For then *flesh* rules *spirit,* and you have subverted the order of the living God, Who has called you and still calls you, by your spirit to govern your fleshly desires, and the lust of your eyes.

Then you dishonor your divine childship that as child of the world you might satisfy your cravings.

Then you go away from God, and turn to the paths, where Satan awaits you, to entice you and to tempt you.

This our fathers have felt and realized, and for

this reason they have insisted especially in daily life upon sobriety, upon soundness of sense and simplicity.

At times they had their feasts, and then they enjoyed the abundance of life with thanksgiving. But ordinarily they purposely applied themselves to quiet simplicity and a sober manner of life. And in that way God the Lord has doubly blessed them. With a blessing after the *spirit,* by withdrawing them from the enervation of luxury and by steeling their power of will. And no less with a blessing after the *body,* by as much as nothing is more healthful than a daily life in sobriety and common-sense order.

God's child has pleasure in God's law, and uses the world. But the godless takes his delight in daily luxury, and uses his God to save him from and after death.

And therefore among all God's children *this* must serve as rule of life, that each, in accordance with the requirements of his station, in ordinary daily life shall love simplicity and sobriety, and on the other hand find daily luxury for their soul in the hidden walk with their God.

THERE is a power in the world, which, under the name of fashion or custom, endeavors to make the law for God's children, as to how they shall live. And especially in our days this evil power demands ever yet greater luxury.

So it was at the close of the eighteenth century, and it lasted until the terrible revolution broke out in Paris, and Napoleon was sent out as scourge of the nations. And then that recklessly inflated luxury was done for at once, and even by the higher classes sometimes there was suffered literal want.

But this should not be necessary for God's child. He has another power, by which to resist the tone-giving power of the world. And with the law of his God he must keep himself free from the slavery of the world.

In us must be found courage, holy, spiritual courage, to ask, not the world, but God, how we are to direct our life, how we shall dress, what we shall eat and drink, and what shall be the proper forms of our recreation.

Even heathen nations have experienced all too bitterly, how the spirit of sturdiness which maintained itself, so long as luxury remained excluded, at once retreated and ended in ruin, when extravagant luxury gained the upper hand.

Also the middle class of the Romans, once by sobriety strong and great, went under when luxury had weakened and unnerved the spirit.

And therefore it is the calling of Christendom in our times to be also in this sense a salt that saves from corruption, that it should not yield to luxury, but resist it by sobriety.

Possessing as *not*-possessing, and in all things *stewarding* as before the face of the Lord God.

XLII

A Time to Laugh

CHEERFULNESS

IN our sin saturated life, laughter stands in such bad repute with us, that the very thought that the Lord our God can laugh, is distasteful to us.

If it were not written in Scripture, and if there you did not read in so many words: "He that sitteth in the heavens, *shall laugh*," it would never have come to you, so much as to suggest "laughter" on the part of God.

Laughter and seriousness form to our perception so sharp a contrast, that, according to general opinion, in holy things *seriousness* alone has a place, even such *somber* seriousness, as excludes every inclination to laugh.

We know indeed that there is such a thing as an innocent laugh. And that all laughter as such is by no means to be condemned. But yet to our perception, laughter belongs exclusively to life in the world, and is excluded from life in the sanctuary.

And in part this perception is correct.

In our broken nature, only as yet restored in its incipiency, we incline involuntarily to relax ourselves by laughter, to get away from the deep seriousness of life, and to lose ourselves more in what is light and trivial.

If you were able to gather up all the laughter of a village during four-and-twenty hours in a phonograph, and then analyze what gave rise to this laughter, into what mood it brought people, and what it effected, you would find that in nine cases out of ten all higher sense is absent from people's laughter.

There is, indeed, the laugh of inward joy of soul, wherewith the young mother looks upon her babe at her breast. There is the laugh of the poor, at the sight of bread for his hunger. There is the laugh of joy, of those who in faithfulness and love, before the face of God, unite themselves to each other as man and wife.

But these are exceptions.

Most laughter, by far, is laughter of fun and folly, or even the laughter of scorn.

To which is added that universal *note of laughter*, which in some companies dominates all conversation, when wit, that has mostly missed the mark, exerts and exhausts itself, always to be cunning, always to be chummy, and to make the joke pass as currency in our life.

YET he is mistaken, who deems on this account, that laughter is an invention of the Evil One.

If *laughter* and *tears* stand over against each other, it must rather be confessed, that *laughter* belongs to the nature of man, and not *tears*.

He who weeps has sorrow. And sorrow is misery. And there would be no misery among men nor in the whole creation of God, were it not for sin.

In Paradise, before sin entered into the heart of Adam, you cannot imagine him weeping, but indeed laughing with holy joy. And when in the Paradise that is to come, all sin shall have been brought to nought, the hour also comes, when all tears shall have been washed away from every face.

Thus tears there were not, and once shall no more be; they belong to the sinful estate, that separates Paradise that went under from Paradise which we look for from the heavens.

Of God the Lord we are nowhere told that He weeps. Of angels we read that they rejoice, not that they mourn.

Poets may so have represented it, but God's Word does not teach it.

The matter stands altogether different with respect to *laughter*.

Of God the Lord we truly read, that He Who sitteth in the heavens shall laugh, even with a laugh, which often seems to us most sinful, to wit, with the laugh of scorn. For upon this it follows immediately: "The Lord shall have them in derision" (Ps. 2).

And when in His beatitudes Christ applies His "blessed" to those that mourn, He says, that they are blessed, because *now* they mourn, but in the day of glory they shall *laugh*.

So little even is laughter excluded from our nature, that of the destruction of the godless it says: that the righteous shall see it, and shall *laugh* (Ps. 52, 6).

The Lord himself says to the godless: "I also will *laugh* at your calamity" (Prov. 1, 26).

When the people of the Lord return from exile and look again upon Jerusalem, in the triumph-song it reads: "Then was our mouth filled with *laughter*."

Even experience teaches, that too much weeping depresses our physical nature, and that laughter, which shakes the liver, makes the blood course free and fresh again through our veins.

YET the same Scripture puts a limit to laughter.

Undoubtedly, laughter and not tears belong to your nature as God created you; once laughter belonged in Paradise; and shall once belong to the realm of glory; but in Paradise you are now *no more* and in the realm of glory *not yet.*

You are now in a world of sin and in the time of grace, and therefore Jesus says: "Woe unto you that laugh now, for ye shall mourn and weep" (Luke 6, 25).

Also the holy apostle admonishes the people of the world: "Be afflicted, and mourn, and weep; let your laughter be turned to mourning, and your joy to heaviness" (S. James 4, 9).

Even the Preacher from of old already told Israel: "Sorrow is better than laughter" (Eccl. 7, 3).

For the sake of our misery tears are given us, and ability to mourn so long as the root of sin is not gone from our heart and misery goes on about us, is a *grace* loaned us of God.

To see, how the vain world, amid laughter and play, hurries on in the pathways of destruction, is against nature and fills you with sorrow.

Laughter belongs to your nature; once it returns; but key-note of our present existence it cannot be in *this* dispensation.

That mirth, which seeks to predominate all of your life, is a jeer at the misery that cries all about us; a palliation of the sin that roots in the bottom of the heart; worse still, a mocking at the seriousness, which life, with such an heart and amidst such misery before the face of the Lord, awakes in us.

DOES this mean to say, that *all laughter* is therefore amiss, and that piety demands that with sternness and gruffness of face you must disarm every laugh in the family circle?

On the contrary.

Holy Scripture emphatically declares, that there is a time to weep, but also that there is *a time to laugh* (Eccl. 3, 4).

Thus laughter is granted you. Laughter in every-day life at what is cunning. Fine laughter over what interests you by its wittiness. The laugh of kindness wherewith you look your neighbor in the eye. The laugh of happiness over a blessing received. Even the holy laugh wherewith inwardly you jubilate in the hidden walk with your God.

Bannish laughter you need least of all. And when you look at pictures of the heroes among our fathers, who have fought the battle of God, in their strong and manly face, beneath their holiest seriousness, there is ever a play of laughter.

Only, while there is a time to laugh, it must lay no claim upon *all* your time.

Laughter may have its play in your life, but it may not dominate your life. It may render your association agreeable, but must not strike the key-note therein.

Your right to laugh must be captured by showing first that you also understand what it is *to mourn,* to mourn over your own heart and misery and the misery round about you.

AND it is at this point, that with laughter sin comes in.

Lovers of laughter, but who do not know the *sorrow after God* and have never learned weeping from inner assault of soul.

Young and old of days, who by their vain laughter have unconsciously come under the dominion, under the power of the laugh, and thereby have become unsusceptible of higher and holier seriousness.

Men and women, who are together hour by hour, without a sensible word passing their lips, who spend their days in what is called "stuff and nonsense."

An evil ended in the dreadful house of our insane, where sometimes you find madmen, who always laugh and grin and roar with laughter, and can no more escape from the violence of that terrible laugh.

And something of this insanity you observe already in advance in the companies of those who always play, always joke, always laugh.

They literally laugh away the seriousness of life, and solve life into one long-drawn-out play.

And this is not all.

For when once the laugh has overpowered you, and has robbed your heart of seriousness, it soon passes over into an unholy, an evil, sometimes a devilish laugh.

Till at length it becomes the jeering laugh at what is holy, the making sport of him who stands in your way, or the laugh to one's heart's content at the need or sorrow of others.

Oh, one refers so frequently to sin in word and deed, but is it not time, that you should come to a confession of sin committed in *your laughter*: even though with you personally it has not come so far yet as the poisonous laughter of scorn?

Here too, we grant, the drawing of the proper boundary, is, oh, so difficult, for by somberness and peevishness and unfriendly surliness there is equal sin committed against the love of God.

But there is a limit. And we ourselves must reverence this limit. Before this limit we must teach our children to maintain a stand.

In the way of our fathers our domestic and social intercourse must not be one continuous laughter with a single drop of seriousness to offset it.

Neither also one constant seriousness, offset with a forced laugh.

Far less yet, nothing but laughter in the heart with a mask of seriousness before the face.

This can never be according to God's Word, and has ever been despised by our fathers.

No, genuine seriousness worked in us of God, which aims not at *semblance* but at *reality*, does not need the *outside* decoration of a laugh.

From this in God consecrated seriousness comes of itself the generous laugh, but a laugh weaned from sin, and especially *a laugh at its proper time.*

XLIII

Sorrow Is Better Than Laughter

SORROW

EVERY one among us knows that in the so-called "Sermon on the Mount" our Savior has declared and testified: "Blessed are they that mourn," but do we also remember, that ten centuries before this the Preacher said: "Sorrow is better than laughter: for by the sadness of the countenance the heart is made better" (Eccl. 7, 3).

And, do we bring to mind this yet stronger exhortation of the apostle James: "Be afflicted, and mourn, and weep: let your laughter be turned to mourning, and your joy to heaviness" (4, 9).

Test by the principle, implied in this, the ordinary tone of life in families, and you feel at once, that even in our Christian circles this principle does not come to its own.

All too generally the common tone of life is one of gayety, of tense amusement, where people come together, even for a good part from an overstimulated desire to laugh.

Life must be "convivial," "convivial" one's associations, "convivial" the conversation, and under the dominion of this inclination you constantly come into companies, in which almost for hours together it is a cracking of jokes, a play of wits, and in which the high-spirited, overstrained tone does not tolerate almost for a single moment the absence of laughter from the lips.

Mingling in such company frequently affects the nerves so strongly, that it takes a certain period of time to bring oneself back again to the ordinary run of things, or compose oneself to sleep.

It is a "setting-up" of life, a mutual attempt at "forced levity," a strain to work oneself up to a laughing, joking mood, which is not natural, but artificial, and which for the most part makes the impression, as though one would cover up the inner hollowness and emptiness of his presence by witticism and cunning play of words.

When people can so laugh and giggle, and wind themselves up as it were to the point of folly, then they deem themselves to be just really happy, and a household in which this tone predominates, is called "convivial" and "chummy."

But Scripture judges differently.

It discerns the inward untruthfulness of this play of excitement, and therefore it testifies: To mourn is better than *so* to laugh.

For under such laughter frequently the heart suffers loss, while sadness of countenance oftentimes makes the heart better.

Now do not take the meaning of this word amiss; and do not commit the fault of falling from one extreme into the other.

Also in that other extreme is very serious danger.

An extreme, which shows itself in this, that intentionally one represses all freer, happier utterance of heart, lets gall operate upon the blood more freely than the blood upon the nerves, and now takes a certain kind of pleasure, in showing a gloomy face, and sighfully and complainingly to makes oneself a burden to others.

This, too, is unnatural, not commanded by Holy Scripture but avenged.

An affectation, which takes pleasure in making a very spiritual show, and aims to make an intentional impression of piety, which perchance readily degenerates into spiritual pride, and ends in making the heart insensible to the ordinary impression of our human life.

Then there is no thanksgiving and no laugh of gladness, for the many good things that come to us from God.

There is a sigh, but no song of praise.

Always a saying it over of the: "O, wretched man that I am," with never an Halleluiah on the lips.

THIS is no "mourning."

"Mourning" must come from the heart. It must be an utterance of real "hunger and distress" that fills our inner life, and therefore the "mourning" which Jesus calls blessed, has nothing whatsoever in common with that artificial melancholy which has presently become a second nature.

One can show tears. But "mourning" is the tender word of a sorrow of heart, which permits no false show.

Thus whether you mourn or do not mourn depends upon two things. First whether the impressions, that go out to your heart, make you glad or sad, and in the second place whether your heart is sufficiently sensitive to receive that impression, and to undergo the effect of it.

In the blessedness of heaven mourning is unthinkable, because there nothing sorrowful will come into your heart, and everything around you will be abounding wealth and glory. Also in Paradise it would have had no meaning, if before his fall Adam had mourned. His was pure joy and gladness.

In our estate and condition, on the other hand, now that our internal and external life is sunken in and broken, most impressions that go out to us are sorrowful and disappointing. Read your papers, whose influence upon our life is now so great, and confess whether they do not bring you almost every day from East or West, from far off and close by sorrowful news, of thunderclouds that threaten and of cruelties and accidents that have happened, while, oh, so rarely even for one single day nothing but praiseworthy and glad reports fill their columns.

But most of the time the sensibility of our heart is so dulled, that time and again you see a person read his paper, which reports all sorts of murders and suicides, of people that are drowned and people that are burned, of theft and robbery, of cruel immorality and low intrigues, and who then lays his paper aside, and lightheartedly and jokingly resumes conversation, as though his heart had received no single impression.

FROM this you understand already *something*, of that "blessed are they that mourn." For he who lives in the midst of a world like ours, and *in*lives and sympathizes *with* the need and the moral and social misery, which surrounds him, by much and serious thought about it would almost be overcome.

In the measure in which you have *less* love, you have less *sympathy* and thus less pity. All that misery does not affect you. It does not trouble you. And therefore you are always able to jest and to laugh.

Hence this continuous laughter and jesting is proof and evidence of your lack of love and of the apathy of your heart. While he who has *much* love, and is less concerned about himself than about others, is affected with great seriousness, and under the impression of all the misery and all the sin that is abroad, though the eye may not weep, is sadly tuned in heart.

And here we mentioned only general misery, and the dark shadow which as such rests upon our human life.

But to him who lives the deeper life, there is added to all this, not only his personal griefs and disappointments, which he suffered at human hands, and unfaithfulness of friendship, but far more yet concern about the lot and future of people and native land, about demoniac spirits that are abroad, and most deeply of all sorrow over God's Zion, when God's name is put to shame, or His church suffers loss, and His law is trodden under foot.

Bring to mind what the Psalmist sang: "Rivers of water run down mine eyes, because they keep not thy law" (119, 36).

And now, who is there among the children of God, who can say this after the Psalmist, and who *so* loves his God?

THERE is, however, also much good abroad, much that makes for gladness and must be cause for joy.

He who understands what it is *to give thanks,* and does not abuse it as mere *form,* cannot kneel any night in worship, but material overwhelms him. In nature, and in common grace, as well as in the particular covenant of grace the mercies of the Lord are so abounding. Much love also comes to us at the hand of man. Even birds when they sing and the dog that jumps up to us in happy greeting bring something kindly into our life.

Hence he who has a tender, receptive heart, and knows his own unworthiness, and in all honesty testifies: "Who am I, Lord, that all these blessings should come upon me," also truly knows in his heart the deep emotion of joy and gladness, which the apostle had in mind when he wrote: "Rejoice evermore" (1 Thess. 5, 16).

This then is real gladness. No artificial flower, but one of joy budded on the stem of our life. A high gladness and thankfulness, which has nothing in common with the laugh of excitement or of forced gayety.

Not a gliding over one's heart, but a life from his heart, and therefore a being kind to every one and a being thankful before his God, with a gladness which never quarrels with seriousness, which is in perfect keeping with compassion for all that are in sorrow and want.

What we need, therefore, in our homes and in society at large is neither endless laughter and joking fun, no stiffness of melancholy and depression of sombernesses, but a serious tone of life, which is animated by real *love,* which is token of a deep life, not of a gliding over things, but of taking vital interest in everything that pertains to the life of our heart.

Also the generous laugh in its time, and the pleasure of sparkling wit. But these as exception. As a rule such a tone of life as an angel of God would strike, if he came down into the midst of our misery, and at the same time opened his eyes to the rich grace wherewith the love of God sweetens it.

XLIV

In the Midst of Trouble

ADVERSITY

"TROUBLED" is such a fearsome word.

Not when one is troubled from lack of courage of faith; but when one feels "oppressed."

Even in a material and physical sense this is true.

When in a room, where you sit at work, fresh air is exhausted, or becomes overheated, so that it becomes difficult to breathe, the lack of air can give you such a feeling of oppression, that the blood rushes to the head. Or when something internal presses upon your lungs, or the throat is swollen, or asthma bothers you, or a cough leaves you no rest, these bodily ailments can make you feel so anxious and oppressed, that it seems that you must choke.

And yet, such vitiated air and tightness of the chest are not the worst. Sometimes even a person forsaken of God has purposely sought asphyxiation, to escape another, a far more dreadful oppression.

No, the most fearsome troubles do not affect the body and not the lungs, but the soul; the spirit that is in you. For while these altogether different troubles may affect you even so deeply, that they communicate themselves to your lungs, by pressure on the heart, so that with open mouth you gasp for breath, even then this physical oppression is merely accidental, and the real trouble oppresses heart and soul.

Of course most dreadful this inner oppression of soul shall be in the place of the outer darkness, when the fire that consumes you, shall never be quenched, and the worm that restlessly gnaws at the fibers of your heart, shall never, never die; but now there is no such *hellish* oppression yet.

Something of such hellish anxiety is sometimes suffered in the struggle of conversion, when for the first time the troubled soul discovers itself in the full light of God's holiness. But when such is truly the case, Christ at once draws near, with the holy breath of His love to refresh you.

No, what Holy Scripture generally means, when it speaks of troubles, are those afflictions of soul, which can come upon us in our home life, in our business affairs, in our intercourse with people, by reason of our children, by scorn and slander, by financial straits, by wrong done which may be found out, by adversity and constant disappointment, by want of appreciation and by the molestation of people.

Troubles in life, which may be aggravated by all sorts of anxieties of unbelief, but which mostly have an outward cause.

Reason why David outlines them in that striking, but always external figure, when he mourns and moans: "O, *my God, all thy waves and all thy billows go* over me."

INTO such troubles in turn comes *every* child of man, but yet, they come upon us in *unequal* measure. With Solomon you hear almost nothing of them, but how dreadful these troubles were for a Job, and how a man like David labored under them.

Also it makes a great difference, *who* so walks in trouble. For one is so much better able to bear it than the other. One is overwhelmed by it in a moment, while the other sometimes makes the best of it all too lightly. One is, as people say, *sensitive,* i.e. he makes burdens of things, while the other is wrapped as in an impervious garment, which permits no rain to pass through.

Temperament here makes so much difference. He who is pessimistic and somber by nature, suffers so much more. Or when in anxious moments dreadful headache comes upon you, which renders everything dark before you, paint things black to you, and double your afflictions.

One, the moment he falls asleep, has all his troubles taken from him, while the other even in his dreams is pursued by them, till he rises almost yet more troubled, than when he retired.

To one man trouble is as an humming insect, which attacks him for a moment, but which he brushes aside, while the other can not get his thought away from it, and literally *walks in the midst of it* (Ps. 138, 7).

Also one will complain, and make his troubles known to others, and thereby obtain partial relief, while the other will keep it to himself, is silent in the presence of others and practices self-control. But for this very reason when presently returned to the privacy of his own room, in the anxieties and fears that overwhelm his soul, will cry the more bitterly.

Also your environment has much to do with it. When a loved one is near, who watches over you, who sees your suffering and sympathizes with you, trouble becomes so much easier to bear, than when there is no eye that pities you, and sometimes hardness and reproach is heaped upon you, so as to make the cup already full to overflow.

Of course, God the Lord has knowledge of it all, and when no human eye had pity on us, our God has known our path, has watched over us, and, though we did not know it, He has imparted grace to us and comfort.

Who shall measure the mercies of our sympathizing High Priest, Who was tempted in all things like as we?

Who shall say, how near God's angels, sent by Him to us, stand by us, to banish in such moments despair from our heart, to avert desperation from our soul?

Never, never, are we alone, and the dreadful result, when in such pains of death the unbelieving heart was no more able to hold out, and then laid violent hands on self, has *always* been a misappreciation of the commiserations of our God.

ALSO in His Word the commiserations of our God with the afflictions of the soul are so surprisingly great. He who has ever taken the trouble, to read consecutively, what in that Word the Holy Spirit has to say *to* the afflicted and *of* the afflicted and *about* the afflictions of our soul, would not have believed beforehand, that God the Lord would have kept Himself so constantly engaged and in so importunate a manner with the desolate in their afflictions.

It goes deepest indeed, when it says: "*In all their*

afflictions he was afflicted." Especially when there is added: "By the Angel of His presence has He saved them; in His love and in His pity He redeemed them; and He bare them, and carried them all the days of old" (Is. 63, 9).

And that this is true, is the experience and still the certain knowledge of him, who in such moments of torment, when the water reached the lips, looked away from self and from every creature, to turn himself solely to his God.

He who did this, experienced still as Isaiah of old, that in such moments the importunate comfortings of the Holy Ghost can be so tender and abundant, that it seems, as though in our own soul's perception we live through with our God the affliction which He suffers for our sakes.

It is so unspeakably tender, that in *all* our afflictions He is afflicted for our sakes. For then the Holy Ghost prays in us, because we can no more pray ourselves. And He Who searches the heart, understands the meaning of the Spirit, and comforts us and pours balsam in the wound of our heart.

You then do not see the Angel of His presence, but that Angel is there. He is close by. He supports us in all our sorrows.

Until that love and pity go out to redeem us. To make the brass gates against which we would have broken our head, open of themselves before us. To make a way of escape where there was no more chance. And in the valley of the shadow of death with His rod and staff to comfort us.

Yea, when at length the Lord our God did with us, what a mother does, when she finds her child in tears, and our soul realized and blessedly enjoyed, that in such moments of tense suffering our God took us up in His arms and carried us as in days of old.

In such afflictions there is something that *kills* us. They utterly undo us. They make us unfit for our work. They darken our outlook. They shut us up with our anguish in ourselves. And that there truly is a *deadening* power in this, you see in those who die under it or in the frenzy of unbelief lay violent hands on themselves.

And therefore, with those who seek Him, God the Lord goes in against this destroying power, and from the jubilant urge of soul makes the Psalmist sing: "When I walk in the midst of trouble, Thou makest me alive."

We then are going under. Wave-beat after wave-beat rolls over our head. And however much we struggle against the stream, we can at length no longer keep our head above water. No sooner has one wave-beat been faced, than a greater one comes along. And then we give up, and worn out we let our arms grow limp, and the waters would have swallowed us.

That is the death, which hides in the afflictions, and from them casts itself upon us, takes us by the throat and aims to stifle in us all desire of life.

And then, what you need, is that you are made *alive* again. And this, says David, is just what in such moments the Lord does to you.

Even though you have already gone under, His love still draws you back as a drowning man to the shore. And though your life-spirits already seem quenched, He brings you back to yourself. Your God makes you alive again.

In the end you realize that you sank by your own fault. That your imagination had deceived you. That the trouble was not so great, as you thought it was. But this makes no difference. Such and not otherwise was the state of your soul. So darkly did the shadow bend over you. And that now you are revived, lift up your head, and are yourself again, you owe solely and alone to the grace, to the love and to the comforting of your God.

He saw you sink away, and He went down to you in the depth of your afflictions. And from those very deep waters He drew you up again.

O, THE world is so cruel. Not of itself, but because it allows itself to be inspired of Satan. And while this stream of troubles goes on day and night to spread its alarms, now in this home and then under the roof of the next, it takes that glorious Bible out of people's hands. It draws a curtain before the infinite mercies of our own High Priest. And when everything around grows all dark, as night without a single star to give light;—then comes that cruel world and points to a revolver wherewith to shoot oneself dead, or to a cord by which to hang oneself, or to a deep stream, in which to drown oneself.

This Satan does though he uses the world for it.

And when the individual oppressed to the point of being stifled stands between these two, between that touching, saving, all else exceeding compassion of his

God, and that murderous cry of Satan in his heart, why, why are there those who yet grieve the Holy Spirit, and despise His love, and make choice of Satan?

Alas, why else, than that in the day of prosperity they have closed their ear to the commiserations of their God?

Then the God of all mercies still calls, but not they are they who can hear it.

And when in the day of their prosperity they forgot their God, they prepared for themselves the day of evil, in which resistless and strengthless they would fall into the hands of Satan.

XLV

Every Day Has Evil Enough of Its Own

SOLICITUDE

THE fact, alas, can not be denied, that for more than one household the new year that is at hand, will open a new source of trouble and anxiety.

So often one had hoped, that he had reached the point of a turn in his affairs. After the many "lean" years at length the "fat" would make their appearance. The worst was now past. The spring could not be bent lower. And if now there would come but a certain *small beginning* of improvement, it would be for trade and business as the first green in the park at spring-time. A spring, which was prophetic of a summer, and presently after that summer an autumn with *rich harvests.*

Then every one would be on top again. Past troubles would be forgotten. Songs of praise would rise from the dried up throat. And already now, while still in the midst of adversity, one was kept standing by the hope, that soon it would come to this; a hope on which one could not *live* indeed, but which kept up life's courage.

But who can close the eye to the fact, that also the year 1895 has not brought us the first bud of this hope.

Advance there is none at a single point. Not one knot in the great social problem has been unraveled. All through Europe, even across the seas, things are on a tension. And the difficulty of earning an honest living, became ever greater. Competition with its unholy passion, ever more austere. For a dozen and more years we have known a period of prosperity, but it has come to an end.

And though we know very well, that "the Kingdom of God and His righteousness" must be sought first, this does not alter the fact, that the change of year is not an event in *spiritual,* but in *civil* life. And that the question, how to pay one's debts, that are still owing, and improve one's affairs, which are going behind, and at least for one year make ends meet with honor, is a hard question for many, that grips the throat as it were and makes the questioning eye gaze somberly out before it.

And now you may say: "Be not concerned, dear brother, He Who provides is the Lord." But from the Gospel it is evident, that Christ Himself deals with our human heart in its anxiety and in its need in an entirely different way.

For truly, the Lord also said: "Take no thought," but with this saying He also made that other string in our heart to vibrate: *Every day has evil enough of its own* (Matt. 6, 34, Dutch version).

WHAT affects one so cruelly in this saying: "Be not anxious, dear brother!" from the lips of one who is himself in comfortable circumstances, is, that one dismisses thereby the troubled of heart with a *word.* Superficially passes over what to him are bands of death. And thereby shows that he has no *love,* does not enter into his neighbor's trouble, and at heart is weaned of the sympathy of compassion.

And with Jesus you find this to be so altogether the opposite. Something which you perceive at once at the sound of the surprising words: "Every day has evil enough of its own."

He who says this, shows that He interprets human life almost yet more somberly, than he who takes life at its hardest.

Most people take it, that ordinarily life is bearable, without being inviting, and that only at certain times troubles increase to overwhelm our heart.

But Jesus takes it far more seriously and somberly.

No, says your Savior, your life is no chain of bearable days, broken only now and then by a day of adversity. All of life is troublous. Every day a cup is to be drained. Seven times a week a sun sets and there are stars that darken. Or briefly, as the Evangelist has reported it to us: *Every day has evil enough of its own.*

The very reverse, therefore, of what those other comforters say.

Not: "There is no reason to be thus troubled and concerned." But rather on the contrary: "You have no idea yet of your real trouble. For if you fully understood the *evil of to-day,* you would have neither time nor strength, so much as even to think of *the evil of to-morrow.*

That you are already busy now with the evil of *to-morrow* and of *day after to-morrow,* shows that you make light of the evil of to-day, that you do not estimate it correctly, that you do not fathom its depth.

And therefore do not fill your head and heart with evil, that belongs to to-morrow. That comes in order when it is to-morrow. Now you have to look out for the evil of *this* day. And he who is right-minded, feels, that with this he has his hands already more than full.

You have neither time nor strength, to be already now engaged with the evil of to-morrow.

Every day has enough and more *of its own evil.*

Did we say too much, that in this drastic word there is something surprising? Something that at once overturns your deliberations, and makes you face life differently?

You had already accustomed yourself to too much evil. To, oh, so much that really hurt your heart, you had already become indifferent. You no longer called it evil.

And what you continued to be alarmed about, were merely those very bad things and painful troubles, which threatened you from afar.

And Jesus at once calls you back to your heart, and complains about your indifference. That at retiring at night you can say: "Thank God, everything to-day has gone well. Nothing has gone wrong," when, viewed by holier light, *nothing* went well. Neither in your own heart, neither in your family, nor in your associations. And not only your inner life, but your relation to others, and your condition in life was so altogether different, from what this ought to be *in your Paradise,* while, as God's child, you should be able to call everything short of Paradise evil.

But you are all over this. You sit in the prison-cell, and have been dulled by it. You carry heavy chains and it does not trouble you when the links of them cut into your flesh.

That is your self-degradation. Born child of a

king, the beggar's tatters do not offend you any more, which at better and deeper insight disgrace you.

And this letting go of your high nobility, this looking away from your claim to higher happiness, is what estranges you from your God, from your Origin, from your Father Who is in heaven. Thereby anxiety for the future of your God quite overpowers you. And while you have become impervious with respect to the evil of to-day, against which you should battle, you fall down helplessly, and without power of resistance, at alarm for the evil that after weeks or months can come.

AND do not say, that this word of Jesus makes you more unhappy.

This is *seemingly* so, but it *is* not so.

But one reproachfully replies: "With my cares for the future I am greatly burdened. And now you would burden my heart still more by the thought of all sorts of present evils, to which fortunately I had become accustomed, and which therefore troubled me no more."

But experience teaches otherwise, and Jesus' word puts the seal to it.

We *must* know, that our life is "seventy and eighty years, and that it is mostly labor and sorrow." Every day we must feel the raw antithesis between the happiness that God had prepared for us, and the reality amid which we live. Then alone you will know and recognize, that your home above, your native land is with God, that the hard journey, which here we have to make, is the result of our own folly, that we took the wrong way, and thus must turn back upon it, to come out again with our God.

So everything in you becomes awake. You make highest claims to your inheritance for Jesus' sake above, but for this very reason you make no slightest claim, to be well off, already now, here on the pilgrim journey.

Evil is here, it is here every day, every hour, indoors and out of doors, within you and in others. And he who has an eye for this, he lives, he feels the smarting pain in his soul, but energy stimulates him, and in the midst of his wrongs he can be so quiet and warmly thankful for every cup of cold water, that is handed him on his pilgrim journey.

HE who goes through life half blind, and therefore does not see the *evil of each day*, does not know sin, feels no concern about the cause of God, his children do not weigh upon his heart with an eternal interest, the love of Christ and of His Zion does not consume him.

When such a man draws a hundred thousand from the lottery, has no sickness at home and has many friends, he is rich as Crœsus, and would cast all care aside.

Other people's needs, deeper wants, more anxious cares do not move him.

And herein lies the falseness of his condition; for once the hour comes, when no money can offer him any more refreshment, and deadly terror of eternal need overtakes the soul, as he is summoned to judgment, and all this evil of every day, for which he never had an eye, shall as a mighty specter suddenly stand before him.

He who, if he but had money, would lay aside all care, in the inmost part of his heart leans yet more upon Mammon than upon God. Sometimes even his prayer is nothing else than a prayer that God will help him gain the favor of Mammon.

And to cut off this evil condition at the root, Jesus unsparingly calls you back from the evil of to-morrow and of the day after to-morrow to the evil of to-day.

To the evil of *this day.* A day in which you see no evil, because your eyes have been blindfolded. And now Jesus removes the blindfold, and shows all the evil, there is *to-day.* Altogether different evil, much deeper evil. Debts not of money, but debts to God. Debts that make separation between you and your Father Who is in heaven, and therefore rob you of the rest and comfort, which faith in your Father above regarding the future can impart.

Here shines Divine wisdom.

He who enters upon the new year, not to take the care for the future out of the hands of his God, but every day with open eye to see the evil, that there is that day, and do battle that day against it, and that day to overcome it, he comes with every passing day *closer* to his God, and every day he learns a little better the difficult lesson, *to commit to his* God, what that God has anyway already in *His* hand.

XLVI

To Put It Into Thine Hand

REST IN GOD

God's consolations are not written for the *child of fortune.*

He who sees the little stream of his life flow quietly, calmly along from one year's end to the other might not for this reason put God's Word aside; but in that Word he does not find *his* world, *his* life, the reflection of the condition of *his* heart.

A single part from the Sermon on the Mount and from what St. John recorded, might do for him. Also here and there a mellifluous verse. But in its entirety, the Scripture does not meet his case. All those wars, all those struggles, all those penitential psalms, all those war-songs, even in the Gospels those disputations, and sometimes even on Jesus' lips those hard sayings of having to hate one's father and mother, and then St. Paul with his polemics and hair-splittings, and St. James with his attack upon the rich, and finally those dreadful prophecies in Revelation that everything shall be overturned; no, that is not *his* spirit.

According to him the whole Bible, from first to last, should breathe nothing but love, nothing but gentle, gracious tenderness.

There are, of course, exceptions to this rule. A few, whose bark almost always drifted with sunshine before wind and tide, were yet so strongly apprehended by the Holy Ghost, that the storm which they were spared at sea from *without* was suffered in a violent manner in the sea of their own soul *within*, and who are therefore more and more aware of how Scripture addresses them.

But these ever remain *exceptions*; and without fear of contradiction it can be said, that God's holy Word in its pith and kernel, in its depth and height, throughout all ages, has really been tasted, understood and enjoyed by those alone, of whom it is so truthfully stated in Ps. 107, 12 (Dutch version), that "their heart became humbled by trouble," that they "walked in darkness and through the shadows of death" and constantly faced "gates of brass."

In Hebrew 11 the *cloud of witnesses* passes before your eye, as a long procession of men and women, who, "destitute, afflicted and tormented, have wandered in deserts, and in mountains, and in dens and caves of the earth." And they who even as these saints have drained the cup full to the brim of "labor and sorrow" find their own deepest thoughts expressed in Scripture.

With them only in full measure Holy Scripture is spiritually sympathetic.

This is especially true of the Psalms of David, in which again and again all the waves and billows of the Almighty go over the head of God's servant, and yet every time again the servant of the Lord lifts up his head from those waves, and asks: "Why art thou cast down, O my soul?" till quieted and restored the soul turns itself again to the God of her strength, and declares: "Thou, Lord, seest it, for Thou beholdest the 'labor and sorrow,' *that one may put it into thine hand*" (Ps. 10, 14, Dutch version).

The "labor and sorrow" are so broadly ramified in the earth.

You do not observe this in the note of gay levity in our streets, in our clubs and several societies, nor at our festal boards, simply because as a rule they who are cast down of heart keep themselves in the background, and mourn in solitude. Again as a general thing, one shows himself outwardly brave, though storms rage within. And it is not the least tender, who hide their grief, and purposely allow no one to surmise it.

So here you must not go by *appearance*.

There is so much excitement, so much affected hilarity, so many mouths that laugh, when complaint is at the lips.

God has also opened in our human heart by grace an almost inexhaustible fountain of quiet hope and courage, which ever and again triumphs over disappointment.

But what even our marriage formula whispers with so great and solemn seriousness in the ear of bride and bridegroom: "Whereas married persons are generally subject to many troubles and afflictions," is commonly far more true at heart, than the language of flowers, which at every wedding prophesies only love and pure joy.

When one is young, he does not believe this. And elders do wrong when they impose the burden of their troubles too early upon the shoulders of the young.

If from the first the plant had to carry the whole burden, it would never be able to bend its stalks upward to full fruition. You see this with many a child, that loaded down too early by trouble and disappointment, was broken down before he had a chance to develop.

But though the young may have extension of time, acquittance of "labor and sorrow" comes to but very few.

As a rule, the thorns and thistles of life wound the feet of every one in turn, till he, too, has marked his track on the pathway of life with his blood and his tears.

AND therefore it is so Divinely blessèd and comforting, when our Father Who is in heaven, comes to us and testifies in His Word, that He looks down upon us in Divine pity, and *beholds all our labor and sorrow.*

Of course this is nothing to the external and the superficial, who knows nothing of the "hidden walk."

Such an one knows from experience nothing of what it is, to see the hiddenness of the Lord hover above his tent, and in turn himself to flee for refuge into his Fortress, his Rock and his high tower.

To him everything is flat, level ground, and lies enclosed within the narrow pales of his own narrow horizon.

Even though such an one still confesses, that there is a God, that God does not *live* for him, and he not for that God.

God is to him a name, a sound, a term, but no full-blessed Reality, and far less a Fountain of all good, a Spring of eternal life.

But when from your own deep experience of soul,

at the reading of God's Word, you really understand something of the *Love of God,* of the majesty of His Divine compassions, and of the fathomless depths of grace in His Father-heart, then indeed, that blessed knowledge, that your God beholds "your labor and sorrow," is everything to you.

When you are maligned, and God hears it; when you are insulted, and your God observes it; when by trouble you are brought low, and the grief of heart makes you succumb in distress, and you realize that you can shed no tear, but your God gathers it, by this simple knowledge your burden is already lightened by half, and in the midst of your trials, even though under your cross you fall to the earth, you can still glory in the "God Who sees" and Who is of impenetrable mercies.

BUT then these comfortings of your God must result in His honor and at least have this beautiful effect, *that you put it into His hand.*

For the Psalmist links the one immediately to the other: "Thou seest it, for Thou beholdest the labor and sorrow that *one may put it into Thy hand.*"

This you do not do, when you prefer to go on bearing the "labor and sorrow" *yourself;* when you take a certain delight, as it were, to bend low under it; and lack moral courage of faith to separate yourself from it.

Our nature inclines toward this.

Then our thoughts multiply themselves within us; we continually dwell upon our grievances; we muse, we brood over them; we think on them again and again;

and at times it seems that we cannot part from that abyss of the woe of our heart.

That deep, somber stream draws and entices us, and it sometimes seems as if that stream opens itself before us, that we should cast ourselves into its gaping abyss, and sink away in it.

Just watch the heavy-hearted, the melancholy, the atrabilious sufferers, and ask, how more than one at length came to put violent hands on themselves.

And all this is against God's appointment.

He comforts, but to the end that your bowed-down soul shall be relieved, to take the burden of woe from you upon Himself, and, as regards your labor and sorrow, to reveal Himself to you in Christ as your merciful High Priest.

MORE still.

When God the Lord beholds your "labor and your sorrow," you turn in upon yourself.

Then you do not stare yourself blind upon that cross, that lies before you in the way, but you inquire into the *purpose* for which God appointed you that cross.

This can be connected with *your own sin and guilt,* so that a golden trace of God's righteousness runs through it, to discover you to yourself, and to humble you before your God.

Or it can be, that your Father Who is in heaven, chastises *you as child,* to make your poor faith the richer, or to press out the grape that ripened on your branch into the cup of His glory.

You shall put it into His hand, also means, that

amid your labor and sorrow God appears before you, stretches out His hand to you, and says to you: "Place your sorrow upon Me, put it here into the hand of my Divine compassion, and let me bear it for you."

There is also this blessing in it, that all too often in our labor and in our sorrow other people are involved, who brought this labor and sorrow upon us.*

And when this is the case, the heart readily inclines to resentment and reproach. So that love becomes minished and feelings of bitterness cross each other in our heart.

And this goes on, and becomes ever worse, the longer we carry the burden of our labor and sorrow ourselves.

Something from which so frequently thoughts of revenge and of retaliation germinate.

And with an eye to this, God's Word says to you, that you do *not* stand alone, that you are *not* forsaken, that all things are known unto the Lord, and that He shall set all things right, so that also what people do unto you, you should not retaliate, but *put into the hand of your God.*

* Then "labor and sorrow" is, as King James' Version has it, "mischief and spite."—*Tr.*

XLVII

The First Isaianic Woe!

LOVE OF MONEY

THE well-known "*Woe unto you's!*" of the prophet Isaiah are six in number, with the *Woe* unto you! against the service of Mammon, i.e. against the love of money, the mania to have and to save, as starting point of national self-weakening.

Loose capital there was almost none in Isaiah's days. There was no other great possession thinkable than in fixed goods, i.e. in houses and in lands.

This gave to the first *Woe unto you!* a peculiar tint.

Just listen. Thus sounded the *Woe unto you!* against the eagerness for riches: *Woe unto them, that join house to house, that lay field to field, till there be no place, that they may be placed alone in the midst of the earth* (5, 8).

This is the form of sinful covetousness, from which the preposterous system of land-nationalization borrows its strength and its truth in part, and explains how pious children of God could for a moment dream the dream, that from land-nationalization would dawn the salvation of the future.

Though this system as system is more to be feared than hailed, it must frankly be conceded, that back of the aspiration it evinces, there is a dynamic of truth.

The over-large possession of lands springs from sin; runs counter to the ordinances of God; and ends in the break of the Divinely appointed relation between the land and the dwellers on that land.

Already in days of old, Calvin pointed out how foolish it was, to enlarge one's house, till all sorts of chambers stood unoccupied, while others scarcely have necessary room. And how senseless it is, "to add so much land to land, as to necessitate the removal of those, whom God has put there, while the earth indeed was given us for our common dwelling-place."

In like sense wrote a prince among exegetes of our century, Delitzch: "They, the insatiables, do not rest, before every small landed-property is swallowed up in the large landed-property. A sin the more atrocious in Israel, where the Divine legislation had instituted an equal division of lands."

In Isaiah's utterance there is a definite and sharp judgment of bringing large landed estates into the possession of one owner.

This must not be.

Even the State should not tolerate it.

And yet, the first dreadful *Woe!* from which presently the other five follow, does not turn itself against wrong possession of land, as such, but against the sinful spirit that expresses itself therein.

The first *Woe!* condemns in every man and in every nation, the sinful inclination of making wealth the ideal of life, and of always getting more property, more money.

It is a *Woe!* against the unholy fever of capitalism.

A *Woe!* against Mammon, and against every one who as priest or choir-boy at the altar of Mammon dances the dance of covetousness and penuriousness.

THAT there is also a protest in that *Woe unto you!* against the old, sinful custom, of taking a whole street, with over-sized houses and gardens in possession on the part of well-to-do families, while the numerous households of the humbler classes are assigned to cellars, shacks and slums, goes without saying.

Calvin chastises this practice justly as covetousness and vanity and unmercifulness, which we likewise must condemn. Yea, already Chrysostom did not hesitate to scourge his Byzantian hearers with the words: "Your covetousness goes so far, that at last you would rob the poor even of sunlight and free air."

And it has actually come to this. And the present movement, to provide better houses for the laboring classes, where he who has little, can at least have God's dear sun and better air, is doubly worthy of the hearty support of every Christian.

But apart from this there lies in this first *Woe!* a warning for every confessor of the Christ, not to seek good in large houses, nor in building of semi-palaces, nor in laying out of large country estates, but to be contented with a moderate residence, which offers room for necessary use.

Also in the choice of a house the *use*, and not the ambition to live on a grand scale, must be the standard.

For therein vanity has play, and the desire to push others back, is evident.

FOR the root of the sin of covetousness is, that every one is bent upon securing privilege for himself, and to realize this end, pushes others to the wall.

The prophet makes this sharply prominent in the words: So long do you join house to house and lay field to field, that at length there is no more room for other dwellers, and you dwell all alone.

Truly, it does not come quite so far, because they fall short in power, but yet, as Calvin says correctly, "as far as they are able, they go to work indeed, as though they want to push every one out of his place and eject him from his possessions, so that he must either live under the open skies, or move elsewhere."

In the capitalistic fever works the motive of brother-envy.

For of course, though it is pure folly, in a world of men, in which by power and disposition one is altogether different from the other, to dream of equal possessions for all, yet this inequality has *certain limits.*

Poor and rich there will always be, but this does not take away the fact, that one is too poor and the other too rich; and it is this grievance which covetousness and miserliness refuses to reverence.

The one ever increases store, though he knows, that by adroitness and cleverness the other is outdone.

He who dares to do this and succeeds, comes to power. That power has honor and distinction. The great masses go out of the way before it. And in this way, the effort to make money, to lay up fortunes, to be mighty owners of vast sums of money, like a poisonous fever attacks the entire national constitution, and thereby tears it away from every higher ideal and holier calling, and so brings the *Woe unto you!* of almighty God upon the whole national existence.

Until even the purest that is known on earth, the love between husband and wife, and the sacred honor of marriage ends by coming under that *Woe!*

One chooses a wife, not because he loves her person, her soul, her real self, but because he loves her money, her house, and the landed estates she brings with her.

AND do not say, that this occurs among the higher classes, but that such eagerness for money and property, such passion for possession avenged of God, at the sacrifice of others, is not found among ordinary burghers and farmers, or among the lower classes.

For facts deny this assertion.

Among the children of God there is indeed among the lower classes a most estimable group of people, who truly live soberly, labor diligently, earn reasonable wages, and lay nothing by, but, at least comparatively, *give* and *communicate* with a generous hand, and take more pleasure in *generosity* than in *hoarding*.

But that is not the national spirit.

And he who overhears our young men when they talk of their future, and our merchants when after their work is done they freely express their mind, and our farmers when they make plans for the future, and our fishermen when they put out their eel-baskets in the water, observes, alas, all but too surely and too constantly, that in the blood of our people the fever of money-greed and covetousness throbs all too excitedly, even ever more so.

If anywhere the fever-thermometer at this point indicates most ominous figures.

One thinks of money, dreams of money, chases after money.

In more than one company, and in more than one house, it has already come to pass that not the man has money, but money the man.

THIS is extremely dangerous, because the boundary between what is conformable to duty and what is *admissible* on one side, and what is *sinful* and what is *accursed of God* on the other is not clearly evident.

Am I not right in my business to be on the alert? And the answer is: To neglect it would render you guilty. You must be zealous, and be zealously on the watch, in the calling wherein God has placed you.

And so it is asked: Am I not permitted to earn money and lay by for wife and child? And again the answer sounds: He who merely looks out for himself, and at his death, by his own fault, leaves wife and child behind in destitute circumstances, stands guilty before God.

But further along, comes in the difficulty.

One lives, a family lives. Those persons are creatures of God, and they have no thought of the Lord their God. They have a soul, and that soul they leave to starve, to become barren and impoverished. They are on the way to an eternal fatherland, and up to their death they are merely concerned about houses and fields, about money and goods, here on earth.

They think of nothing else. They speak of nothing else. In their beds they dream of it.

So are father and mother.

They beget children. Those children drink in that selfsame Mammonistic spirit. The poisonous money-fever takes hold of them also.

So the entire family becomes a small Mammon-temple.

With neighbor at the right and neighbor at the left it goes the same way. So the city-spirit is corrupted. Presently also the spirit of our towns and villages. In the end the spirit of the nation as a whole is infected.

And then comes the *Woe unto you!* from the Lord Jehovah upon such a people, and ripens it for destruction.

ONLY one spirit goes in against this, and offers an antidote.

That is the Spirit of Christ, that is the Spirit of God, Who speaks in his interpreters and witnesses, the Spirit of the Word.

And therefore it is so dreadful, when Christians also are infected by this insatiable, deeply ignoble spirit of Mammon.

For then there is no more deliverance. Then the horror has penetrated into the sanctuary. Then the altar of Mammon is carried into the holy places, and by His own children God the Lord is provoked to His face.

Let it be said therefore to all Christian households and be bound upon the heart, to testify against that unholy spirit, to banish that unholy Mammon-spirit from their midst; to make not money, but God their *highest good;* and not less than by large, generous, if needs be extravagant generosity to lift the *ban,* which *because* of money and *through* money rests upon so many a Christian household.

XLVIII

The Second Isaianic Woe!

LUST OF WEALTH

THE first *Woe unto you!* turned itself against the ever ground-gaining pursuit after wealth, goods and money, against the insatiable lust of adding house to house, and joining field to field.

Thus not merely against *money-wolves;* but against the love of money which increased hand over hand among our people, and finally infected the most godly.

Consider well, it is always God's people, against which these bitter *Woes!* are pronounced. Always after the rule of our poet Bilderdyk: "When on account of sin a people must perish, in church begins the soul's corruption."

Listen further to the second *Woe!* of Isaiah, not this time against the slavery of money, but against *wealth* and *wantonness,* which comes from it.

Woe unto them, so speaks the seer of the Lord:

"Woe unto them that rise up early in the morning, that they may follow strong drink, that continue until night, till wine inflame them! and the harp and the viol, the tabret and pipe, and wine are in their feasts; but they regard not the work of the Lord, neither consider the operation of His hands" (5, 11, 12).

This second stage of a people's degeneration and moral decadence of a nation does not begin with evil intent, but is the unavoidable and the of itself following result of too great an accumulation of money and the large growth of fortunes.

For the man himself, who accumulated the money, is as a rule more saving than extravagant, and still holds himself to the simple manner of life, in which he had his early bringing up and training. But when he dies, and the money comes into the hands of his children, it takes in most cases the opposite course.

They do not know their father's attachment to money; but desire and longing goads them on, *to enjoy* that money.

In that money there is magical power.

That money will buy worlds of sensual pleasure and delights.

And that hidden virtue of money, is what they want out of it. Their father accumulated it, but they, his children, must bring the value of it into evidence.

And then simplicity departs, wealth begins to practice its enchantment, and wantonness is the ash that remains of the charred wealth.

So it was in Egypt and Babylon, so it was in Samaria and Damascus, so it went on in Athens and in Rome; and so, to come nearer home, the Netherlands declined, when reviving from the struggle for freedom against Spain, the treasures of East and West were poured into our laps, and as a consequence asking after God became ever *less* and asking after *gold* ever more insistent.

For then in our land also upon Mammon followed wealth, and after wealth came wantonness, until in the second half of the last century in our stately houses and old-fashioned country places life became one not of honor but of shame, to which God has brought an end, by letting the French carry away our treasures from us, and by sending Napoleon to us as our scourge.

And now you see the same process again.

Especially in the latter part of this century, money has become plentiful again, and even now, before the century is ended, you see wealth increase again hand over hand, and wantonness follow after in wild drinking-bouts and in a sort of theater exhibitions and books that make mockery of all chastity and shame.

Understand well, that this is not said, because here and there you find a single excessive plutocrat, or a few conscienceless debauchees.

Such disgraceful characters have always and everywhere been known. This, however, does not destroy the nation, so long as the public conscience still reacts and protests resiliently against it.

No, what is avenged, and against which the *Woe unto you!* goes forth from the Lord of hosts, is when that wealth infects the nation itself in its broader circles, including even the followers of the Lord, and in the public market of life the serious life-tone of sobriety must more and more lower the flag before the din of sensual pleasure.

Then among all ranks and stations play and recreation become the sole object at which one aims, the booty of every chase.

And then the people has entered upon the *second* stage of its corruption, and against this second form of corruption is sounded once again, reproaching and recalling, the penitential trumpet of the second *Woe unto you!*

This corruption can only be arrested in its course, either by the judgment which God sends forth and turns riches into poverty, or by the preaching of the Word, that loudly sounds the penitential trumpet, arrests people in their wild course, and from heathen morals that creep in calls them back to a quiet, domestic life, as becomes Christians.

Improvement does not come from so-called "ennobling of public entertainments," and still less from vain attempts to exalt the Stage by fine art.

All this sort of means is nothing more than so much mortar, with which one plasters over the crack in the wall of national life, to hide the approaching corruption from sight.

A people, thus sliding down the incline, can no more save itself. For this in its wealth weakened system it lacks courage and elasticity.

It groans under the mode, and as slave of the same, it must run along and follow, when wealth passes by on the road.

No, salvation of a people lies in that heart of the nation alone, which maintains the faithfulnesses, and still trembles at the Word, and holds itself fast by its God.

Jesus Himself testifies: only in that kernel is *the salt,* that can avert corruption.

Not because as people they are so much better than others, but because *the Word* still has an hold on them, and God's Holy Spirit is still at work in them.

But this arrest is not brought to effect, save as the power of the Word reveals itself in the *households.*

Faithful church attendance becomes an empty show, when from church the mind of the Lord is not conveyed to *the home.*

Therefore it is so beautifully significant that God teaches His people *to give,* exercises them ever more and more in the practice of *giving,* makes them give ever more richly and more generously and more abundantly, because by that giving just so much money goes out from the purse, and thereby so much fuel from the furnace of wealth.

He who gives generously and bountifully to the cause of God in the world, does not have much left for luxuries, and holds himself aloof thereby from those companies and associations, in which wantonness keeps the bells of the fool's cap ringing.

The sounding of this penitential trumpet in the preaching of the Word, must direct itself therefore to two things in particular: first . . . *much and always yet more giving,* and again separation from the world, in which wealth and wantonness strike the key-note.

The old and tried wisdom of life on the part of all sober-minded Christians, to resist gambling, dance and theater, as inimical powers, that stand over against the honor of God's people. To give the Sabbath to God and not to the world. And in civic virtue and quiet simplicity to seek real delight of life.

A wisdom of life, which even yet will stand the test of fire, provided father and mother are not so egotistic as to think: If I but control myself, all is well.

No, especially to the children and to the rising generation must the discipline of life be applied.

For a stigma in the congregation of the Lord are those evil households, where father and mother truly reverence bit and bridle, but in which the children are left to grow up wild, counting their Baptism as nothing, allowing them to reach maturity not as children of God, but as *children of the world.*

God's child also knows of wealth; but it is an altogether different wealth, *the wealth of soul,* when his heart can enjoy itself in the hidden walk, and in the fellowship of his God.

So it is written in that second *Woe unto you!*

A people, that lets itself be carried off as prey by the wealth of the world, "regard no more *the work of the Lord, neither consider the operations of His hands.*"

When the artificial light of the world still blinds our eye, the glory of the firmament hides itself from us in the dark. So, when the wealth of the world has captured our heart, there dies away in us the taste and the sense for spiritual enjoyment, and we miss the eye, to delight ourselves in considering the wonders of the Lord.

This is the righteous punishment, that follows at the heel of the gleam of earthly wealth. It shuts you up in the world, and renders the sky-line of the eternal, the horizon of the glory of our God, invisible.

So *gold* takes a people away from their God, and earthly wealth removes them from God's glory.

They sink away ever deeper. They become ever more obtuse. They lose ever more the gold-dust from their wings!

And so they must either be brought to a stand, that they might convert themselves to the living God, or with ever quickening strides they hasten on to judgment in perdition.

A *Woe unto you!* is no complaint, and no mere warning.

When God pronounces His *Woe unto you!* upon a people, that *Woe unto you!* itself is the bolt of the lightning, wherewith presently He sets that people on fire.

XLIX

The Third Isaianic Woe!

FRIVOLITY

WITH *love of money it began.* From possession of money *Wealth* was born. With his third *Woe!* the prophet assails the child of luxury, named *Frivolity.*

How from exaggerated and wanton *luxury* of itself *frivolity* is born, you can readily trace from your own experience.

Now and then you took part in some festivity or marriage-feast. And that was right, for at Cana your Savior set you the example. But however stately and conventionally the marriage, which you attended, was conducted, you knew, that things were different from ordinary life. Cares had been put aside, there prevailed a more relaxed humor. Even though excitement was avoided, there was a lighter, more cheerful tone in the general conversation. Tongues became more loose. Voices became more musical. Witticisms were in demand. In brief, on such an occasion you were in a freer and happier frame of mind than in your everyday life, and with your fellow-guests you forgot the somber, dark side of life, to satisfy yourself with the lighter side of it.

But even though you were kept thereby from sinful dissipation, yet you felt, on coming home, that you had more or less become a stranger to yourself; that ordinary restfulness and calm were gone; that excitement of senses and nerves did not go well together with the ordinary seriousness of your life.

And it took you a little while, before you were yourself again, and the occasion left you conscious, that you would not like to get away too often from the *restfulness* and *seriousness* of your ordinary mood.

Such wedding-festivity is good, but it must remain an exception.

Every day, or even every week, to help celebrate such an occasion, would be impossible.

And yet just this, is what amidst exaggerated luxury life soon runs into.

That superabundance of food and drink and sensual pleasure that makes a wedding-banquet, and which an ordinary person allows himself at most once in a great while, takes place in those circles of wealth every evening anew.

Also the over-strained tone and the light-hearted joke is in those circles no exception but rule.

And so it comes to pass, that light-heartedness banishes seriousness; that the sense for the holy becomes dull and blunt; that constant excitement estranges people to themselves, and that *Frivolity* presently turning into mockery becomes a predominant power, and which they can not resist.

THIS condition of a person living in luxury, who at last is *overpowered* by Frivolity, Isaiah portrays in bold outline.

You can readily picture to yourself a valiant, strong horse, which, holding its head high, and not without quick gracefulness, heroically draws the heavily laden wagon. A horse that is fiery and wants to go ahead, but . . . harnessed with cords and traces to the loaded cart, cannot go forward, without it pulling the cart along.

Well, says the prophet, a luxurious and over-excited sinner is like such a horse.

"Woe unto them that draw iniquity with cords of vanity, and the sin-wagon as it were with cart ropes" (5, 18).

Such is the slavery of this sin.

Over-excitement knows no rest. When by exhaustion unharnessing would follow, at once swish goes the whip of the driver of the wagon of sin.

On, on it must go, and on it goes.

In the midst of wealth the rich man has lost dominion over his own spirit. Unobservedly wealth has bound him with *cords,* and wantonness has put him in harness.

He is still conscious that sin is a burden, but a burden as of a wagon which he must draw.

And as a courageous horse he pulls at the cart, and with this burden of sin he makes ever greater advances in the way of sin.

There is no opportunity granted to come to one's senses. There is no such thing as a standing still.

And when at times in a moment of sobriety and of return of seriousness he would liberate himself, he realizes all but too speedily that those *cords* are too strong and those *traces* too thick to be broken.

And so he runs along, always in over-excitement, always with the driver behind him.

And as once he ceased to have *money,* because money *had him,* so now it is no longer he who has *wealth,* but *wealth* has become his evil master.

The punishment of sin has run after the sin, and has made this rich man and this luxurious child of the world a *slave of sin.*

And so the *seriousness* of life has fled him forever, and *Frivolity* is the cancer that consumes him.

AND then of course mockery of the holy could not remain wanting.

He who still has *seriousness* in his soul, still trembles before the Almighty, and still fears the Judge of quick and dead.

But the slave of Frivolity laughs with loud sallies of hilarity sacred seriousness in the face, and defiantly taunts God: *"that He make speed, that He hasten his work, that we may see it, and that He let the counsel of the Holy One draw nigh and come, that we may know it"* (v. 19).

To such taunting of God and bold and reckless calling in of judgment, it does not come at once.

Only drop by drop the poison of evil is let into the veins of our soul.

The first time hearing *some one else* say it, and self half shrinking back from it, but keeping silent.

A next time that dread already gone, and joining others in laughing at the language of the scoffer, as though it were witty.

Then invite it, so as to make some one else hear it again.

Gradually himself taking *a single phrase* of it on his lips, to be hailed for it by others.

Ever bolder, ever yielding more recklessly to this unholy urge.

At length leading others in it.

And finally *taking pleasure in it,* bringing younger people, who have not advanced so far in sin, out from their innocence, purposely poisoning their soul, and enjoying it, when one who first trembled at the sound of such mockery, is at last overcome, and now himself first *laughs* with others, and then himself *takes part* in it.

How many young men there are, who once learned to pray at mother's knee, who were filled with awe for the holy, and with righteous indignation called for revenge when they heard derisive speech, and who now sit down in the bar-room and in clubs amidst sponging scoffers, reveling in it, when that God of their father and of their mother, before Whom once they themselves knelt, is derided, with blasphemy and vilification is defamed.

AGAINST nothing therefore do the people of the Lord have to watch so zealously, as against the ever-menacing danger, that the demon of Frivolity enter stealthily into their own circle and in the circle of their households.

That demon tries to do this by means of a seductive *book,* which is most interestingly written, or by an *acquaintance* or *friend,* who charms by his appearance or clever way in presenting himself.

And when such a book is then read on the sly, or such a young man scoffer is listened to with certain delight, the poison is already operative, and the evil plague enters into the blood.

And therefore it cannot be urged sufficiently that Christian parents keep all such books away from the home, and forbid the visits of all such seductive friends, even though they are members of their respective families, and for the rest most agreeable and polite.

All such books and persons are tainted, and they communicate the taint to you and to your children, when, otherwise than in passing, your family comes in touch with it.

Forget not, that a scoffer hides also in your own heart and in the heart of your child, and the desire, to pull the sin-wagon along by cord or rope, lodges in our sinful blood till death.

Therefore frivolous *books* and frivolous *talkers* have no place in your home, and *you* have no place in their *houses,* and by intercourse or attendance upon parties you must not accustom your children to the association of the frivolous.

If you have the courage, if you have command of speech, when they come to you, or when you are with them, to resist them at once and stop their mouth, then freely erect the barrier, but then count with it that the intercourse is soon ended.

Such sternness must be practiced; not because we deem ourselves holier than others, but because God has said: *Come ye out from among them,* and because sin in your own heart renders the danger of taking part with them so great and serious.

Go out from Babylon, saith the Lord, and that world of frivolity is *Babylon.*

What prevails in those circles, is the spirit of Belshazzar at his brilliant banquet, where all present caroused and made the rafters ring with their sallies of laughter and they scoffed, till the "*Mene, Tekel, Upharsin*" in flaming characters appeared on the wall.

For though in our times God does not strike with terror in so wondrous a manner the frivolous in their frivolities, once they too in bewilderment of dismay will see that "*Mene, Tekel, Upharsin*" gleam before them.

Not just before their dying.

Even not always on their death-bed.

But certainly *as soon as they have died,* when they open their dull and glazed eyes in eternity.

L

The Fourth Isaianic Woe!

CALLING EVIL GOOD

Too great possessions led to luxury. Luxury brought forth frivolity. But the jocular language of mockery does not end it. Even the scoffer in turn knows how to become serious. So the fourth stage of this unholy process of sin is reached, in the equally wanton, but now *reasoned* wickedness.

Then what is bad is said to be good. Of *evil* a *theory* is made, for the unholy a high-sounding *system* is set up. And so everything is subverted. What thus far you took as light was really darkness, and what seemed darkness, when carefully examined, proves to be real light. And this is demonstrated, and is accounted for, and is brought to your understanding, and it is reasoned out before you in a manner at which you stand aghast.

And therefore Isaiah offers no reasoned argument in return, but briefly cuts off the folly with his fourth *Woe!* saying: "*Woe unto them that call evil good, and good evil; that put darkness for light, and light for darkness; that put bitter for sweet, and sweet for bitter*" (5, 20).

In our poor land you need but name the name of *Multatuli,* to call to mind the object of this *Woe!* provided you but understand, that this wandering spirit would never have spoken as he dared to speak, or would have exercised an influence, such as he did, had there not been at his very coming already a considerable number of our people that had reached this fourth stage of national decadence.

When the *Money-fever* broke out, old morals, at least outwardly, were still maintained. Even at the Exchange the white cravat was still in demand, to carry a certain impression of solidity.

When *Luxury* increased hand over hand, in common conversation one still had respect for form. One courted the reputation of being honest and a man of good morals.

At the outbreak of *wantonness* the standard of what was holy and good, was lowered somewhat at times; but as a rule it was left alone and was merely made sport of, after the manner of a child, that hankers after what is forbidden, and when he succeeds in violating the command, takes pleasure in the wantonness of his daring.

But since the period in which *Multatuli* became the hero of the day, this is all changed.

Now one has begun to *reason*. Now it is asked, why the foundations of human society cannot be turned around. The ideas, and the morals and customs which were derived from these ideas, were based merely upon human opinions, but of old-fashioned people, of people who came from the night-boat, and understood nothing of modern life.

What then more simple, than that for the theory of those old sleepy-heads other theories, other ideas, other principles were put in place, and these so put together as to dovetail with the playful, wanton, light-hearted morals of the man of the world.

So *they* were the good, the enlightened people, that would enjoy life, who now in their turn could laugh to scorn the stupid, antiquated paragons of virtue, as folks who do not understand their world, were handicapped by their narrow-mindedness, and in no particular up to the times.

AND to this it has now come.

In former times they called the man a rake and laughed him to scorn as he passed, even all those who had the insolence to go contrary to God's Word. *Now* on the other hand to oppose God's Word is a sign of high development. And he who still holds fast by God's Word is called narrow, backward, beclouded by darkness.

Undoubtedly in former times sins were committed in the seductive domain of the senses, the same as now. But one was ashamed of it. In public opinion marital fidelity and chastity were held in honor. *Now*, on the other hand, all feeling of shame is cast aside. It is argued in public, that free love is more honorable than marriage. That for young people to remain chaste is playing with health, and thus is sin. In all sorts of pamphlets, even in dignified magazines lust of the flesh is openly advocated. On the stage nothing is spared. Even women begin ever more shamelessly to take part in this chorus. And he who now is laughed to scorn, and held up to public gaze, is no more the libertine, but the house-bodies, the illiberal, the narrow-minded woman, who has scarce any more count, who still esteems her modesty her honor, seeks her happiness in quiet marital faithfulness and finds the world of her wealth in the mystery of the household.

So everything is turned into its contrary.

Not father and mother teach the children, but the children come home with all sorts of latest novelties in morals, and try to bring them to the understanding of their parents.

Mother cannot enter into it, and father is too dull-headed to grasp it, but they, young men and young maidens, they know.

Father and mother in their old-fashioned way had imagined that their children should honor them, but that is altogether amiss. Children are under no obligations whatever to their parents. What was called parental love, is nothing more than pure egoism. And parents may indeed be thankful, when notwithstanding their backwardness and narrow-mindedness their children, if they do not honor and love them, at least still endure and tolerate them.

THUS, what in his fourth *Woe!* Isaiah censures, is none too vigorously drawn. You literally find it again in your own land, in your own literature, in the conversations of the rising generation, in the theories that are broad-cast.

All bands are cast off, every bit and bridle is thrown down. One lives according to the desires of his heart, and fights shy of no single sin. And while thus actually a life is lived in direct opposition to the ordinances of God, one first persuades himself, and then tries to prove to others, that thus it is not sin, that it is entirely natural, that so it is only really good, and that he who still holds to those old-wives' tales of virtue and chastity and modesty and piety, deserves no better name than that of *narrow-minded obscurantist.*

So he who walks by the light of God's Word, is called an *obscurantist.* He who walks in evil ways, prides himself that he alone *sees* the good and directs his life according to this clear insight.

Formerly sin was called bitter, and the *sweet of life* was tasted in the virtuous life of family and circle of friends. But this, too, is now all turned about, and, according to this reversed taste, that former *sweet* of life, even the very sound of it, arouses a *bitter* feeling of nausea. Such a home-bird. Such a back-number. No, now is known another sweet, and in the end you see the young woman, in young men's clothes, publicly by the way kick the football into the air, and in all the papers her name is blazed abroad, and from ambition she *enjoys* what with better morals in the eye of all would be her shame.

ESPECIALLY the lowering of womanly standards is an evil omen.

In times past a sportive youth would propound foolish theories, but mother would frown upon it and the sisters would look at him with an injured feeling of seriousness. And this never failed of its effect. Conscience spoke again. The wild notion was curbed. And in face of the loose talk of the man, the woman, true to her calling, continued to keep watch over God's holinesses.

But when a people grow decadent, it is a sure sign in national disease that, at last the moment comes, when woman too is poisoned in her soul; instead of offering resistance, she first begins by taking part, then to join the loose talk, and finally, carried away in the unholy stream, to outdo the man.

And then the last dam is broken, and the entire field of life is inundated by these unholy waters.

Against the ordinances of life appointed of God altogether different ordinances are enacted.

He who then still holds to God's ordinances, is laughed to scorn. To court popularity one must vigorously and boldly denounce those ordinances. No book so bad but one dares to read it before others, or talk about it with whoever else read it, yea, counts it pusillanimous and small, when some one yet declares, that he does not read such books.

AND so we come back again to the Christian home, as the center from which this evil of arguing and by arguing calling evil good can be resisted and healed.

When in the family *God's holy Word* remains the foundation of life, the only authoritative Word, by which we let ourselves be led, this evil arguing and calling sin good has no hold on our heart. And whether one laughs us to scorn, we keep on calling evil evil, and what is darkness darkness, and enjoying of the sweet of life, as God has apportioned it to us.

But then let the mother in the home be level-headed and watchful, let the daughter understand her sacred calling, and let not the father imagine, that life is salvable by mere dogmatic steepness.

The conflict against the mysteries of our faith is already far behind us. Against *the Word* itself the weapons of the world are now turned, not to overturn your doctrines, but to bring under foot the ordinances of God, to push aside His holy Law, and to put over against the law of God the law of the new, the light-hearted life.

Give no respite in this conflict for a single moment, neither to yourself in your conscience, nor to your children in their training, nor to your servants in their companionships, nor to yourself with those who visit and associate with you.

Continue faithful to the God of the fathers, and let *His* Law be the rejoicings of your heart.

And though the strife be bitter at times, and victory *scarcely* possible, still here also it applies, that who shall have fought faithfully to the end, cannot be vanquished, and that the crown which eternally blooms, awaits him at the hand of his King.

LI

The Fifth Isaianic Woe!

PEDANTRY

THE last but one of the Isaianic *Woes!* is of this content: "*Woe unto them that are wise in their own eyes, and prudent in their own sight!*" (5, 21), a sin, to which no people is so strongly inclined as the Dutch people.

Yet the evil, against which this fifth *Woe!* turns itself, is by no means limited to any one people or national character. On the contrary being wise in one's own conceit has its root in nothing else than in the common sin of our human heart.

Reason, why the Proverb-poet opposed it, when in Prov. 3, 7 he wrote: "*Be not wise in thine own eyes:* fear the Lord, and depart from evil," and likewise the holy apostle Paul opposed it, when to those in Rome he wrote: "Be of the same mind one toward another and *be not wise in your own conceits*" (12, 16).

From this you learn at once, how this being wise in one's own eyes is a twofold wrong. On one side one commits the sin of self-conceit, when he presumes to set up his own ideas over against the pronouncements of God's Word. And on the other side this sin is evident in the love of giving the play alone; in what the Germans call the will to be the *Einspänner;* always to sing the *solo* and never being willing to join the chorus, or if you like, in always putting one's own ideas over against the counsel and the discretion of others.

Either self-conceit, because one will not give in to the *Wisdom of God;* or self-conceit, willfulness, high-handedness, because one always deems himself to know better than the *wisdom of men.*

In the chain of the six *woes* it is linked together, that first from frugal diligence comes the sin of *Money;* from the sin of Money in the second generation the passion of *Luxury;* that presently Luxury breaks out in *Levity* and *Wantonness;* that after that the frivolous generation will call evil good and *argue,* as for instance, that *free love* is superior to *marriage;* and that from this self-made moral law, which then begins to be predominant, in the end the tendency is born, to oppose also the moral law of that particular circle, and so allow every one a world-view of his own.

Such in fact is the process of sin.

First God's law is in force, and while one sins against it, he adapts himself to it. Then one refuses longer to become shamefaced, and with the common consent of the frivolous sets up a godless moral over against the moral that brings honor to God. When once this step is taken, comes Babylonian confusion of speech. Then every light-heart in his way claims again to know better. When one no longer bows before God, and thus takes the reins of authority in his own hands, why should he go out of the way of his fellow-men?

Perhaps the other one is wiser, sees further, and is of better insight. But what of that? I am as good as he. I, too, have a rooster that can crow. And I put *my* insight, or rather *my* fancy and notion, squarely over against the opinion of whoever it may be.

THAT the germ of the sin also hides in the human heart, you not infrequently observe already in the nursery.

"He is a dear child," so whispers the mother in confidential tones, but it is "too bad the boy is so self-willed."

And there are such among children.

Children who always contradict. Who always know better. Who with everything they are told, have some objection to offer. Children with a wisdom of their own, which soon turns into self-conceit, and which at last makes it unbelievably difficult for father and mother to keep house with him.

Though this sin links itself directly with *reasoned* wickedness, yet in most instances it is overlooked, how at this pass *haughtiness* and *pride* mingle themselves in this otherwise *sensual* process of sin.

Money-greed, wealth, frivolity are sensual of nature, and setting-up a reasoned theory of sin over against God's Law similarly sprang from the passionate desire to be free with respect to one's own sensual impulses.

But when it comes to self-conceit, willfulness and high-handedness, the *spiritual* sin of pride enters in. Then it is no longer calling sin good, the more to be at liberty to sin, but taking delight in contradiction, pleasure in pedantry, satisfaction in putting obstacles in the way of others, and presently being too stubborn and too unruly, to remove the obstacle again out of the way.

This begins in the nursery, from the nursery this evil is carried into the sitting-room, from the sitting-room it goes along to school. From school it goes out into life. And so this miserable condition is born, that in church, in State and in society almost nothing can be built up and nothing can be permanently established, because every time again one stumbles upon this pedantry and contrariness, which holds back, unnerves and paralyzes, and wastes elasticity in mutual bickerings instead of using it in prudent assault on the enemy.

So you become conscious of the coherence of this sin of *pedantry* with the "confusion of speech at the Tower of Babel."

Yet ancient Rome was already aware of this evil, when they spoke of *tot capita tot sensus,* a proverb borrowed by us in the saying: "So many people so many minds!" Or as we also say: "Every one has a hobby of his own." Sometimes, even if unfair, translated into that other proverb: "Every bird sings as it has been voiced."

This does not take away the fact, that the further North one travels, the bolder this driving of the will becomes, and the mind of one's own dear self. A Northern thinker zealously maintains, that opposing everything and everybody, and always insisting upon having his own way and will, is the inexorable condition of forming a sharply defined character.

Among us, too, our fathers understood so well, that this pedantry was in our blood, that by way of warning they put a bundle of arrows in the lion-claw on the coat of arms, with the first part of the proverb: "By unity the smallest state reaches the top, by pedantry the mightiest goes under," as legend.

Concordia res parvæ crescunt, discordia maximæ dilabuntur.

Something which we preached, but Rome brought into practice, continually to score off us Christians of the Reformation.

Now this demon, for this sin of pedantry is really such, would never exert permanent influence, if it did not so seductively present itself as an angel of light.

From that Northern thinker you already learned, that what he is after is character. What is more beautiful than character that is well defined? And what lack is more deeply felt in our times than the scarceness of strong characters? Is it not then worthy of admiration and of praise, for the sake of this substantial character-formation, to cherish and caress one's own mind and one's own will?

In addition to this, a brother who always says: Yes, what good is he? Such a nonentity, who always goes with the crowd.

Every man has his own nature, his own way of looking at things, his own calling, and from this course of reasoning, which by itself is perfectly correct, a single-track minded Hollander will at once form the questionable conclusion, which he expresses by the word: *idiosyncrasy.*

An *eccentric* man is what becomes of the pedantic school-boy, which shows that what seemed *wise* ends in stupidity.

But the most dangerous temptation to this sin is still something else.

To row against the stream is sometimes duty. To tack against the wind can sometimes be a holy calling.

To offer resistance, even at the cost of convenience and position, can be duty of conviction. So to stand was the honor of all prophets, the glory of the holy apostles, and the Reformers have borrowed strength from it.

Not in *uniformity,* but in *multiformity* the splendor of human life comes to light.

And from this as starting-point this demon whispers in your ear, that upon close consideration, always to want something different from the other, is highest wisdom of life, and to tickle your vanity, he adds in underbreath, that you indeed are not the kind of man, passively to follow along with the rest.

Thus the sin of *pedantry* covers itself by the prophet's mantle of *hero-courage.*

He who was himself tempted by this, tempts in turn again others.

And in the end this sin of pedantry breaks all unity of strength, unravels the bundle of arrows, and makes a people go under in faction-mania and wicked bewilderment.

AND therefore the duty is imperative, with the training of our children at once to nip this evil in the bud.

This conceit and pedantry must if needs be driven out with the rod, since for corruption of fruit there is almost no evil that can be compared with the fruit of this poisonous seed of pedantry.

Here too *faith* is the God-given antidote.

Faith, which on one hand deeply engraves it upon the soul to bow before God and never before men, and which enables and steels you to row against the sinful stream of the world. But simultaneously on the other hand gives you oneness of life's root and of fruit with the brethren, and by the communion of saints prunes your unholy self-conceit.

In *faith* are the two powers which both Solomon and Paul put over against conceit.

For Solomon said: "Be not wise in thine own eyes, *but fear the Lord.*"

And to this Paul added: "Be not wise in your own conceits, *but be of the same mind one toward another.*"

LII

The Sixth Isaianic Woe!

BRUTALITY

ISAIAH's last *Woe!* turns itself against *Brutality*, which arising partly from *recklessness*, partly from *love of mischief*, is thus outlined by the prophet: "*Woe unto them that are mighty to drink wine, and men of strength to mingle strong drink: which justify the wicked for reward, and take away the righteousness of the righteous from him*" (Is. 5, 22, 23).

So the six links of this dreadful chain lie before us. First love of *Money*. From love of money comes *Wealth*. Wealth entices to *Wantonness*. From this by soberer consideration wilful *Falsification of ideas* is born. Moral falsification of ideas terminates in *Pedantry*. And finally pedantry stimulates what we call *Brutality*.

Brutality has two forms, one as regards the *person himself*, and the second which indicates how he treats *his neighbor*.

Brutal with respect *to himself*, is the man who is past all bounds, and now seeks honor in shame and glories in evil. And *brutal* against his neighbor is he who as judge withholds righteousness from the righteous and condemns the guiltless.

This accounts for the fact that Isaiah includes this twofold utterance in one *Woe!* One selfsame *Woe!* upon him who boasts that he can drink so and so much, and at the same time upon the godless, who sits as judge and violates justice.

Consider well, how at the end of the road all this vile wickedness turns back into its original. With love of money it began, and in violation of justice for the sake of *money* it ends.

Money, it is said, is the nerve of war, but it is also the nerve of sin in its evil development.

Under all its forms of development love of money is and remains a root of all evil.

So long as the struggle between good and evil goes on in man, he may indeed run after sin, and when he can overtake it he may rejoice in it, but with it all he prefers, that it be not noticed, and he ever does his best to establish a good reputation for himself.

As often as he perceives, that he is esteemed as an ordinary, but honorable man, it is to him a matter of congratulation. While on the other hand, when he becomes aware, that with respect to him people shrug their shoulders, or that there are shady reports of him abroad, it fills him with anxious apprehension.

The reason of this is, that in this first stage of sin man still reckons with his *conscience*, that conscience punishes him and so keeps him small in his own eyes, and that by this humbling operation of conscience recklessness is held in check.

But when he arrives at this *last* stage, things are altogether different.

He is then long past listening to his conscience. A madness has come upon him. His moral taste, his rational sense is falsified. He is no longer his former self. Evil bewilderment has made itself master of his heart.

His good name is now lost. He understands all the more clearly how people regard him. And in the end he refuses any longer to lower his eyes. He also dares. And henceforth he will brutally look his critics with their annoying remarks, in the eyes. What can they do to him?

He is at least as good as they. Or properly considered, the slander only came from sneaks, who were afraid to sin, and who have no courage to surrender themselves to sin. Small-souled and narrow-minded cowards.

Such a coward, he is not.

He is *daring.*

In him is courage, recklessness even, before the eyes of all to dare to sin. See how much of a hero he is, to drink himself drunk with wine, or to stimulate himself with strong drink.

AND do not say that this brutality of recklessness is an exception. For it is a fact that especially among the young, it haunts all worldly societies.

To be known among his comrades as a dare-devil, to dare what others do not dare, one makes a boast of it, that he can drink like a trooper. That he knows immoral resorts by name and surname. That he can swear and taunt like the roughest. That in brutality against his masters and superiors he is worsted by no one. That in wicked games of cards he is a past-master. That in meanest ways he gets rid of his friends or his debtors. That he knows how to get money out of his father. Dares brutalize virtuous maidens. And that especially in the matter of religion in scorn and in denial he far excels the purest atheist.

This is boasting of oneself in evil.

This is making one's honor of his shame.

And then this goes so far, and he is so enamored of it and in such unholy circles one makes so notorious a reputation of distinction by it, that in the end he even boasts of sin, as though he had actually rendered himself guilty of what he has *not* committed.

That is braggadocio, priding oneself on it, swaggering in sin.

Ever stronger forms, in which *brutality* reveals its devilish nature.

WHAT evil this brutality has wrought with respect *to one's own person,* is unbelievable.

Sometimes with boys of fourteen or fifteen years of age the soul is murdered by it.

Such boys are somewhat ambitious. Among their acquaintances they love to play the first violin. And they see, that nothing is in such demand, as this *daring* to sin; to go out of the way before no one and nothing; by nothing to be daunted.

At first the conscience still troubles them, and they hesitate.

But let one who is already dyed in the wool, unfortunately say: Come on, if you dare! just the suggestion, that there is something they would not dare to do, so that they would be looked upon as lacking in courage, as being pusillanimous, is so unbearable to them, that they rush in against it, and are now bound to make a *show,* and so they glide down into the depth of sin.

With women this evil daring wakens commonly at a later age.

But still you are mistaken when you deem, that this brutality of sin only occurs with boys and young men.

With our married men, and women, it is encountered equally well, be it in a less boisterous form.

Once in a while you even find a man of gray hair, who still takes hellish delight, in encouraging this brutality of sin among the young.

Think also of *navy* and *army.*

From of old brutal talk about sin and in brutality of sin outdoing others, has been part of the moral philosophy of a *man-of-war* and *barracks.*

When once this brutality of *recklessness* has struck root deep enough, it turns into the brutality of love of mischief, which is aimed *at others.*

It begins among boys with teasing one another, to laugh at, to provoke, and finally, in popular parlance, to play Judas. A hellish game, in which many a young boy of well-to-do families has made incredible advances.

When one grows older, and obtains an independent standing in the world, this wantonness of brutality turns itself against every one over whom he has a certain authority, against his wife, his children, his servants, his creditors.

So in his small domain this brutal man becomes a tyrant.

If this already is shameful, it becomes most shameful only, when such a wanton and brutal person becomes clothed with larger authority. A land-agent over tenant-farmers; a foreman over factory-hands; a lieutenant over his troop; a mayor over a town; a judge over one who seeks justice or who on account of misdoing is prosecuted by law.

Then this selfsame wantonness, this tyrannical disposition, this brutality that spares nothing, tempts all such persons, to let *arbitrariness* pass for *justice,* high-handed approval for reasonableness, and in their love of mischief take delight, deliberately to violate the right, which should be *holy.*

All prophecy shows, that God the Lord points to arbitrariness in the judge, as the certain, positive sign, that the downfall of a nation is at hand.

Whatever totters and vacillates, as long as justice is held high, there is yet hope. "The king," says Solomon, "by judgment establisheth the land" (Prov. 29, 4). "Zion," thus saith the Lord by Isaiah, "shall by judgment be redeemed" (1, 27). And as token of His good pleasure, He promises His people: "I will restore thy judges as at the first" (Is. 1, 26).

And therefore, when sin goes so far, that in brutality, from love of mischief, it deliberately violates *justice;* worse still when it uses this violation of justice as a shameful means to benefit itself; then there is nothing more that can stop the evil; then operates a poison *against which there is no antidote.*

For do not forget, this evil never enters into the

courts of law, except as it has been bred at home and in school and in all sorts of associations.

All brutality is in its root, that one boasts of the fact, *that he spares no man.*

And he who spares no one, is always in the last instance an audacious man, *who in his heart also does not fear God.*

LIII

No One Shall Say: I Am Sick

SICKNESS

THE wise man of our age, who is ever yet as over-bold and proud, as the "wise of the world" in the days of St. Paul, simply refuses to have any knowledge of a relation between "sin" and "death."

Dying, he declares, is a necessity of nature. Death is the toll which each of us has to pay to Fate. Everything comes and goes, appears to disappear. Constant change of matter is the law, which governs all existence, and solely and alone because man is under this law, he must die.

And yet, however flippantly one may say this after the other, in the conscience of the nations a holier perception continues to protest against this lie.

No, death is *not* natural. Dying goes *against* the nature and the inclination of our being. And though he who fears God, in dying will humbly bow the head, yea, though one who loves his Savior, can even long to depart, yet the transition itself remains something appalling. The valley of the shadow of death is ever something somber and dark. He who is Christ's may once heroically and jubilantly triumph over death, but even in that triumph death is *his enemy*, whom he holds down as he sings and offers praise.

Scripture declares it so definitely and strikingly: "The last enemy that shall be destroyed is death."

And this solemn word: "death is our *enemy*," finds

an echo in our heart for the reason that in most cases by far dying is introduced by *sickness* or *illness,* and that at least with a somewhat alarming sickness, it is so keenly felt by the patient, and by those who stand around his sickbed, that in this attack upon more than his body, it is not a natural process, but a *disturbance* of his natural existence that takes place, the entering into him of a power from without, which aims at his very life.

Especially the fact, that not *all* suffer sickness, excludes so positively from sickness every idea of necessity of nature.

In death we have to do with a suffering that early or late comes upon all, but sickness overtakes one to spare the other.

There are sick people, who almost all their lifelong must bear the trouble of illness, but over against these unfortunates stand those vigorous constitutions, who until death never lie on a sickbed. And it is this *inequality* of lot, which at the time of sickness at least puts the enthusiast of natural law to silence.

Sickness can never have been intended of God in His creation.

Illness must, outside of God's original plan, find its cause in sin.

Hear what prophecy testifies of the holy city in which there shall be no more sin.

Because there shall be no sin there, therefore there shall *no inhabitant any more say: I am sick, for,* thus saith the Holy One of Israel, the people that dwell therein, *shall be forgiven their iniquity* (Is. 33, 24).

"SICKNESS" and "death," however closely allied, are therefore clearly distinguished in this, that death is the portion of *all,* sickness only of *some.*

This is especially evident, when we take "sickness" in its widest range, and thus understand by it not alone tubercular cases, cancer patients, etc., but also *blind* and *deaf.*

Almost every one *sees* and *hears,* and only a very small minority are sorely afflicted, to be deprived of sight or hearing, the latter frequently aggravated by dumbness. Were our love strong enough, the thought of the deprivation and suffering of these bereft ones would embitter our own life. For no words can express what a deaf person misses and a blind person goes without. Misses and is deprived of not merely for a short time or for a few months, but year in and year out until death.

And though the more real sicknesses cover a far broader domain, yet you see, that *real great sickness* is no rule, but much rather the exception. Less so in our civilized lands, where health is impaired, but very positively among the more distant nations, among mountaineers, and in part even in the country. There small indispositions may occur, but for the rest serious sickness is seldom seen.

Unequal also in this respect is the division. The angel of sickness passes one by and prostrates the other. Something that is specially evident with diseases that are hereditary in families. Then two families live side by side, in one every rising generation has the glow of health in the face and in the other children are almost born with the mark of death upon the countenance.

What applies to the blind and deaf really applies

to all sickness, even in epidemics: Sickness is not the lot of *all*. It prostrates one and leaves the other unharmed.

And He Who here makes dead and alive, or if you will, makes sick and conserves health, Who is He but the Lord, Who also in this respect doeth with the children of men according to *His good pleasure?*

NOT man by sin, but God's sovereign good pleasure alone, determines what generations, families and persons *are* and are *not* visited with these diseases.

We would even remain true to Scripture, if we were to include *plagues;* for of Jehoram it is told in 2 Chron. 21, 18: "And after all this the Lord *plagued* him with a disease, that was incurable."

It is not a *few* guilty ones in the midst of *saints*, who are smitten with disease, while saints are prospered with health and strength.

One rather sees, on the contrary, in many instances that sinners, who defy the Lord, are as the Psalmist says in Ps. 73, 5: "not in trouble as other men"; and who has not frequently found among blind and sick people gentle pious souls, who made no show of the mark of their election, but who unconsciously exhibited the same.

Also in this respect it ever was and will be: the *suffering* servant of God.

All sickness is because of sin. Without sin no sickness would be thinkable. But the guilt is *from Adam*, is the portion of *all*, belongs to our *race* as such. And where God can smite all, it is *His grace*, and nothing but

His grace, that spares the thousands to chastise with His plagues merely the hundreds.

No one of us has for so much as one day of his life a claim to health.

To be sick and to languish away till death is the lot we have all deserved. And when in mercy God the Lord spares most of us this bitter suffering of sickness, to lay low but a few of us, should these few murmur that they do not go out free?

Do they ever bear anything else than what fully as much as others they have deserved? May not God the Lord bring upon them what is ever yet less than their righteous punishment? Yea, would not these few, if they feared God, in the midst of their suffering be *refreshed* by the love of God that spared others?

Does not this sparing of others waft toward them also the fragrance of God's love? If all were laid low, where would be the ministering love, the heart that brings comfort? And if this sparing of others is a means in the hand of God, to mitigate their suffering and to refresh their soul by love, confess, should not then also amidst bitterest suffering praise and thanksgiving ascend from the heart of God's sick child for this tender disposing love of God?

So glistens high and glorious also here the appointment of God's ways, provided they who are in health do not begin to say: Because God brought this affliction upon *you,* therefore *you* are the sinner.

The sufferer himself will confess this in quietness to his own soul and to his God. For every serious sickness is a call to give account. And he who in his sickness feels the aftermath of the guilt of Adam, the guilt of the sin of his whole race, recognizes on this very account not least the personal investigation wherewith the Lord comes to his soul.

What Jesus said to the impotent man (St. John 5, 14), "Go, sin no more," finds its echo with every child of God that feels the waves of sickness and weakness go over his head.

Yet this is and ever will be the personal transaction between God and his heart. What concerns all is the grace of God, which in *not* smiting all, but only a *few*, where *all* are guilty, becomes evident.

For now there discloses itself in this wondrous sickness a mystery, whereby our Father, Who is in heaven, quickens from all sides the moral, holy powers of life to the honor of His Name.

It is true that in his sinful pursuits man can make even sickness end in *spiritual evil*, and that by no means all sickness works out *blessing*.

But this does not take away the fact, that from its nature sickness is disposed to make small what was too high, to turn self-confidence into confidence in God, to place our own work and God's work in more accurate proportions before the eye of our faith, and no less to awaken the pity and compassion of others, the love and sympathy of many, to rouse into action what lay slumbering in the brother-heart, yea, above all, along these ways to make great and glorious the Name of that Knower and Operator of hearts, Who through the dark cloud of suffering makes to shine forth so sunnily and cherishingly the glow of His holy compassion.

To which is added, that *when it pleases Him,* God

the Lord sends out the spirit of prayer. And not *because* of the prayer of many, but yet not outside of connection with what He Himself worked in the heart, sometimes takes away again the plague and heals the sick.

The faithful Shepherd, Who first Himself drove us into the valley of shadows, and now takes us by the hand again and leads us back, and brings us to the fields of light.

Glorious prophecy and blessed anticipation of what it shall once be in the resurrection of the dead.

From dejection reviving, and presently reborn to new strength.

When He, the Lord, multiplies strength to him who had no more strength, and in that renewal, as with an eagle's youth, is felt what once it shall be, when this corruptible shall have put on incorruption, and everything shall bloom in eternal youth in the Jerusalem above, *where no inhabitant shall any more say: I am sick.*

LIV

Forsake Me Not When I Am Old

OLD AGE

By the four seasons of the year God creates four worlds in one, and by the four *periods of life* our God brings out in one selfsame human life four altogether different lives.

It is one selfsame world, which through all the months of the year turns itself upon its axis before the face of God, and just because God withdraws somewhat the glow of the sun or makes him approach a little nearer, He makes that world four times appear in an altogether different form, in an entirely different aspect, every time with a beauty of its own and with a particular speech of His majesty.

The world *in winter* is something altogether different from that same world *in summer*. But he who has an eye for it, sees in both a special glory, such beauty as from God's hand alone can be poured out upon the creature.

This is the richness of the Lord Jehovah. This is the mark of His Divinity. From an almost unnamable small cause such wondrous effect. An effect which penetrates everything, and which already in the mere *snowflake* and in the *water-drop* presents and symbolizes two altogether different worlds, which even as the snowflake and the water-drop themselves are one in essence, and unobservedly pass over the one into the other.

In a similar way God deals with your life. Take it

to be eighty years. That is the full measure of a period of twenty years, four times round. First your spring, till you are full grown. Then the summer of your life in the fulness of your strength. After that the harvest till your sixty years are ended. And finally, with whiteness of snow on the head, the winter of your life, till God calls you away, and you are carried out to the grave.

As with the seasons so here the transitions are scarcely observable. Each of these periods of time imparts to your human life an entirely other existence and appearance. And yet in every one of these four periods life has an excellency of its own, in which your God and your Creator glorifies His creative majesty.

UNDOUBTEDLY of these four periods of human life old age is least desired. In the wealth of spring to flourish and to be young; as man or woman, ripened and altogether matured, to count along with others in life; and so likewise to live the years of autumn, in which the fruit loosens itself from the branches; all this animates and charms. But when old age and grayness arrive, there is the beginning of the waning of strength, of the cooling down, of the shrinkage of life, and above all, when provisions are none too bountiful, there are few days so dreaded and feared as the days of old age.

And there is reason for it.

"Old age has its infirmities," says a proverb. And it cannot be denied, that to feel one's vital powers fail, to feel the light in one's eyes darken, and to be conscious of loss in keenness of hearing, and to be hindered in freedom of motion, does not appeal to the heart, but goes against the urge of our nature.

Especially at the end this becomes irksome and oppressive, when it comes to what the Preacher sang about already thousands of years ago, when "the keepers of the house (legs and arms) shall tremble"; when his walk becomes unsteady and the grinders cease because they are few; when "the two doors toward the street (our eyes) shall be shut"; when sleep is gone and the old man wakens before it is day, "at the voice of the bird"; when the daughter of music, i.e., your voice, shall be brought low; when the almond tree white on your head shall flourish; and he is fearful by the roadside, until at length bent and trembling "as a grasshopper he wanders about, and all desire shall fail him."

Herein is suffering, a going out of the lamp of life until it is extinguished. A slow dying, before yet the hour of death strikes.

A taking of last steps on the pilgrim-way.

For man goeth to his long home, and his dust shall return to the earth, when his spirit returns again to God Who gave it.

THUS is the way to our Nebo, to that high mountain-top, from whose summit God shall show us Canaan.

Though you yourself have climbed no Nebo or Hermon, you can readily picture to yourself the course of such an ascent.

First walking for hours amidst flowers and through orchards, to reach the foot of the mountain. Then an easy ascent of slopes through forests of oaks and pines, image of midlife *summer*-strength. After that the forests behind you, and now the high uplands, where no tree can flourish. And from this *autumn*-nature, you ascend at length to the snow-field, that never melts away, and the cold of the ice-field numbs the skin. This with mountain-climbing is your *winter,* image of old age. And then it goes ever higher to the top, until finally there is nothing more that breaks your visual line, and on that top you kneel in adoration, to glorify your God, Who alone is great, in the majesty of His creation.

Below, in the tablelands of earth, the fostering glow and the wealth of vegetation. But on the heights ice and snow, and a chill that makes you shiver. But yet on that frozen mountain-top, amidst that bareness and nakedness of rocks, *nearest heaven,* the broadest outlook upon the glory and the greatness and the majesty of your God.

If such your old age might be, you feel indeed the cold, and are conscious of the emptiness around you, and you learn to pray more fervently: "O, My God, now that I am old and grayheaded, forsake not thy servant, forsake not thy handmaid" (Ps. 71, 18), but you will also find in that old age itself a bundle of blessings hidden by your God, and for that old age you will be able to offer Him thanks.

Always if you *believe.* If your hope stands forever sure. If your seeking eye may gaze toward the gate of the new-Jerusalem above.

For truly, an old man, who unconverted and with his heart hardened, continues anxiously to hold himself fast to the world, and trembles at the thought, that "the silver cord is being loosed," as Solomon describes it, *he is miserable.*

Everything he had set his heart upon slips away from him. The world, in which he sought his life, in the end laughs at him, and is the first to put him to a side and then in the corner. Until finally he is still endured for a while as a burden of life, and then is laid away in the grave.

But when back of the eye that has grown dim, the spark of heavenly light may glisten, God makes old age to be so entirely different to us, so rich in many ways, a continual refreshment of soul.

A blood, that courses less fast, and therefore silenced the storm of temper and passion, whereby in former years the struggle was so hard and so bitter before the face of God.

Sin still creeping after, but yet as fruit of much godly exercise and rich experience of soul, more easily resisted, and the danger of being taken unawares by Satan's guiles, considerably lessened.

Looser from earthly goods, and in one's own self less irritable. Thereby calmer of nature and more restful in mind. More equable day by day. More used to carrying the cross, and thereby no longer so readily succumbing under the weight of the same.

In the Word of his God more deeply initiated. More at home in His holinesses. The soul more accustomed to the still waters of His salvation.

So following after the Good Shepherd, by His rod and by His staff comforted. Inwardly rejoicing in God's hidden walk. His blessed fellowship less distant. And dwelling more continuously in the tent of His Divine presence.

By reason of this known of God's people. More fervently loved by his own. Not abandoned, but sought for wiser counsel. And because of the peace that radiates from him loved by all those whose heart goes out to the eternal.

Meanwhile each day gazing more clearly into eternity, to the fatherland above. Ever more irresistibly drawn. And already now enjoying a foretaste of what once it shall be with Jesus above, in the congregation of the just made perfect, in the unbroken fellowship of his God.

To whom it is given of God's free grace, thus to grow old, there is a holy beauty about old age, which he would on no account exchange for a return of the days of his youth.

He who thus may be old, continues, aged though he be, young of heart.

He feels, indeed, that the outward tabernacle of his life is being dissolved, but life within does not grow less, but more, becomes not poorer, but richer. He observes that far from being at the end of things, he only now approaches the mountains back of which the eternal morning spreads beams of glowing light. Yet a while, a few more mile-posts, and his *real* life, his life, that shall never die away, *begins*.

Only let him who would have such a green old age, not wait to prepare for this until old age is upon him, but already in the days of his strength lay foundations for such a beautiful decline of life.

Let him understand well, that nothing burdens old age more bitterly, than the pitiful remembrance of sins that have been dragged along, of deeds of infidelity, of denials of his Savior, of the urge of love choked in the urge of self.

So many aged men, so many women of years do not know the glory of old age, because in earlier years they have demanded too much of the body, have neglected health, have tainted the soul, have spotted the conscience, and have lived their faith too much on their lips, and too little in their heart.

And for this even in old age there is medicine to be had with the Only Physician. Jesus, Who on earth never knew old age, is ready to refresh aged people with the fruit of His offering. Simeon with his snow-white hair, holding the infant Jesus in his arms, and saying: "Let now thy servant depart in peace, O Lord, according to thy word, for mine eyes have seen thy salvation," remains the enticing image of the aged, who comforts himself in his Savior.

But yet, he who first, when he is old, when his strength is more and more broken, seeks Jesus, faces a hard battle. Also the members of the soul with people of years are no longer supple, but stiff and rigid. A man of sixty and more years, who converts himself to his Savior, is very rare.

And therefore he who when old age is upon him, would not wander about abandoned of his God, let him seek his God while He may be found.

Not first when he is old, but in the days of his youth, in the years of his midlife strength.

LV

Who Have Fallen Asleep in Jesus

OUR DEAD

EVERY family, every circle has its dead, those that have passed away, those that have been carried out to the grave, who were once their own, in whose love they rejoiced, and *whom God took away.*

Is there not something lovely in it, when after such a dying, the memory of him who went from us, lives on in such a family and among such friends?

That indeed they are gone, but that they are held in mind, and sometimes in sad reflection, in inquiring imagination, or in hushed conversation you almost have glimpses of their form.

You might say: This must of itself be so, this must be the case with all.

Who would forget his beloved dead?

And truly, when the day after the demise you see sometimes the overwhelming emotion of pain of heart, and that passionate outcry of grief, you would think that *forgetting* would be impossible.

Yet experience teaches differently.

Of course there is difference here. Difference of all kinds. No rule can apply to *all,* nor with respect to *all* the dead.

A young infant, that is transferred from the cradle to the little coffin, cannot continue to live in the memory, as the child, that grew up and matured under you, and whom in his riper years you lost.

According as the inner life of the family is emotional or reserved, the impression of a loss by death is deeper or less deep.

The place which your dead occupied in your heart, can have been greater or smaller, and as thereby the measure of your loss was determined, the measure of your mourning keeps pace with the measure of your loss.

The man, who at once returns to the busy world, is more readily diverted from the remembrance of his dead, than the woman, who sits pensively down in her chamber or wanders about the house.

With those who are younger the outbreak of grief at first is generally more passionate, with those of older years not so abundant in shedding of tears, but for this very reason sometimes the more lasting.

And so memory, that under the stimulus of mourning affects the heart, is generally defined by three data, i.e., by the actual worth of him who died, by the gift of appreciative love on the part of those who remained behind, and by the nature of all sorts of circumstances of life.

MEANWHILE, apart from the cause, the complaint is surely not too exaggerated, that the remembrance of our dead is rather too weak than too strong.

There are exceptions. In a *too* sentimental family even less fortunate exceptions. When all sorts of things which the deceased left behind are kept as relics, if not openly exhibited. When all sorts of pictures set in wreaths of immortelles decorate walls. And a picture of the grave is placed by the side of it. And at the grave a sort of brief ritual is celebrated. Whereby a certain cult of the dead originates, so altogether in conflict with Jesus' saying: "Let the dead bury their dead, go and preach thou the Kingdom of God."

This is a sickly utterance of sentiment, which fortunately is but rarely seen among us.

But for the rest at one funeral service after another it is confidently stated that, though he is dead, the deceased shall *live* in the grateful remembrance of all. Yet there are few words that by later developments are so bitterly given the lie as this grandiloquence at the grave.

It is rather to be wondered at, within how short a time after the funeral the name and the remembrance of the deceased is dropped from conversation and from mind. And when you come two or three years later, a new member in the circle would scarcely perceive, that only so recently a death occurred in that circle, and that at an open grave there had been such passionate weeping.

It was with this, as with the stone that broke the mirror of the water. A momentary plump *into* and a bubbling up *of* the water. Then a circle forming itself around that point, and ever widening itself. Until in its widening it became ever fainter, and less observable. And it did not take long, before the waters flowed on and on, as though never a stone had been sunk in them.

ESPECIALLY in our days this is grievous. The quickened pulse-beat of life makes the blood circulate too hurriedly, so that there is no time for thought. The present day crowds out the remembrance of yesterday. What time then is left for pensive remembrance of those who were with us years ago?

Yet the complaint about that speedy forgetting of our dead has come to us already from antiquity. In all sorts of lands and under all sorts of religious forms it has been tried to bring an end to this evil.

In ancient Rome the ashes of the cremated body in a stone vase reposed on a shelf in one's reception-hall. The service of the *Penates,* as it was called.

In China all the holier sense of the people was directed to such religious ritual and veneration of the dead.

Before all things else Radboud at his baptism thought of how he might come to his forefathers.

By costly graves, and visits at those graves, and beautifying of those graves similar remembrances of the dead are kept alive in all southern lands.

And how by her "All souls," and by masses for the dead, the Church of Rome has tried to work in like direction, is known by all.

Altogether efforts, which, though they ended in wrong paths, yet provisionally sprang from the need, to strengthen the remembrances of our dead, to revive and to maintain them.

It is so hard to be obliged to think: "When to-morrow I die, in a year's time perhaps there will no one think of me."

Also the family-tie became so loose by this frequent sinful forgetting.

And, moreover, did not our love among the living become suspect, when that love, put to the test by death, so quickly allowed its flame to be extinguished?

ALSO among us, Christians of the Reformation, tenderness in this respect might well be somewhat greater.

When Jesus stands at the grave of Lazarus, and deeply moved *weeps* over the death of His friend, there is least of all in this an approval of that coldness and callousness that so frequently marks behavior among us at the bier and at the open grave.

And when the apostles of the Lord so frequently speak of those who have gone before and have fallen asleep in Jesus, it is clearly evident, that thought of our brethren and sisters, who have fallen asleep in Christ, is inseparable from the drawings of love in God's child.

Undoubtedly, he who lives from the spirit of our fathers, maintains also at the grave the high commandment, that God alone must be great, and that even the most dearly beloved dead for no single moment may cast a shadow across the honor of God's name.

Therefore we do not decorate our graves, we deem flowers offensive on a casket, and in death we will see *death*, in the grave *the grave*, both in serious reality before us.

That seriousness we dare to face, because we are of Christ.

And so with the thought of our own dying it is not longing in the first place, to see our dead again. When the heart is right, and at times home-sickness after heaven draws, it must be a desire to "depart *and be with Christ.*"

David sang it out in his song, not that he would delight himself with the likeness of his dead, but that he would eternally delight himself *with the likeness of his God.*

The great and first and high commandment admits of nothing else.

In life and death our Lord's, and therefore in life and in death God the first and God the last in our thought, in our imagination, in our remembrance, in our home-sickness.

That, that alone, at the grave, at the approach of death, and at the remembrance of our dead, after the spirit of the fathers, is life according to God's holy Word.

But along this very way the remembrance of those who have fallen asleep in Christ, of itself springs up within us, especially where those early dead were ours, and were given us of God.

About those who did not fall asleep in Jesus, we are silent.

We do not judge. Even where we did not observe that they fell asleep in Jesus, no one of us can say, what in the latest gasp took place between God and that soul.

The mysteries of the soul and the mystery of God's grace lie so deep.

To Him, and not to us, the judgment.

But when he who dies, so far as we know died

away in his sin, without faith, then there also is no tie for us between the deceased and our God, and in our expectation of a heaven, which is entirely lost in God, the thought of our dead can have no place. Even if this were possible, it would draw us away from God, which must not be.

Surprises can, and surprises there will be at our awakening in eternity. Also, alas, bitter disappointments. But this remains till later. Here on earth in our remembrances we may not do otherwise than count with what we can believe.

And then it is they "who have fallen asleep in Jesus," who of themselves are present with us in our devotional lifting up of soul to our High Priest, and through Him to our God.

Not merely: I shall die, and then be with God, as though Christ were *alone*, and thus no count with the mystical body of Christ is necessary, but God in Christ, and for His sake the just made perfect. Seth, Enoch, Noah, Abraham, Peter and John and Paul, all anointed and justified, to us they are not dead, but they are all alive, and we shall live with them (1 Thess. 4, 14).

And to that company of redeemed of earlier ages are joined our own beloveds, who went away from us, for so much as they have fallen asleep in Jesus. A father or mother, a brother or sister, a child, sometimes known but for a moment, a friend who was a bosom-friend. All that numerous company of pilgrims, who walked with us by the way, and before us entered the gate of heaven.

In them mingles then your *faith* with the personal love of your heart, to keep their remembrances alive, and through them make yourself conversant with heaven above.

On earth ever poorer with respect to loved ones and friends, as the wind blows across the fields and every time again makes a flower drop from its stem.

But in the eternal, on the other side of the grave ever richer, until here at length you no longer feel yourself at home, but at home above, where your God in Christ is, and with and around Him all God's elect, and among those elect also they who are yours, who here below you were permitted to possess but for a little while, that you might love them forever before the face of God.

LVI

His Name Shall Be Propagated from Child to Child

GRACE IN THE GENERATIONS

IMAGINE, that Prince William the Silent were still alive, and after having founded and delivered the Dutch nation, had happily ruled over them all these centuries, and still ruled them, and was sure, as long as sun and moon endure, to wield the scepter over them,—would not the tie between such a prince and the people founded, saved and made happy by him, far excel every idea of fondness and devotedness.

With Prince William this was not possible. For even if the base crime of Balthasar Gerards had not cut him off early in life, he would long ago have paid his toll to death. Even the first Orange-prince was mortal, and not by him in person, but only through the House that is named after him, could his generation continue in the fatherland.

Israel, on the other hand, has very really dreamed this wondrous dream. What is more, it has received the sure prophecy, that a permanent King would come. And finally, in the fullness of time, at His resurrection from the dead, has begun the Kingship of that Prince of Heaven.

To this Prince it is said in Psalm 45: "Thy throne is for ever and ever." It is of that King that in the song of Solomon it is sung (Ps. 72): "They shall fear thee as long as the sun and moon endure, throughout all generations," yea, that at the end of the psalm it is said:

"His name shall endure for ever; yea, so long as the sun endures, his name shall be propagated from child unto child" (Dutch version).

A SUPERFICIAL Bible-reader sees nothing special in this.

For, thinks he, also the names of King David and of King Solomon have been handed down now almost thirty centuries from generation to generation. Of Nebuchadnezzar every child knows. Of Cyrus and Alexander every high school boy can tell the story. And though Prince William *lives* no more among us, his illustrious name shall never be forgotten.

So, it is taken as a something strikingly common, that also the name of the Messiah lives on and on; and the Psalmist said nothing out of the ordinary, when he proclaimed, that His name, so long as the sun endures, shall be propagated from child to child.

But he who speaks thus forgets, that there stands with it: "They shall fear thee as long as the sun and moon endure." One can hold a deceased prince in thankful remembrance, one can visit his tomb and immortalize the memory of his deeds in the epic; but a deceased prince one cannot *fear.*

To fear a king takes for granted that he still lives, bears rule, and can still bless you.

And so in Psalm 72 in the days of the Old Covenant this glorious ideal is held before the faithful people, and this rich promise given, that once a King should rise, who would not *die,* whose Kingdom would have *no* end, who would not merely rule for a while, but for ever and for aye, and whose name as that of an ever ruling and ever blessing Prince would be honored not merely in one generation, but through long series of generations, and in that sense be propagated from child to child.

The people ever changing, but always over that people the one and selfsame King.

We still live under the sweet dominion of this of God-anointed King. Age after age went by, sometimes stormed along, but whatever fell and whatever tumbled and changed, His throne stands for ever and aye; He, our King, lives and still reigns.

There is even now no prince on earth comparable with this King, as little in the extensions of His domain, as in the faithfulness wherewith He rules His people, and in affectionate love wherewith that people swear loyalty and fidelity to Him.

At the glory of Jesus' crown every prince on earth becomes little more than a pseudo-king. So brief, so limited, so little impressive is their power.

This kingship of Jesus stands so high, because it never is anything else than *real.* Over no one is He King, but He rules in his heart, over his person, over his whole existence, and He lets not go, until every one of His subjects becomes partaker of the full salvation.

What is the course pursued among us, with respect to this propagation of His name from child to child?

Does it mean merely, that you tell your child the

story of Jesus? Is this purpose reached, when at school your child sings in chorus with other children: "How sweet the name of Jesus sounds?"

Propagating that name from child to child, is it done, when there is a Christian school, where from generation to generation our children hear of Jesus and sing praises to Him?

When His name lives on the lips, and dominates in the memory, and you do not subscribe to the foolish notion, of "*silently* bearing witness to Jesus," is His name then propagated in the sense of Psalm 72, from child to child?

So that nothing else is implied herewith, nothing deeper, nothing more real, than a keeping in mind of the name of Jesus, keeping His name from passing into forgetfulness, and at most a continuous utterance of that name with certain reverence and childlike veneration?

So the Bible-reader would have it, who does not understand the depth of Scripture, and has never been enchanted by its rich ideals.

But God's people must not rest content with such superficial interpretation.

No, propagated from child to child the name of our King is only, when generation after generation, children, and presently from these children men and women rise, who will glory in that King as *their* Prince and Lord, and when century upon century, so long as the sun endures, the genuflection of Thomas repeats itself with the worshiping exclamation: *My Lord and my God!*

Because He is an eternal King, His name cannot be propagated, except by him who wills to be a *subject* of that King.

And therefore, propagated from child to child the

name of this King only is, when from child to child there are not only always those, who hold this name in mind, but also such as *confess* it, and apply that name to themselves, acknowledging Him the King Who also bears rule over and in their heart.

THIS is the high end, toward which all Christian training must be directed.

In holy Baptism to receive the mark of this King, and, as soon as consciousness wakens, to acquaint the child with that King, as with a King Who bears rule eternally, Who also must bear rule over him, and to Whom likewise every child given us of God in His favor, owes submission as subject, and the tribute of praise and worship.

So only do you come to the generation-idea of faith.

Not merely to the prayer, once saved to enter the palace of that King; and not to commit the child you love to that King; but from the passion of faith not to see in your own generation the subjects of King Jesus die out.

A vain man investigates his pedigree, that perchance he might come across some ancestor of name, some person of fame among men. But a true child of God asks rather and far more, whether among his forebears there were those who were "known of the Lord." And he feels rich, and overjoyed, when two or three centuries back he comes across a concatenated succession of men and women, who continued faithful in the fear of the Lord.

Not to have an earl or a duke, but a *martyr* in his old family, is then highest and richest genealogical glory.

So *backward* in history, but also *forward* into the future of our generation. Every one in his own.

No one of us knows, how long the Lord will yet tarry, before the Maranatha goes into fulfillment.

But suppose, there will yet ten, yet twenty generations come after us, then *this* quickens our ambition, to be able to prophesy that children of God, sprung from our loins, as with holy links, will form one great chain, which from now on until our Lord's return will propagate *our generation,* not merely in the life of the world, but also among *the people of God.*

As long as the sun shall endure, from child to child, also among the children, that shall come forth from you.

This you have not in your own power.

But in increasing measure this becomes the content of your most fervent prayer. And because you so learn to pray, you develop a far more glorious efficacy in the bringing up of your children.

LVII

The Book of the Generation

OUR GENERATION OF GOD

OUR holy Gospel begins with *a Book of generations,* which commences with Abraham and ends with Jesus.

By this one move Scripture sums up the whole history of our human race, as ending in Christ at Bethlehem, and after that starting out again from Christ on Golgotha.

Everything that took place from Adam on to the Patriarchs, merely serves as a pedestal on which to place the *Father of all the faithful.* And when Abraham departs from Ur of the Chaldees, the course of history straightly directs itself to the Womanseed.

So every idea falls away, as though in the generations, succeeding one another, there was but a monotonous repetition of always other people, who were born and died. Such for the sake of sin it might be in Africa among the negro-tribes, where these many centuries a sea of humanity undulates hither and thither, without aim. But so it was not with that part of our human race, which held fast to the fear of God. The generation that fears God has a *history.* That is to say, with such a generation there reveals itself a plan, a counsel of God. Therefore our believing fathers placed a family-register in their Bibles. Something to which Scripture itself invited them; for it gives us both in Genesis for the *Old,* and in SS. Matthew and Luke for the *New* Testament, *a Book of generations.*

More still.

Matthew the Evangelist calls attention to the fact that in that stream of living beings, which we call *an historic generation,* there is not merely the monotonous succession of father and son, but also a certain grouping.

Abraham, David and Christ, the three names, whereby that grouping is indicated, while the Babylonian exile as an incision in the course of centuries indicates to us the humiliating fall of the once so far-famed generation.

So you receive the impression, as though all that lies back of Abraham, simply tended to have Abraham appear; as though everything that lies in between Abraham and David, has no other plan than to bring forth David; and as though everything that came before, in and after David, merely served as shadow, to make the light in the Christ of God to break through.

The Evangelist even took pleasure, to introduce some sort of rhythm therein. From Abraham to David there were *fourteen* generations. Therefore from Judah's kings he only names *fourteen.* And equally *fourteen* descendants of Jechonias after the Babylonian exile.

The effort to take the sacred *seven double,* is here too perspicuous to need further explanation. Evidently the Evangelist wants to make us feel, how the stream of this sacred genealogical line flows onward with three broad wave-beats evenly from Abraham to Christ.

Everything tending to show how in this succession of generations it is not the individuals that follow one after the other, but God's command and counsel that makes the history.

AND if you ask, in what light the Evangelist places this Book of generations before us, we answer: Truly not in the light of human greatness.

You see this in three particulars.

First in the mention of Tamar and of "her who had been Uriah's wife."

Not one great, mighty act of Abraham or Jacob, of David or Solomon is mentioned. Regarding everything that can exalt man, this Book of generations preserves *absolute silence*. But what is recorded, are two dreadful human *sins*. Altogether in harmony with the prophecy which presently follows, that Christ should come to save His people from their sins.

And not the little sin of a forgotten kind, but the terrible transgression of a Judah and the atrocious fall of King David are again immortalized by this Book of generations.

Even Bathsheba's name is not mentioned, but her dangerous person is indicated as the seductive "that had been the wife of Uriah."

Secondly you observe the human insignificance of this generation in the many, for the most part altogether unknown names, which are recorded here. What do you know of Esrom and Aram, what meaning has Azor and Achim for you? What promise of greatness regarding Christ is there in that series of men, that have come and gone, leaving little else behind them, than the memory of their gradually bastardized name?

For their names also, by the intermediary of the Greek translation, have gradually in pronunciation become almost irrecognizable. Hezekiah is called Ezekias, Perez (in Dutch version) has become Phares.

Even their name has no permanence.

To which is added in the third place, that all this once so celebrated and princely generation of Abraham and David, at length in the Babylonian exile goes under altogether, till in the days of Emperor Augustus you find Prince Joseph back again in forgotten Nazareth, with a leather apron over his knees and a wood-plane in his hand.

AND while this Book of generation so makes you see the sin and the sinking down into insignificance of the children of men, so that God's counsel alone unites them into a generation and in their generation effects a history, this now is the glory, that into this generation the Holy Ghost descends from above, and so presents Christ to the world.

Herein alone this Book of generations finds its rest, that the virgin Mary *was found with child of the Holy Ghost.*

Of this patriarchical generation in the end *nothing* came. What was wrought in Abraham, was sinned away by Judah, and what seemed regained in David, was in David himself covered with the scum of sin.

So this generation does not *climb,* but *sink.*

Sinks ever deeper and ever more sadly.

And all that remains is *the promise of God,* which through all the stages of humiliation and self-disdain, keeps accompanying this chosen generation.

But when it comes to the point, the outcome shows, that there was *nothing* in this generation itself, by reason of which it was chosen, and that this election aimed solely and alone at what would be wrought *by God*

Himself; not from below but from above; not from human efficiency but by the holy God.

Not this princely generation of David had borne a fruit of salvation for the world.

On the contrary, the stem of Jesse lay cut off. Only its root still hid in the earth. There was no branch and no leaf and no more blossom to it.

And yet a rod came up out of the barren earth.

God came to us. A virgin is become pregnant. And so the world received her "God with us," her Immanuel, her Savior, Who would save her from death.

ALSO among men such family-records used to be made. One knows how far even a poet like Bilderdyk lost himself in this vanity.

We say in *vanity.*

For by itself of course it is good and praiseworthy that one honors his connection with the past, and attaches value to what lies in the interbraiding of the generations.

But the vanity of it is this, that such family-records are almost exclusively made, to show to what a *noble* family one belongs, with what *great* historical figures one is related, and to what *remote antiquity* one can trace the origin of his race.

This other people cannot do. Self can. And so these family-records tend to distinguish oneself, as belonging to a sort of *higher* race of beings.

And so it should not be.

In every generation one should have a family-tree in his Bible, and that family-record should be kept for

God's sake. For his sake, in Whose eye a day-laborer is of no less account than a prince of royal blood; and Whose providence-care is over the successive generations of poor and rich.

For the sake of *the Covenant* one should make record of his generation, and that Book of generations should preserve the memory, not chiefly of the high titles and quarters which human vanity had formed, but far more of what God's grace and God's favor had wrought, to enrich such a generation spiritually, and, as blessing in the external, from *nothing* to make it *something.*

As family-records now are, they for the most part stimulate human pride and are kept outside of God's ordinance and the honor of His name.

So altogether different from this Book of the generations in Matthew's first chapter, in which you see man in his sin and in his insignificance from generation to generation climb when there is fear of God, and deteriorate when the fear of God was lost, in order in the end to see the heavens rend, and from the throne of grace see the Salvation come down, for which this generation of Abraham and David has served in the counsel of God.

LVIII

Without Me Ye Can Do Nothing

OUR DEEP DEPENDENCE

ORDINARILY with our fruit trees the *small* and delicate twigs do most; for from those *thin* branches you pick in autumn the best fruit. Thus what neither the heavy trunk nor the thick branches could do, this, when summer is over, those freshly budded twigs have done; they have produced the grape-bunches; and from that thin twig the muscatel is plucked.

Those little twigs therefore can do very much; yet under one condition, and that is, that those small, thin twigs are fixed firmly to the tree. For when in some moment of carelessness you break that little twig, it is ended at once, it withers, and there is nothing more it can do.

Thus every tree in nature speaks to all its little twigs and branches, saying: *Without me ye can do nothing.* Cut off from me, or just broken off, you feel no more the flow of my life-sap. Firmly grown in me, you can make fruit ripen, which fruit, when presently fully ripe, will fall into man's lap. But broken away from me, at once all your strength is gone, you can make no single blossom bud, no single fruit can longer set itself. Remaining fixed in me, as a fruitful branch, you can do all things, but without me, because I am your tree, as twig or branch you can do *nothing.*

This, especially with regard to the vine, is what our highest Prophet and Teacher has observed. Being in the vine, the branches can bear abundant fruit, but without the vine, outside of the vine, and loosened from the vine, they are nothing but kindling-wood, and as regards bearing fruit, they can absolutely do nothing.

This was not something which, as a new discovery, Jesus told His disciples. On the contrary, that this was so, the disciples also knew; as every boy among us knows this now. Who would think of picking up a little twig, broken off by the wind, and keep it in expectation of fruit that it might bear.

With this, therefore, Jesus said nothing new. He rather supposed that each of his disciples knew this well, and thought of it as He did.

And the new only came in when Jesus applied to Himself this very ordinary thing from the life of tree and branch, of vine and twig, and in other words said to his disciples, in them to all His church, and in His church to each of His elect: "Ye are the branches, and on your twigs fruit must bud, set itself and ripen, and this is possible, for this you have been made able. Abundantly to bring forth fruit, and presently when it is ripened, to cast it off for the honor of your God and for the salvation of your neighbor. *This you can do;* provided . . . and this condition is inexorable . . . provided with the spiritual fibers of faith you continue fixed in Me as your Vine. For, and consider this with all seriousness, if once you are removed from Me, or have broken away from Me, so that from Me the life-sap ceases to flow out to you, no single fruit can ripen any more on your twig. Without the life-sap from the Vine the branch, and on that branch the twig, can absolutely do nothing."

FROM this you see, how often this definite and striking word of Jesus: "Without me ye can do nothing," is misunderstood.

In many instances it is taken by itself, apart from the connection in which Jesus said it, and then it is made to point to the Divine assistance, which of His grace Jesus is bound to lend us, that our plan may prosper and succeed.

It then obtains the like meaning, as though some one said: "Without God I can do nothing."

It is then understood of our creaturely impotence; and the powerless creature can never succeed in anything, except the almighty and everywhere present power of God supports and carries him.

So this beautiful, rich saying: "Without me ye can do nothing" (St. John 15, 5), is taken in the sense of Providence-faith, and so seems to urge us, in nothing to forsake prayer and supplication, but with everything we undertake, to invoke the mighty help and unconquerable assistance of our God in Christ.

But however true all this is, it has *nothing* to do with what Jesus here says.

He does not speak of this.

He speaks of something altogether different.

Not of your plans and purposes, but exclusively of your high calling, to bear fruit, for the honor of your God.

Not of His gracious help, as to Whom all power is given in heaven and on earth; but exclusively of the life-sap of the soul, that must flow out to you from Him, as your Vine.

Neither also of your creaturely limitation and impotence as creature; but exclusively of your absolute inability, as believer, to bring forth any fruit of faith, outside of the spiritual tie of life, wherein with Him, as the Head of the Body, your soul must stand.

He who is one planting with Me, Jesus means to say, of himself bears fruit; but likewise, he who as a broken off twig or branch comes to lie alongside of Me as his plant, is absolutely incapable of bearing any fruit.

"Without Me ye can do nothing" means: Without vital communion with your Savior, you lack every capacity to produce even the very smallest fruit of faith.

THE correct and sharp insight of this clear meaning of Jesus' saying is by no means a matter of indifference.

If you take the word amiss, and in connection with it think of the gracious help of Jesus toward the success of what you undertake, it only comes to mind, when you prepare yourself for the execution of a new plan.

But if you take it in the clear sense, in which Jesus intended it, then it is a word of faith *for every day*, which every morning at waking is sounded in your ear, and which every evening, at retiring, either comforts or pronounces judgment against you.

For faith must *bear fruit* by no means merely with what you undertake for the church, for missions, for schools or for the care of the poor; but you must *bear fruit*, even first of all, in your *daily* life, in your *calling* and in your *home*.

No day, what say I, no morning, no midday and

no evening may pass by that you bear no fruit for the honor of your God.

All of your life, on Sunday and in the week, and all those days long in every occurring event, that bearing of fruit must go on.

There must be a fruit bearing of faith in *everything.* In all your labor, in all your associations, in all your difficulties, even in all trouble and all suffering that overtakes you.

Fruit of faith, fruit to the honor of God in your association with yourself, in the forming of your character, in the development of your spirit, in the bridling of your passions, in the restraint of your hot temper and mood, in the renunciation of vanity, in subduing your haughtiness and pride, in purifying of your heart.

Fruit of faith, fruit to the honor of your God, there must be in your relation to your husband or wife, in your care for the children God gave you, in your association with your brothers and sisters, in your relation to your employees, or, if you are an employee yourself, in your attitude toward those that have been placed over you.

And so also, fruit of faith, fruit to the honor of your God, must blossom and ripen on the twigs of your soul, in the acquittance of your life's task, in caring for everything committed to your keeping, in accomplishing the task of daily life, in bringing to a finish what each day is laid upon you as a task.

In and with all this, as believer, as a child of God, you will not satisfy yourself with a fruit of civil righteousness, but you will bear a fruit of faith. And each day is played away and sinned away, on which the heavenly Husbandman does not find this *fruit of faith* on your branches.

So with this deep word: "Without Me ye can do nothing," Jesus turns in to you, in your house. He looks you up with it in your home. He calls it out to you every morning and every evening. He accompanies you with it at your work. He whispers it to you in every difficulty, which you come to face in everyday life.

Nothing without relation of life with me. You, as believer, have no standing by yourself alone. You are not yourself a tree, with a root of your own, but only a branch, a twig, a shoot. Not in yourself, in me alone is the root, and from that root alone can the life-sap of faith come to you. What would ye do without Me?

Be it thus, that you live a moderate life, and quietly do your work, and keep peace with those that are about you, yet all this, when it springs up from yourself, when in your own strength you wrought it, is never a fruit of faith.

You then produce nothing else than a sour, bitter, wormy fruit, which your God does not pick to His honor, but as unusable casts away; just as in autumn you throw away the unripe, the spoiled fruit, to gather only the good, ripe fruit in your baskets.

And therefore, if yours shall be a *life* of faith, and bear a *fruit* of faith, all this work of your own shall not once come into consideration. Only that will count what from Jesus came into you, and through Him, by His fellowship, by the life-sap from Him flowing out to you has been made into a *fruit of faith.*

FROM this it follows, that all your zeal and all your endeavor cannot prosper, unless daily that communion with the Vine is sought by you and established.

You do not lead the life of a Christian, of a child of God, when you confess that Christ is your Savior, and for the rest direct your life, spend your day and finish your task outside of Him, and without His fellowship.

Christian is he alone, who is implanted in Christ, and once implanted in Him considers this implanting every day, counts with it, and lives from it.

And therefore it does not avail, whether, at some individual difficult matter that presents itself to you, you take refuge with your Jesus. For then you are not accustomed to Him. Then He is to you as a stranger. As a Savior, Who is far distant from you, and now, for this one moment, must come to your help.

No, to live as a child of God, your life must flourish *every day* from the root, which is in Christ. *All day long* it must be dominated by the superior power which the Vine has over the branch. The fact that you are implanted in Christ must *all your life long* carry you.

Without Me ye can do nothing is not merely a warning, not to begin anything without Jesus, but also a stimulus, which enters into your soul, to say to you, that there must be *fruit of every day,* and that therefore every day of your life you must seek that intimate fellowship of life with your Savior, from which alone the power comes to you, to bear fruit to the honor of God.